SPORTS and GAMES

NEW REVISED EDITION

SPORTS
AND GAMES

BY HAROLD KEITH

THOMAS Y. CROWELL COMPANY

New York

For Johnny

FOREWORD

I SHOULD LIKE to acknowledge several debts I owe in connection with the preparation of this book.

Extensive help and criticism were cheerfully given by Charles ("Bud") Wilkinson, University of Oklahoma football coach; Lawrence ("Jap") Haskell, former University of Oklahoma baseball coach; Bruce Drake, University of Oklahoma basketball and former golf coach, and Bob James, University of Oklahoma golf coach; Larry Armstrong, University of Minnesota hockey coach; C. H. Winston, coach of the Houston, Texas, Y.M.C.A. volleyball team; John Jacobs, University of Oklahoma track and cross-country coach; and Paul V. Keen, former University of Oklahoma wrestling coach, and Tommy Evans, assistant coach.

I am indebted also to Brad Scheer, member of the Oklahoma badminton doubles championship teams of 1938 and 1939; Charles Saulsberry for aid on the bowling chapter; Jack Davis and Matt Mann, swimming coaches at the University of Oklahoma; and to John Breeden, basketball coach, Montana State College; Jack Baer and John Heath, former University of Oklahoma baseball players and Robert T. Jones, Jr., and the American Golf Institute for advice on specific problems.

I should like to thank Robert W. Henderson for per-

{382

mission to quote from his bulletin, *Baseball and Rounders;* also Everett Morris, basketball editor of the *New York Herald Tribune* and Jack Frank, the *Herald Tribune* photographer; Parke Carroll, sports editor of the *Kansas City Journal-Post,* and Chuck Taylor; The American Sports Publishing Company and John T. Doyle; Sec Taylor, sports editor of the *Des Moines Register;* Tom O'Hara, head caddie master of the Denver Country Club; H. R. Palmer of Ann Arbor, Michigan; Al Wesson, sports publicity director of the University of Southern California and photographer Joe Mingo; and Harold Tacker, University of Oklahoma photographer. Dr. Gustav Mueller, associate professor of philosophy at the University of Oklahoma, kindly translated a description of the ancient game of *Faustball* from German encyclopedias.

Permission to quote material was cheerfully given by Robert H. Davis, author of *Ruby Robert* published by Doubleday, Doran and Company; Babe Ruth and G. P. Putnam's Sons; Little, Brown and Company, publishers of Donn Byrne's *Destiny Bay;* A. S. Barnes and Company, publishers of *The Control of Football Injuries,* by Dr. Mal Stevens and Dr. W. M. Phelps; G. P. Putnam's Sons, publishers of *Kicking the American Football* by the late LeRoy N. Mills; Matt Mann and Prof. Charles C. Fries, who wrote *Swimming Fundamentals,* published by Prentice-Hall; and the *Atlantic Monthly.* I also found the University of Oklahoma library a splendid source.

HAROLD KEITH

CONTENTS

CHAPTER 1

BADMINTON

IN 1873, the Duke of Beaufort gave a house party at Badminton, his country estate in Gloucestershire, England. A severe storm forced the guests to remain indoors. Among them were some British Army officers home from India; they fell to discussing poona, a native Indian game centuries old. To illustrate the game, the officers took a champagne cork, stuck one end of it full of feathers, and began to bat it back and forth across the table with tennis rackets. Soon all the guests were enthusiastically playing and found the new sport a fascinating means of escaping the boredom of their confinement.

That was the birth of badminton, which took its name from the duke's country home.

The sport spread quickly in England, particularly among the upper classes. They enjoyed it not only for its exercise but also because of the comic spirit which was expressed in the twisting, darting, floating course of the shuttle and the amusing efforts of the players to hit it. The original poona rules called for a quick shove of the bird and depended upon placements, but in 1887 these were abandoned by the newly-formed Bath Badminton Club and the present game, which combines grace and smash and extreme activity, was introduced.

It became tremendously popular and circulated all over the British Isles. In 1899 the all-England badminton tournament at Westminster, which now corresponds to the famous Wimbledon world tennis tournament and draws almost as large an international entry, was started and today there are thousands of clubs in the British Isles.

Badminton came to Canada about 1890 where it flourished so amazingly that it now rivals ice hockey as the Dominion's most popular indoor sport. In 1922 the Canadian National championships were introduced and it is generally conceded that Canada's crack players today are as skillful as the best in England. When World War I ended in 1918 the game expanded all over the world. In 1948 the first Thomas Cup matches were held and badminton had become a truly international sport.

In America, the game had at first a slow growth. It was introduced here several years before the turn of the century and worked its way down from Canada through Boston and New York, but after a few seasons of mild popularity became almost completely forgotten for thirty-five years. In the late 1920's it suddenly burgeoned all over the United States, chiefly because of exhibition matches played in armories, gymnasia, on the stages of prominent theaters and in excellent moving picture shorts.

Today hundreds of thousands of Americans play the game
and in 1937 the American National championships were
begun. Although the English and Canadian game is unquestionably faster and more highly developed than the
American, because of its tremendous head start in those
countries, the United States, after 1937, enthusiastically
concentrated on badminton and began to advance toward
the Canadian superiority.

Unlike tennis, its parent sport, badminton is entirely
a volleying game in which the "ball," called a shuttle-
cock or bird, does not bounce but must be struck in the
air over a net five feet high. It is hit on its rounded end,
which usually comes flying foremost with the feathered
end following behind, like an arrow. The court is small,
only 20 x 44 feet for doubles and 17 x 44 for singles, but
the player is kept very busy covering it. Points may be
made on service alone, as in handball, and if a rally is
won by the receiver, he gains only the right to serve.
Games go to 11 points for ladies, 15 for men, with doubles
sometimes traveling to 21. Victory in tournament play
usually goes to the player who first wins two sets.

A badminton racket is delicate and fragile looking, as
though it had been built by some skillful fairy workman,
and yet it is a marvel of lightness and strength. It resembles slightly a tennis racket, for it is tightly strung with
gut that pings like a mandolin string. The head is much
smaller than that of a tennis racket, its shaft is slender as
a pipe stem and it weighs only about five ounces.

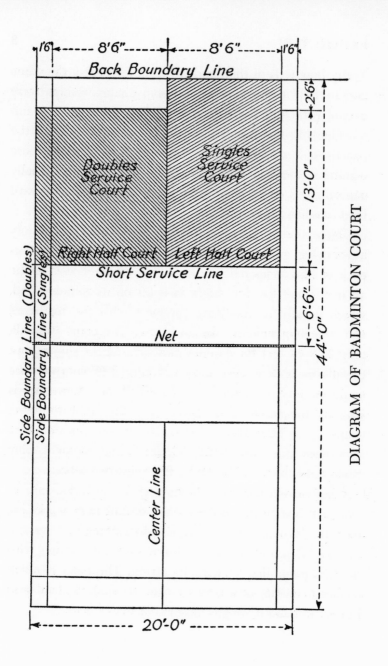

DIAGRAM OF BADMINTON COURT

The shuttle or bird is made of kid-covered cork about one inch in diameter. Into one end of it are studded and sewn fourteen to sixteen feathers approximately two and one-half inches long. These feathers come chiefly from the tails of Czechoslovakian geese. If the feathers are pointed the shuttle is fast; if they are rounded it is slow. The whole shuttle weighs only a fraction of an ounce; that is why it "acts up" when struck by a skillful player; it buzzes low across the net like an angry bee, zooms high like a sky rocket, or flits along like a butterfly. Plastic shuttles, which last longer, are sometimes used for instruction.

In England and Canada badminton is primarily an indoor game, for the season starts in October and continues six months. In America it is a popular summer outdoor game and a heavier bird is used to combat the breeze. Because it is so easy to learn and its court surface so small it makes a fine social or family game, and children and middle-aged women pick it up very readily. Another reason for its popularity is its inexpensiveness. A complete set of rackets, shuttlecocks, nets and posts may be bought very reasonably.

EQUIPMENT: It is best to buy a good, tightly-strung racket. With care it will last three years and can then be re-strung. Select one with a flat handle, for it is easier to grip. Buy a press, too, and always put your racket in it when not playing. Keep it in a room that is neither hot nor damp and stand it against a wall or lay it flat on a shelf instead of hanging it on a hook or nail.

Shuttles are easily damaged, often by beginners who carelessly bat them along the floor when relaying them to the server and thus injure the feathers. It is best to throw the shuttle over to the server or bat it to him cleanly. Keep the birds in a box where they will have some humidification; otherwise the feathers will break if they dry out.

The best poles are those with metal bars at the base that can be screwed to the floor, but poles with weighted bottoms will do. The spot for an indoor court should have at least four feet clearance on all sides and at least thirty feet overhead. The background on the ends should be dark, if possible, so the white bird may be easily seen against it, and all windows at the ends should be blocked out. Dark floors should have white lines painted on them and vice versa.

Tennis shoes and white clothing are suitable while playing, but a jacket or topcoat should be worn while the player is sitting on the sidelines awaiting his turn.

FOOTWORK AND BODY BALANCE: Play most shots, particularly all long ones, with the body quartering toward the net and the feet comfortably spread. The left foot will be nearer the net and advanced when you hit a forehander, the right when a backhander is attempted. Don't take a shot with the feet together if it can be helped. Transfer the weight of the body from the rear foot to the front at the moment of hitting the bird.

In moving backward to get a high lob driven over the

head, run with short steps, leaning back sharply and keeping the eye glued on the bird. Practice running backward rapidly, learning to control the feet so they will be placed correctly when you strike the shuttle.

Don't jump into the air when playing a smash.

Advance with short steps to meet the shuttle, striking it at almost full arm's reach from the body for both forehand and backhand. Don't hit with the elbow bent or power will be lost. Arthur Devlin, who was for six years the all-England champion, says that a player's reach is farther than he realizes, for it consists of the length of the racket, the arm and one stride, or about seven feet.

HOLDING THE RACKET: Grip it with the right hand as though shaking hands with it, and be careful to hold it at the bottom of the handle so that the base won't protrude and impede the wrist action. This is the accepted forehand grip. Hold it with the fingers. Don't let the butt slip too far back in the palm or your stroke may be locked.

When changing from forehand to backhand, use the opposite face of the bat for the backhand stroke and slip the thumb up the back of the handle.

Keep the grip loose and relaxed. This is done by grasping the bat with the fingers and not the whole hand. However, at the moment the racket hits the bird, tighten the fingers automatically. There is a jingle that will help you to remember this: "If the knuckles are white, the grip is too tight."

No two persons hold their bats exactly the same, but

the two methods described are the most practical for beginners.

WRIST FLEXIBILITY: As in golf and baseball, wrist snap is vitally important in badminton hitting. Arthur Devlin says the secret of all badminton hitting is learning to play with the wrist and not the whole arm, of bending the wrist back and snapping it forward as the bird is hit on every stroke. A player with good wrist action can hit hard with little effort and also mask the direction he intends to strike the shuttle.

Hitting an old shuttle against a wall is good practice. It sharpens the eye and exercises both forehand and backhand as well as teaching the importance of snapping the wrist on every shuttle which is hit. Try to hit each stroke squarely in the middle of the racket. And at all times keep the eye on the bird. This is most important in badminton for the shuttle darts and cork-screws like a green-winged teal trying to make a sudden landing in a marsh.

STROKE

SERVICE: The server in badminton is on the defense because he has to hit the bird up and clear a high net, instead of smashing it down overhanded over a low net as is done in tennis. Therefore it is well to learn and constantly practice many different types of serves and get them off deceptively.

First practice the two main serves: (1) the low short serve that just skims the net and falls inside the front

service line; this forces the foe to return the bird underhanded and gives the server the attack; and (2) the high
lob to within a few inches of the baseline in the backhand
corner of the receiver's court. Unless both are hit just right,
the opponent may smash the bird back for kills.

In serving, the player stands on his side of the middle
line four feet back of the front service line. This facilitates
flattening out the short service, causing it to start dropping sooner and thus making it harder for the foe to smash.
Don't face the net but turn slightly to the right with the
left foot and the left shoulder a little toward the net so
that body pivot can be added to the serves and both corners commanded. Bend forward slightly, bring the shuttle over the right foot and hold it by the feathers; then
drop it instead of throwing it. Take plenty of time. Look
at the opponent before serving. However, when in the act
of serving, look only at the shuttle and try to use the
same swing for both the short and long serves in order to
confuse the opponent.

Keep the head of the racket up and the wrist cocked
back. Always remember that the serve must be underhanded and that the shuttle must not be struck higher
than the server's waist at the moment of striking; also the
head of the racket must be lower than the server's hand.
Snap the wrist on all serves. This will not only give direction to the bird, but will permit the long serve with a
minimum of swing, and thus help to disguise it.

After each serve, and also after each stroke, court position should be recovered by retreating to a spot in the middle of the player's half of the court about two-thirds the way from the net to the baseline. He should be totally relaxed and alert for his opponent's return. Because it is easier to move forward than backward the player should go back almost two-thirds and not midway back on the court. Service alternates from right to left-hand courts and back again.

In receiving service, stand within five or six feet of the front service line, with the left foot slightly advanced. On a short service, step up and smash the bird for a kill if it is more than six inches above the net; otherwise try a high lob to the baseline or a drop-shot away from the server. On a high deep serve, the best return is a high lob to the foe's backhand, or a drop-shot to his forehand corner.

LOB OR CLEAR: This is badminton's outstanding defensive stroke. It has to be hit high and to within inches of the opponent's baseline or he will smash it back for a kill. The lob is usually employed when the opponent has the player on the run. If it is hit high and deeply enough, the hitter will have time to recover his important middle court position two-thirds the way from the net to the baseline and will tend to put the opponent on the defense.

In lobbing it is far better to overdrive the distant baseline than to hit short. A short lob is easy to kill, and so is a crosscourt lob that isn't hit high. The lob becomes an effective offensive stroke if the opponent has been drawn close to the net, in which case it should be pushed just high enough to clear the opponent's racket, as in tennis, instead of lofting it so he will have time to run back and get under it.

In receiving, the lob should be killed if it is short, or if it is hit sharply crosscourt. Sometimes a reply may be made with a drop-shot, lob or drive.

DROP-SHOT: A drop-shot is any stroke hit some distance away from the net in which the bird is struck either overhand or underhand so that it barely clears the top of the net and immediately falls short in the opponent's court. This makes him hit it upward if he reaches it at all. It is usually hit horizontally at half speed.

The purpose in hitting this most delicate badminton stroke is to impart a sharp downward angle to the bird. In the overhand forehand stroke, this is done by striking the bird as high as possible. Even more important, it should be hit far enough in front of the player so that his bat has already started its swing downward before it meets the shuttle. Place the feet as for other forehand strokes; then snap the wrist and follow through.

The player must be careful not to clear the net too high or his opponent may smash the bird back for a kill. Every drop-shot or net shot, no matter how lightly hit, should be definitely stroked. By stroking it, the player avoids having it rebound from his racket.

In playing net shots hit by the opponent, it is well to

take them while the bird is close to the top of the net. However, if the player strikes the net with his bat, he loses the point. If the bird just skims the net and can't be reached in time to play it high, it is best to let it fall below the bottom of the net before the return, which should be a high lob hit as far back as possible, varied with an angled drop-shot, is sent back. If it carries several feet from the net, the player can lob, drive or play another drop.

DRIVE: This is a hard-hit horizontal shot in which the shuttle is kept as low as possible. It isn't a fundamental stroke (as in tennis), but rather a placement stroke. It is usually hit in a straight line to an open spot in the court, or straight at the opponent. When hitting a drive from the back of the court, it is important to place the feet correctly; the left foot should be not only well in advance of the right but pointing almost at the right sideline so that the player's back is to the net. The arm should be as far away from the body as possible, to enable the player to employ a full wrist-snap, body pivot and follow-through. Always strike the bird in front of you. This stroke calls for power and is tiring unless the player uses his feet and wrists properly.

SMASH: The offensive stroke most apt to win points outright is the terrifically hit smash, which is almost impossible to return when hit from the forward half of the court. Bend the knees a little, hold the weight on the right foot, and use a long slow preliminary swing. Take the bird high in the air a little in front of you at the extreme limit of your reach and hit it down. Do not hit this stroke behind you or when you are moving backwards. You must be behind the shuttle when you hit it. Follow through so that the racket is pointing at the ground after the bird is hit. Don't smash blindly but use your wrist to turn the smash down the center, or to the sideline.

Do not give your opponent a weak stroke, and he will have little to smash. However, once the smash is hit at you, you may be able to lob it to the baseline or reply with a drop-shot.

SINGLES

Although the singles court is only seventeen feet wide, you will have to keep moving to cover it. Consequently it is necessary to develop your backhand game together with your forehand so you can take shots on either wing. Singles are far more strenuous than doubles.

First, perfect a high long serve to the opponent's baseline, preferably to his backhand corner. This stroke will be too deep for him to smash effectively, will tax his strength to lob, and will probably be too deep for him to combat with an accurate drop-shot. Use these deep, high serves frequently in singles; vary them occasionally with shorter ones to surprise your foe and pull him to the net. Always bear in mind that in singles you can serve the full twenty-two feet to the baseline, but in doubles the back service line goes back only nineteen and one-half feet.

Always try to keep the attack. Make your opponent do the running, if possible.

Learn to hit at those parts of the court which are most difficult to cover: deep down the sideline or close to the net. Hit straight at your opponent if he is playing close to you.

Return to your defensive spot on the center line, two-thirds the distance from net to baseline, after each stroke, service or otherwise, to await your foe's reply. Even when you think you have hit a winning stroke, always go back and be ready for a possible miraculous recovery by your opponent.

It is obvious that drop-shots should be played when your opponent is too deep. Clear him with lobs when he is up too close. However, do not use too many net shots in singles, for you must cover both net and baseline.

During a game, breathe through both mouth and nose, stay relaxed and conserve strength. After a hard rally don't hurry to the next service. Save yourself for the climaxes. After you hit a stroke, hold your bat loosely in your right hand, and let the left hand support the neck. Concentrate upon form and strategy rather than winning and you will be a far better player in the long run. Learn to think during action.

DOUBLES

There are several ways of playing doubles: the *front and back* method in which the weaker player stays near the net and the stronger in backcourt, the *side by side* method in which each player takes care of his own half of the court, and the *revolving method.*

In the front and back method, the front player, ranging in the front third of the court, handles all shots falling over the net. He straddles the middle line and remains just back of the short service line so that he can get a better view of the speeding shuttle before it can be driven past him. His partner covers the back two-thirds, taking the deep hard shots. His defensive position, to which he should return after all shots, is on the middle line, two and one-half feet from the baseline.

In the revolving defense, the receiver in the right-hand court stands about halfway between baseline and net, four feet to the right of the middle line. He is responsible for all shots close to the net except those that drop near the left net post. He must also take any shot hit to his deep forehand corner. The receiver in the left-hand court stands within three feet of the left sideline, and about four feet farther back in the court than his partner. He is responsible for all shots hit deeply to the baseline except those to the deep forehand corner, and he must also be ready to go up for the short ones that fall near the left net post. The two receivers cover each other. For example, when the right-hand receiver is pulled up to the net, his partner quickly occupies his vacated position and the right-hand receiver, after hitting his net shot, hurries back to the left-hand receiver's original position. The same thing results when the left-hand receiver advances or retreats to answer a shot in his zone; his partner covers him.

Good teamwork is necessary in any style. For example, if one player has a particularly good stroke, e.g. a smash, his partner should create openings for it by making drop-shots at the net. Thus the opponents must hit up to the smasher.

Partners who play side by side should always be ready to come to each other's rescue. For instance, if a player smashes from fairly close to the net or hits a short service, he should follow it up for net play and his partner should have the court sense to cover the space behind him. If a player smashes from a deep position, his partner should be moving forward with the stroke to handle a possible net shot by the opponents.

The best doubles service from the right-hand court is hit from a position five or six feet back of the service line, standing almost on the right sideline. The server should shoot a quick straight horizontal stroke that skims the net and drops below the receiver's shoulder, deep to the receiver's backhand corner. This service may be alternated with a short service to the receiver's front forehand corner, thus keeping him in position. The best doubles service from the left-hand court is hit from the middle of the left service court, standing about six feet back of the service line. From this position, the server should direct the bird at varying depth along the opponent's backhand, shooting each time to within inches of the right sideline.

Avoid using the lob in doubles save as a defensive stroke. Use smashes and drops to force your opponents to hit the shuttle up and thus surrender the attack. On all shots down the middle, the player in the left court should be responsible since he can play them off his forehand.

Know and observe the "wood shot" rule. It is a fault if the *base* of the shuttle is hit by the wooden frame around the head of the racket. It is also a fault if the shuttle is caught and slung instead of being distinctly hit.

CHAPTER 2

BASEBALL

SEVERAL years ago Ty Cobb, the veteran manager of the Detroit American League baseball team, put on his gray uniform and walked onto the field at Yankee Stadium, New York City, an hour before a scheduled game between Detroit and New York. He was alert, aggressive, and keen-eyed, nearing forty years of age. He had to walk past the New York dugout where the World's Champion Yankees were sitting.

"Howdy, gentlemen," said Cobb.

"Howdy yourself," retorted the Yankees.

Then Urban Shocker, Yankee pitcher, decided to have a little fun.

"Isn't it time to take off that uniform, old man, and quit kidding the public?" he razzed. Cobb laughed tolerantly at this sally and went to the plate for hitting practice.

"Hit one into left field," one of the Yankees shouted, and thereupon innocently precipitated an exhibition of baseball place-hitting that old-timers still talk about.

"All right!" said Cobb. He promptly faced the hitting-

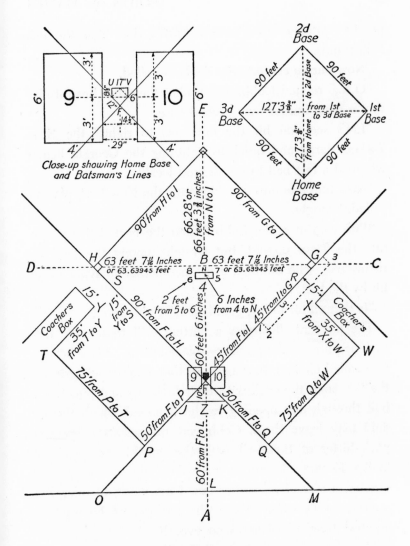

Close-up showing Home Base
and Batsman's Lines

DIAGRAM OF
BASEBALL DIAMOND

practice pitcher and drove a terrific liner into the left field stands.

"Now one to center!" the Yankees yelled.

"O.K.," replied Cobb, and timing the pitch beautifully, shot a grass-burner over second base.

"Let's see you hit the next one to right!" the New Yorkers dared and quick as lightning the Georgia Peach whipped a fast ball to the desired locality.

"Now foul one into your dugout," the New York players called, jokingly.

With a grim smile, Cobb fouled the next delivery, not into the Tiger dugout, but straight among the Yankees themselves, who tumbled over one another to avoid being hit by the ball.

"Is that all for today, gentlemen?" Cobb asked.

The incident illustrates a batting skill that every boy can acquire with practice—place-hitting. Place-hitters, also called choke hitters because they choke their grip on the bat, snap the stick with their forearms and punch the ball through any opening in the diamond which the infield may leave them. Cobb was probably the greatest place-hitter of them all with the possible exception of Willie Keeler, diminutive marvel of the old Baltimore Orioles, a star of an earlier era. I am going to refer frequently to Ty Cobb in this chapter because he was the greatest baseball player who ever lived.

Place-hitting, for reasons that will be explained later, is not seen very much any more. Swing hitting is the common practice nowadays. Swing hitters grasp the bat on the extreme end of the handle and try to knock the ball over the fence. They usually hit to just one field. Included in this class were such well-known professional swatsmen as Dan Brouthers, Joe Jackson, Lou Gehrig and the incomparable Babe Ruth. And Ted Williams of a later dynasty.

A comparison of Cobb's and Babe Ruth's batting forms is interesting since these two players, both left-handed hitters, were probably the outstanding exponents of the two batting vogues. Cobb used a choke grip with hands apart so that he could better control the bat. If he kept his hands apart on the handle, he could hit to left or center. By sliding his hands together as he swung, he could hit to right field. Of course he sacrificed power, but hits were what he wanted.

Ruth's style was different. Ruth took a terrific swipe at the ball, using a golfing swing, loose and easy with a slight upward motion. Ruth stood with his feet fairly close together in the back of the batting box, and took a long stride forward as he swung. He hit with his entire body coming around on the swing, which gave him tremendous follow-through. Most of his home runs were towering flies that simply carried out of the park, but they were the longest flies any man has hit before or since.

And yet Ruth declared that Cobb's batting stance was soundest. "I'm paid to hit home runs," the big walloper of the Yankees declared in his book on baseball. "In a way, that's a handicap. I've got to hit from my heels with

all the power in my body, which isn't good batting style.
And the greatest tribute I can pay Ty Cobb is this: If I
wasn't expected to drive the ball out of the lot every time
I came up to the plate, I'd change my batting form to-
morrow. I'd copy Cobb's style in every single thing he
does."

Let us examine the art of batting:

OFFENSIVE BASEBALL

HOW TO BAT: Given good eyes and average
physical strength, any boy can learn to bat. First find a
bat you can grip and swing properly. Always choose ash
or hickory and look for a smooth even grain. Ash is probably better because it is lighter, but both are good, tough,
springy baseball woods. John McGraw, former manager of
the New York Giants, always maintained that most boys,
and also many professional players, use bats too heavy and
too long for them. "A light bat, used with intelligence
and accuracy, will do more damage against a good pitcher
than a heavy bat," McGraw said. He also advised boys to
select bats with small handles suited to their grip.

Position at the plate is next in importance. The batsman should stand, comfortably relaxed, a little nearer the
rear of the box than the front; his front foot (the one
nearest the pitcher) should be closer to the inside line of
the batsman's box than the rear foot. The feet should be
a foot or so apart. He should face the pitcher and not the
plate so he can gauge the pitcher's speed better and deter-

mine what kind of curve he throws. The bat is held loosely and there must be no tightening of the muscles before the ball is hit. The shoulders and hips should be level both before and during the swing. Very little back swing should be used. Hold the bat back in position to swing as soon as the pitcher prepares to throw. Only when the pitcher releases the ball should the bat be gripped firmly.

As the ball comes through from the pitching mound, the batter, watching it keenly, takes a short easy stride forward with his front foot (the rear foot is never moved), swings the bat level. Hitting off the rear foot, he meets the ball and follows through, shifting his weight from the rear to the forward foot. He keeps the hands away from the body while swinging. He doesn't stop his bat when it hits the ball, but brings it on around, completing the arc. When the swing is entirely completed, the batsman should be balancing on the toe of his rear foot.

Don't be a one-lane strider. Always hit the ball where it is pitched unless a place-hitting situation is on. The stride of the front foot varies with the pitch. If the pitcher throws an inside ball, one that passes close to the hitter's body over the inside corner of the plate, the hitter, if he is right-handed, should step slightly to the left with his front foot and try to drive the ball into left field. If the hitter is swinging at a ball over the heart of the plate, he should stride straight forward with his front foot. This type of hit usually goes to center. If the hitter swings at an outside ball, he strides in a right oblique direction, shooting for right field. The purpose is to sense where the pitch will cut the plate and learn automatically to step into it correctly.

Always be set for a fast ball. Then you are ready to hit anything the pitcher throws.

Confidence is necessary to good batting. This does not mean blind, wishful confidence. The batter should step to the plate with a cool eager assurance, born of long practice against all kinds of pitching, that he can hit any pitcher who ever lived. If a batter goes to the plate feeling that he won't hit the ball, his chance for doing so is very slight. If he is weak against curve ball pitching, he should practice batting curves until he has overcome this weakness. Then his confidence in himself will be genuine and his batting will improve.

BATTING FAULTS: Crouching with the knees bent, striking at bad balls, dropping one shoulder in the swing of the bat, taking too long a stride forward, and pulling away from a curve ball are common faults.

This latter fault, sometimes called "stepping in the bucket," can be cured in several different ways. The batter may draw a line in the dirt from the back of the heel of the front foot parallel to the plate and concentrate on not stepping over that line. Or a box or two-by-four may be placed along this parallel to force the batter to keep his front foot within the striding lane. Sometimes a player can break himself by spreading his feet farther apart as he takes his stance at the plate, or by deliberately allowing two or three pitches to hit him, thus erasing the fear of being struck by a pitched ball.

Any boy who wants to play baseball should take good care of his eyes. Eyes are extremely important to batters. Ty Cobb always refused to try to read on a train because the shaking motion of the cars strained his vision, and he was careful, even when reading in his hotel, that the light was adjusted correctly. Rogers Hornsby, the right-handed slugger of the St. Louis Nationals, was even more extreme. Hornsby believed that watching motion pictures was bad for his eyes and since baseball was his business and he needed his eyes for hitting, he didn't go to the movies. William J. Clarke, former Princeton baseball coach, maintained that all kinds of artificial lights hurt the eyes and advised his players to do their studying in the daytime or in the early part of the night, if possible. Boys afflicted with near-sightedness or far-sightedness have trouble hitting but sometimes can solve their difficulty by taking their batting position a step nearer the pitcher, or a step farther back.

PLACE-HITTING: Boys can learn to hit the ball to a certain field just as if they were professional players. The idea is simply to shift the feet properly (already discussed) and to change the timing of the swing.

For example, if a right-handed batter wants to pull a hit into left field, he shifts his front foot slightly to the left and gets out ahead of the ball, hitting it approximately a foot in front of the plate. If he wants to drive a ball to center, he strides straight ahead with his front foot and makes his bat meet the ball exactly as it crosses the plate. If he wishes to hit to right, he strides a bit to the right with his front foot and hits late, letting the ball get still farther across the plate.

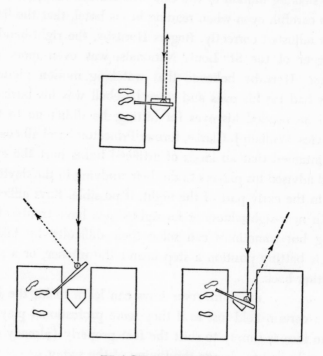

PLACE-HITTING
(illustrating position of front foot and angle of bat)

1. When hitting to center, stride straight ahead and meet ball directly over plate. 2. When hitting to left, stride toward third base and meet ball in front of plate. 3. When hitting to right, stride toward first base and meet ball slightly behind plate. NOTE: Don't move the back foot. Pivot off it.

With the bases empty, hit toward third base where the throw is longer and the baseman, playing closer, can't cover so much ground. With a runner on first, try to hit to right field so the throw will be longer if the runner tries to go from first to third. Also your hit to right will have a better chance to go through on this situation since the first baseman must leave a gap while hugging the bag to hold the runner. Perhaps the safest place of all to hit is through the pitcher, who is stationed too close to the hitter to field hard-hit balls properly, and who has no infield coverage behind him.

HIT-AND-RUN PLAY: As your place-hitting skill improves, you can shoot for the hole left by the shortstop or second baseman as they cover second base on the hit-and-run play. The hit-and-run is a clever offensive stratagem used to advance the base-runner. It is built around place-hitting. For example, suppose there is a runner on first. The hit-and-run signal is flashed, usually by the hitter, who may have gotten it originally from the manager or coach. As the pitcher starts his motion, the runner on first breaks to second and the hitter tries to drive the ball through the gap left by the enemy second baseman or shortstop, whichever leaves his position open to take the throw at second base from the catcher. The hitting team usually learns early in the game which infielder covers second base on a threatened steal. The idea is for the base runner to secure such a long start and be running so fast that he can advance to third base on any kind of a hit, or at least reach second safely and avoid a double play, even if the batter is thrown out. Usually the batter waits for a 2–0 (two balls and no strikes), a 2–1 or a 2–0 situation when the pitcher has to put the next ball over to keep from issuing or setting up a base on balls, before signaling for the hit-and-run. Obviously the batter has a much better chance to hit this type of ball. Failure to hit the ball dooms the runner. Or if the batter slashes a line drive to an infielder, a double play results. If the ball is hit high into the air, the runner has time to get back to the bag. A good place-hitter is invaluable as a hit-and-run man. Willie Keeler, famous little outfielder of the Baltimore Orioles and top batsman of the nation from 1894 through 1905, immortalized this play. "Hit 'em where they ain't" was his motto. Incidentally Keeler used the smallest bat in the history of baseball, thirty inches long (the rules permit a forty-two inch bat) and only two and one-half inches in diameter at the barrel end. Remember this the next time you buy a bat.

HISTORY OF BASEBALL

Baseball is older than the American nation itself. There are tales about Abner Doubleday's "devising" the game at Cooperstown, New York, in 1839. But long before General George Washington struck out Lord Cornwallis at Yorktown, sports-hungry American colonists living along the eastern seaboard were playing it. Robert W. Henderson, a sportsman who is also an executive officer of the

New York Public Library, has produced unimpeachable evidence to show that the game is closely related to the old West England sport of rounders, and that there was a baseball game in England as early as 1744.

Henderson's exploding of the Doubleday myth has been thorough and his evidence reliable and voluminous. For instance, George Ewing, an American soldier in the Revolution, wrote in his journal that at Valley Forge on April 7, 1778, he "exercised in the afternoon in the intervals played at base." The students of Princeton University were prohibited in 1787 from playing "with balls and sticks in the back commons of the college." When Colonel James Lee in 1846 was made an honorary member of the old Knickerbocker Baseball Club, he claimed that he had played baseball as a boy. This would have been about 1800. So popular was "ball-playing" in the streets of Worcester, Massachusetts, in 1816 that the city council forbade it by ordinance. Thurlow Weed, in his autobiography, speaks of a "base-ball club, numbering nearly fifty members," which was organized about the year 1825. Dr. Oliver Wendell Holmes, in his later years, said he had played baseball at Harvard, and he was graduated in 1829.

The game quickly worked its way over the Allegheny Mountains and across the western prairies until soon it obtained a permanent footing in every town and village in the land. It achieved its most lasting popularity before radio and paved roads destroyed the isolation of the

American small town. In those days baseball was the most popular game at recess at the little frame country school and also the two-story brick town school. It also furnished a clean and exciting Sunday afternoon recreation for hundreds of active young men who had no other outlet for muscular energy, and also for thousands of spectators who proudly followed their nines to the small plank grandstands at the edge of the village or in the vacant lots of the cities, and, while supporting them zealously and vociferously, acquired for themselves health and pleasure and an escape from the routine boredom of their own lives that was an invaluable tonic as they faced their jobs the following Monday morning.

Now its rootage and growth are even more vast. The game has a terrific following among boys of grade school age. Hundreds of thousands of them are playing in Little Leagues all over the country in summer. High school baseball is flourishing in Oklahoma, Arizona, California and the Carolinas. The biggest high school tournament in the nation is that held one week end each April at the University of Oklahoma where games are played simultaneously on 14 diamonds with approximately 100 teams entered. Jack Baer, Oklahoma baseball coach, has skillfully organized this tournament, using his varsity and freshman squads as umpires. Every major league club in both the National and American leagues sends scouts to watch the 1,500 schoolboy players in the three-day meet.

Other nations also have adopted baseball. The Japanese

player is learning fast. Already he is a skillful fielder and
an alert base runner. American teams touring Japan re-
port that nearly everybody there is playing baseball. Japanese youngsters are on their way to the baseball grounds
early in the morning and play all day. A game was played
in the rain as early as 1934 at which eleven thousand
spectators knelt in the outfield in water up to their hips.
Twenty thousand saw this game and some were at the
gates as early as five o'clock in the morning.

There have been three general trends in the history of
American baseball. First came an era of free hitting and
high scoring that is unprecedented in the history of the
sport. This was a baseball period of which modern enthu-
siasts know little or nothing, yet it was a very flourishing
time for baseball, for the fans of the '60s and '70s were
just as doting of their mustached heroes as today's spectators are of the modern smooth-chinned ones. Back in
1866, a few months after Lee surrendered to Grant, a
crowd of thirty thousand jammed a park in Philadelphia
to see a game between the old Athletics and the Brooklyn
Atlantics that had to be postponed after one inning because there was not enough room for the players. As early
as 1871 teams began to travel in railroad sleeping cars; in
1874 two American teams made an enthusiastic tour of
the British Isles and in 1888 further introduced the game
to foreign nations with a trip around the world. The
sharp free hitting of these early days would have put
modern slugging to shame. For instance, in 1868 the Niag-

ara Club of Buffalo, New York, established the record
score of all time, thumping the Columbias of the same
city 209 to 10 and scoring 58 runs in the eighth inning
alone. In 1867 George Wright, great shortstop of the Cin-
cinnati Red Stockings, hit seven home runs in a single
game and two years later batted .518 over the season's
span. The fact that pitchers then were required to throw
a straight ball under-handed, and that few parks had
fences to stop the rolling ball contributed to the heavy
cannonading.

However, as the game grew older and the overhand delivery and the curve came in and were perfected, scores
declined sharply and the Golden Age of Pitching was
ushered in. From approximately 1900 until 1919 most
games were little else but low-score pitching battles with
place-hitting, base-stealing and such beautiful machinations of team strategy as the hit-and-run, sacrifice, squeeze
and double steal being emphasized to secure the run or
two that was usually adequate for victory. Records of the
professional leagues prove this unquestionably. During
this era were set most of the great pitching feats still standing today. For example, in 1913, Christy Mathewson of the
New York Giants hurled sixty-eight consecutive innings
without giving a base on balls; in 1908 Ed Reulbach of
the Chicago Nationals pitched a double-header shutout
against Brooklyn the same day; in 1916 Ferdinand Schupp
of the New York Giants allowed only 0.90 earned runs
per game over the season's span and in 1916 Grover

Cleveland Alexander of the mediocre Philadelphia Club of the National League pitched sixteen shutout games. Base-stealing also reached its zenith during this period. In 1915 Ty Cobb of the Detroit Tigers set the present modern record of ninety-six stolen bags. In 1912 the American League established an all-time record by stealing 1,810 bases. (Today only one-third that number are stolen by the eight American League clubs in one season.) It was also a time of low-hitting marks; the National League reached its all-time low with a league-hitting percentage of only .218 in 1907 (compared to .292 in 1922) and the American League crashed only 142 home runs in 1916. (Each league annually has nearly three times that many home runs today.)

Then came the third or modern era, making a partial return to the old heavy-hitting free-scoring mode of the 1865–1900 period. Three principal factors brought it about. In 1920 the spit ball and other so-called "freak" deliveries were prohibited, for they gave pitchers an unnatural hop on the ball by discoloring, marring, roughing or moistening it. Introduction of the livelier ball about this time added to this new advantage for the batter.

Also it was during this time that Babe Ruth, big left-handed pitcher of the Boston Red Sox whom the New York Yankees bought and transformed into an outfielder, began to break all home run records. Soon the other players in both leagues were trying to copy Ruth and hit the ball over the fence, too. And that is the fashion today.

However, none of the old pitching masters equaled the feat of Don Larsen, New York Yankee right-hander, who in the fifth game of the 1956 World Series pitched a perfect no-hit, no-run game against the Brooklyn Dodgers, champions of the National League, cutting down 27 consecutive batsmen and permitting none to reach first base. Larsen pitched without a windup. He threw three balls to only one batter, Peewee Reese in the first inning. He mowed down such formidable Brooklyn hitters as Duke Snider, Jackie Robinson, Gil Hodges, Carl Furillo, and Roy Campanella. It was the first no-hitter in 307 World Series games dating back to the first one in 1903. And the ball Larsen threw was far livelier than the one the old-time aces pegged. Millions saw the dramatic feat on television and heard it on the radio.

Baseball came of age in the late 1940's when Branch Rickey of Brooklyn brought Jackie Robinson, a fine Negro player, into the National League. A flood of great Negro players followed Robinson through the breach Rickey cut in the dam of segregation. Another development was the widening of major league geography. Milwaukee, Los Angeles, and San Francisco replaced Boston, Brooklyn, and New York in the National League. Kansas City purchased the Philadelphia franchise and Baltimore acquired that of St. Louis in the American. The airliner makes today's transcontinental-team travel practical.

THE BUNT: Every baseball player should learn to bunt. A hitter who can't bunt is like a long-driving golfer who can't putt. His offensive equipment is not well-rounded and he cannot be of much value to his team. That is why players, in batting drills, practice bunting the ball as well as driving it out.

There are two purposes in bunting. First, the bunt may be used as a sacrifice to advance a base runner even at the cost of sacrificing the batter. Or it may be used to upset the infield and put the bunter on first base. When sacrificing, if the base runner is to be advanced from second to third base, the bunter should dump the ball down to the third baseman, forcing him to handle it and leave the sack open to the base runner. However if the runner is to be moved from first to second, the bunt should be softer and only about halfway down to third base so the pitcher will have to field it, turn around and throw.

A *drag* bunt is a ball pushed on the ground toward first base just out of the pitcher's reach and slow enough to keep the second baseman from handling it. About the only way to stop it on a fast man is for the first baseman to dash in and handle the ball while the second baseman covers the bag. Whitey Witt, a teammate of Babe Ruth on the New York team, beat out thirty-two bunts for hits one season and when sports writers questioned him about it, he explained it as follows: "I'm conservative. I believe in saving distance. Those thirty-two bunts, laid end to end, would just about equal one of the Babe's shortest home runs. Yet he got only four bases on the distance and I got thirty-two. Science pays off, boys, science pays off."

The execution of the drag bunt for a left-handed batter is as follows: After the pitcher starts winding up, the batter moves his rear foot up behind his front and as he bunts the ball, steps right obliquely with his front foot. The method for right-handed hitters is as follows: After the pitcher starts winding up, step back with the right foot, slide the right hand up on the bat and with the same motion lay the bat on top of the ball. Right-handed batters will find it almost impossible to drag-bunt inside balls. The batsman should avoid bunting straight toward the pitching mound. A right-handed batter should bunt outside balls down the first-base line and inside balls down the third-base line. Left-handed batters should bunt outside balls to the third baseman and inside balls down the first-base line.

SACRIFICE BUNT: Mechanically, the bunt is not difficult but requires practice. For example, in the sacrifice bunt, the bunter must always hide from the enemy team his intention to bunt. He does this by assuming his natural batting position until the ball is pitched. Then, watching the ball keenly, he suddenly steps back with his front foot until his body is facing the pitcher. At the same time he slides his top hand halfway up on the bat, using it as a fulcrum; he utilizes the lower hand to guide the bat, which he holds on a level plane as far out in front of him as he can. Above all, he grasps the bat loosely, so that the ball won't be bunted too hard, and tries to meet the ball on its upper side to avoid popping it into the air. He does not try to run before the ball is bunted. A good bunter picks out only strikes to bunt, unless, of course, a squeeze play is on. In this case the batter must try to bunt a previously agreed-upon pitch, no matter where it comes.

A good sacrifice bunter is an outstanding team player and is highly valued by his coach, captain and team-mates. He is like the expert blocker in football or the passer in basketball—he does not get much public adulation but he is the key man on the play. In baseball, the player who successfully executes the sacrifice bunt is never charged with a time at bat and is given credit for a sacrifice. Eddie Collins, who started playing second base for Philadelphia back in 1908, was the greatest sacrifice hitter in the history of baseball with 509 to his credit. No other player has ever made more than 392.

SQUEEZE BUNT: One of baseball's most daring and beautiful plays, the squeeze, is built around the sacrifice bunt. The squeeze is ordinarily used only when third base is occupied and one run is needed to tie or win. When the squeeze is on, the runner on third dashes for home when the pitcher's arm goes down, getting a tremendous start on the defense. Ordinarily the catcher would have time to glove the pitch and tag the runner out by ten or fifteen feet. This is where the batter's work is useful. He knows in advance on what pitch the base runner is coming down and how fatal it would be to let that pitch go through to the catcher. So he lays down a slow teasing bunt, and while the enemy infield is falling over itself trying to handle it, the runner scores standing up. Everything depends upon the bunter. The play cannot miss if the batsman bunts the ball properly. The infield does not have time to reach the ball, handle it and catch the runner at home. However, the play is dangerous; therein lies the thrill. If the batsman misses the ball, the runner is doomed. If the batsman pops the ball into the air while trying to bunt, an easy double play results. If the batsman bunts the ball too closely to the plate, the catcher may have time to pounce upon it, dive back and tag the runner. If the batsman bunts straight toward the pitcher, the latter may have time to throw the base-runner out at the plate. Any of these four possibilities is fatal, because the runner cannot turn back.

The squeeze flourished as an offensive weapon during the second, or 1900–1919, period of big-league baseball when the scores were low and a single run loomed big. But today scores are higher and the squeeze has largely gone out. Bunting is much poorer than it used to be.

Jap Haskell, former Oklahoma coach, used the squeeze with telling effect at any point of the game. He argued that a run is a run no matter when it is scored. Even when his Oklahoma teams were safely ahead and in the midst of a hot hitting spree, Haskell frequently ordered the squeeze to cash sure runs from third and to demoralize the enemy infield. Nearly all his players were good bunters, thanks to constant practice. Babe Ruth says college boys are quicker and more willing to learn "inside" baseball than the average non-college man.

STEALING BASES: Base-stealing remains the most daring and exciting play in baseball, in spite of the fact that big-league players today pilfer only one-third as many cushions as the skilled base thieves of twenty and thirty years ago. In professional baseball, just as in the field of crime, the percentage is all against the thief. The smart pitcher knows how to hold the runner near the first-base bag, the average catcher can whirl and without yanking off his mask, bullet the ball ankle high to second base several feet ahead of the sprinting runner. The average second baseman or shortstop knows instinctively how to catch the ball and, while waiting alertly at the bag, dab it on the runner as the latter reaches for it with his fingers or his spiked feet. But occasionally the bold runner gets through safely.

Surprising as it may seem, speed on the paths is not nearly so important in stealing bases as knowing when to start and clever sliding. Ty Cobb, the champion base burglar of all time, was a keen student of the motions of enemy pitchers. He knew the tricks enemy infielders had of covering the bag and tagging the runner, and this knowledge alone was worth to Cobb fifteen to twenty stolen bases a season. "I generally watch the baseman's eyes to make up my mind how to come into the bag,"

Cobb revealed, "and pull my body away from where he is going to catch the ball."

There are scores of tricks used in base-stealing. One the most ingenious was employed by Eddie Collins of Philadelphia, who, upon hitting a two-bagger, would over-run second base a few feet and slow up as if to stop. Then when the outfielder raised his arm to lob the ball to the second baseman, Collins would suddenly streak toward third. By the time the mentally befuddled outfielder could pull his arm back again and change the direction of his throw, Collins would be sliding into third. Cobb himself had a trick, when sacrificed to second, of whirling on to third; so cleverly did he catch the foe first-basemen off their guard that he worked this play of going from first to third on a bunt nineteen out of twenty-one times in one season.

But in spite of Cobb's brilliance, he was once very nearly trapped on this play by Hal Chase, one of the foxiest first basemen of all time. Chase was a left-hander who played with the New York American leaguers. The incident is valuable because of the keen baseball strategy involved. One day when New York and Detroit were playing, Chase fell victim to Cobb's trick of going from first to third on a bunt. Chagrined, the New York first baseman resolved to trap Cobb next time he tried it. In the New York dugout afterwards Chase told Jimmy Austin, his third baseman, to stick to the bag if Cobb reached first safely again. "When the bunt comes to me, I'll play the ball to third without paying any attention to the bunter going to first,"

Chase said. Next day when Cobb went to first on a walk, the New York players put on the play Chase suggested. The pitcher obligingly threw the ball low and Sam Crawford, the Detroit player who followed Cobb, bunted the ball to Chase. True to expectations, Cobb rounded second and broke for third. Disregarding Crawford, Chase lined a perfect throw to Austin and the New York third baseman whirled to tag Cobb. But Cobb wasn't there. He was standing on second and Crawford was standing on first. Both wore wide grins. Later Chase asked Cobb why he had turned back to second base and Cobb explained: Unable to find any ice water in the cooler in the Detroit dugout the previous afternoon, Cobb had walked over to the New York dugout for a drink and while there accidentally overheard Chase and Austin plotting to stop him. Naturally Cobb organized a counterplot among the Detroit players. But Chase's plan was sound and he perfected the check play so well that thereafter Cobb abandoned attempting an extra base on the days Chase played against him.

Cobb was a terror on the base paths. There was no predicting what he might try. He would score from second on a dinky sacrifice or flit from first to home on a single. Wally Schang, Philadelphia catcher, thought he had the right system for stopping him, and perhaps he did. One afternoon before a game with Detroit when Manager Connie Mack was holding a meeting of the Philadelphia players in their clubhouse, he asked Schang, then a youngster: "Now, Wally, suppose the Tigers are one run behind, Cobb is on second and you know he is going to steal.

What would you do?" For a moment Schang scratched his head. Then came his answer: "I'd fake a throw to third, then hold the ball and tag him as he slid across the plate." Not bad strategy!

DEFENSIVE BASEBALL

OUTFIELD: An outfielder should have his mind made up before each ball is pitched to what base he will throw if a hit ball comes to his field. When a ball is hit over his head, he should turn around and run to the place where the ball is dropping rather than try to back up to it. He should catch fly balls above the eye level with the backs of his hands toward his face. Unless he is close to the baseman, he should throw to a base overhand, making the ball take one hop.

An outfielder should watch his opponents in batting practices and try to discover whether they are long or short hitters; then he can play up or back for them in the game. He studies the wind, too, playing closer to the infield if the breeze is behind him, or deep if it blows toward him. He never forgets that a fly ball will curve in a cross wind and that most balls hit to either left or right fields usually curve toward the foul line. Outfielders should back up all bases on all throws made by infielders. They soon learn to back up the base nearest them.

INFIELD: An infielder must know in advance what he will do if the ball is hit to him. On ground balls, he should catch the ball with the hands in front of him, be careful not to get his feet crossed. He should keep his eye on the ball until it lodges in his glove, keep his glove close to the ground on balls that hug the grass, and charge the ball if possible so as to field it on a hop. To become an infielder, practice throwing the ball from the position you field it, with an underhand or sidearm throw if caught below the knees. In tagging a runner, keep your feet on the opposite side of the bag the runner is sliding into to avoid getting spiked. Wait for the runner to come to the bag; don't go out after him. Tag him, if possible, with the ball held in both the glove and the bare hand to insure holding on to the ball. Let the outfielder handle all short flies he can reach, because it is easier to catch a ball when going toward it.

PITCHER: Pitching is about sixty per cent of baseball defense. There is more to pitching than merely throwing to the batsman. The pitcher should wait for the first baseman to reach the bag before he throws to him after fielding a ground ball. Always throw the ball to a baseman, never toss it to him. Throw slow hit balls to first base only. On a high pop fly, step aside and let an infielder handle it, if possible. Back up the third baseman when the batter singles with a runner on first, or hits a high fly with a runner on second. Back up the catcher on an outfield fly with a runner on third.

Pitchers should hold a curve ball in the same manner as they hold a fast one, and keep the ball covered by the glove until it is delivered. They bring the gloved hand straight up in front of the face, when winding up. They study the pitching rules carefully to prevent balks, and they don't wind up with runners on first base, or on second base, or on both first and third base. They conserve energy by not walking toward the catcher after each pitch. They don't pitch slow balls with a runner on first or he will be halfway down to second before the ball gets to the catcher. The first pitch, whether curved or not, should be a strike so that the pitcher can work on the batter's weakness. If the hitter pulls away from a curve, he gives him a low outside ball. Some particular part of the catcher's body or uniform is used for a target, rather than his glove.

Control is all-important. To develop it, the player practices pitching high and low first, and later inside and outside. If, on a bunt situation, the batter assumes a bunting stance while the pitcher is winding up, thus tipping him off, he breaks up the play by throwing high and inside. This type of pitch is most difficult to bunt.

Even though a pitcher doesn't yield any bases on balls, he may still be wild. If he gives the batter three balls, he has to put the next one over and that is the ball a clever batsman waits to hit because it is "fatter," and therefore easier to hit. A good "control" pitcher seldom gets behind on the ball-and-strike count. He stays in front of the batter, striving to work the count to two strikes and no balls, or two strikes and one ball so that he can work on the batter with the pitch he wants him to hit.

CATCHER: The catcher is usually the most valuable man on any baseball team. He is the quarterback and the dynamo of the club and, having the whole field in front of him, is in an ideal spot to direct the team's defensive tactics. He is easily the busiest player on the field. He instructs the infield what to do with rolling bunts and keeps his pitcher informed as to the position of enemy base runners. Not only must he handle the ball on every pitch, but he indicates to the outfielders and infielders how to play each batter, watches the batter keenly for a tip-off on the hit-and-run sign so he can break up the play with a pitch-out, signals for every ball the pitcher throws and has to keep several sets of signals in his head besides mentally tabulating each hitter's weakness and chattering incessantly to generate player morale.

One of the shrewdest catchers of all time was Billy Sullivan, of the old Chicago White Sox. Once Detroit was playing Chicago and had the fleet Cobb on second base and big Sam Crawford on first. With two men out and Detroit two runs behind, Cobb flashed Crawford the double steal signal. Getting a good lead, he dug for third with the pitch, for he thought Sullivan would make the play for him since he was the farthest advanced runner. But Sullivan crossed Cobb up, pegging to second base and throwing out Crawford by a wide margin, retiring the side. It was an unorthodox play but smart. Sullivan won many battles for Chicago with his brains.

Have you ever wondered why there are so few left-handed catchers, shortstops, and second and third basemen in baseball? There is a reason. A left-handed catcher would have to throw over a right-handed batter's head to second base, and since most batters hit right-handed, this would be awkward. Even if the hitter weren't in the way, a southpaw catcher would have trouble making the quick overhand throw with the wrist and shoulder that the catcher must use because few left-handed players have a true overhand throw. Most of them get the ball off side-armed, or somewhere between a side and overhand stance, and have a tendency to curve the ball, which would not allow for quick throwing to bases.

Left-handed outfielders are plentiful. So are left-handed first basemen, whose advantage over their right-handed brethren consists in their being better faced to throw to the other bases. Also their gloved hand is ideally located to catch a quick throw from the pitcher and tag a runner sliding back all in the same motion. But the other infielders should be right-handed so they will not have to turn their bodies to make the throw to first.

STOPPING THE DOUBLE STEAL: A difficult play to stop is the double steal with runners on first and third. We have seen that play dozens of times. In almost all high-school games, and also in a surprising number of college contests, when there are runners on first and third the catcher lets the man from first go down to second unchallenged, probably fearing that if he played the ball to second the man on third would score before the ball could be returned from second base. He is mistaken. To stop this play the catcher should throw through to the shortstop covering second base. Meanwhile the second baseman cuts midway between his base and the pitcher, and watches the base runner on third. If this runner dashes for the plate, the second baseman cuts off the catcher's throw to second and returns it to the catcher in time to retire the runner. If the runner on third bluffs to go home and gets too far off the bag, the second baseman snaps the ball to third, catching the runner. If the runner does not break for home, the second baseman lets the catcher's throw go through to the shortstop, who tags the runner coming in from first. The shortstop can help the second baseman on the play by calling to him: "Take it!" or "Cut it off!" Sometimes this runner, when he sees that he is trapped, will double back toward first. In this event the shortstop must chase him back, keeping

HOW TO STOP THE DOUBLE STEAL

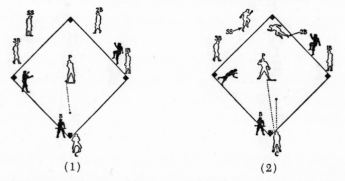

(1)   (2)

1. Base runner on first breaks for second with the pitch. 2. Second baseman runs to his spot and watches baserunner on third, shortstop covers second base, catcher throws on line to second base.

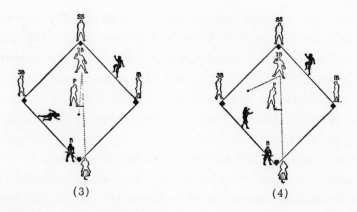

(3)   (4)

3. If base runner on third breaks for home, second baseman cuts off catcher's throw and pegs runner out at home. 4. If runner on third breaks for plate, then stops, second baseman heads him off at third.

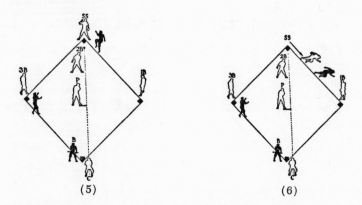

(5)   (6)

5. If base runner on third holds bag, second baseman lets catcher's throw go through to shortstop, retiring base runner at second. 6. If base runner stops short of second and doubles back to first, shortstop chases him back, making put-out at first.

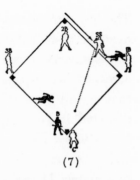

7. However, shortstop must watch base runner on third and be ready to throw him out at plate if he tries to score.

(7)

constant watch on the man on third, and make the put-out at first base. If, during this rundown, the runner on third starts for home, the shortstop suddenly plays him and disregards the base runner between first and second. By practicing all phases of the play over and over on the junior-sized diamond so the throws won't be too long, boys can master it.

JUNIOR EQUIPMENT: Boys under sixteen years of age should use the official junior cork-center baseball and play on the junior-sized diamond, the measurements of which are described in Rule 2 of the official baseball rules, printed in any of the national guides. The diamond is 82 feet between bases instead of the 90 feet of the professional diamond, 115 feet 11½ inches from home base to second base (and from first to third) and 50 feet from home base to the pitching slab. Professional players would not like to play baseball on a diamond larger than the ones the rules provide for them; yet this is no more ridiculous than boys trying to play on a diamond laid off for adults.

The boy pitcher will find that his curve breaks just right over the 50-foot distance and the boy third baseman and shortstop will discover they can whip the ball on a line across to their first baseman on the junior-size field whereas they would have to bounce it across on the professional diamond. It is easy to convert temporarily a senior diamond into a junior one. Move the first- and third-base bags in eight feet on each foul line. Then move second base approximately 11 feet 4 inches closer to home plate, and the pitching mark 10½ feet nearer the plate. The junior diamond is then ready for play.

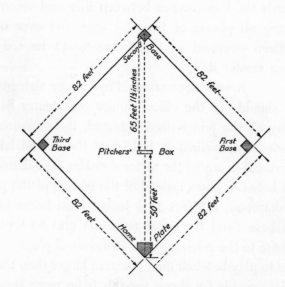

**DIAGRAM OF BASEBALL DIAMOND
FOR BOYS UNDER 16 YEARS OF AGE**

LITTLE LEAGUE DIAMOND: Baseball fields for boys 12 years old or younger are smaller still. Here is a diagram showing a Little League field layout. All dimensions are compulsory unless marked "optional."

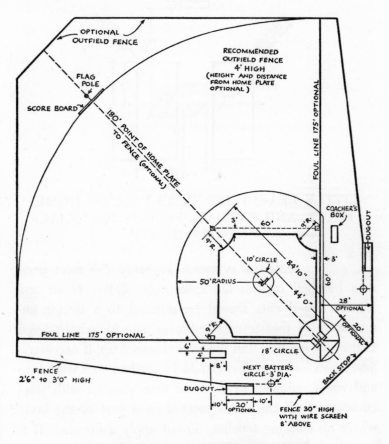

DIAGRAM OF LITTLE LEAGUE
BASEBALL FIELD

Here's another showing official measurements for the Little League pitcher's rubber, home plate and batsman's boxes.

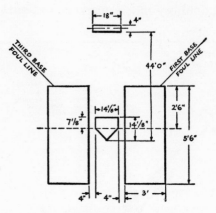

LITTLE LEAGUE PITCHER'S RUBBER, HOME PLATE, AND BATSMAN'S BOXES (OFFICIAL MEASUREMENTS)

BASEBALL INJURIES: Probably the most common baseball injuries are spike cuts, sliding burns and blisters. Deep cuts should be referred to a doctor immediately so that tetanus antitoxin may be administered to prevent lockjaw, and the wound sewed up, if necessary. Small cuts and scratches should be washed well with soap and water, allowed to dry, and then painted with mercurochrome. If the cut is located on a part of the body where no clothing touches, do not apply a dressing. If it is, a single layer of sterile gauze may be fastened over the wound with single strips of adhesive tape and this dress-

BASEBALL

BASEBALLing left on until the abrasion heals completely, provided
there is no infection meanwhile. Treat sliding burns as
you would small cuts and scratches.

Never open blisters, because there is danger of infection. If the blister opens voluntarily and the outer layer
of skin comes off, treat it as you would a minor cut or
scratch, by the method described above. If the outer
surface of the skin does not come off, wrap hand blisters
with adhesive to prevent irritation. For heel blisters, cut
a hole in a small soft felt pad and fasten it over the blister
with adhesive tape. It is important to remember that any
serious or puzzling injury, that does not readily respond
to treatment, should be shown to a doctor at once.

Study the baseball rules carefully. It is surprising how
many major leaguers do not know them. Remember
that a pitcher who accidentally drops a ball while winding up with one or more runners on base commits a
balk, and the runners advance one base. When a fielder
throws his cap or glove at a batted ball and strikes it, the
batter is automatically given a three-base hit. The batter
who bunts a third strike foul is automatically out. The
umpire can call a ball on a pitcher who takes more than
twenty seconds to deliver a ball to the batsman. Even if
the catcher drops the third strike, the batsman is automatically out if first base is occupied and there are less
than two out. If a foul is caught on the fly, a base runner
may be "doubled up" if he does not get back before the
caught ball is thrown to the base which he has just left.

There have been some good stories written about baseball. Although Zane Grey is known principally for his Western stories and his fishing yarns, he was at his best when writing about baseball. Grey was a former leaguer and he wrote two excellent baseball stories called *The Shortstop* and *The Young Pitcher*, each a cloth-bound volume. Ring Lardner's books, *You Know Me Al* and *Lose With A Smile*, and also two of his short stories, *Harmony* and *Alibi Ike*, both of which may be found in his book *Round Up*, are excellent. Also read *Mister Conley* by Charles E. Van Loan, a popular baseball fictionist of a generation ago.

CHAPTER 3

BASKETBALL

BASKETBALL, which annually leads all American sports in paid attendance, is an American game that was devised in 1891 as a means of providing a new and exciting indoor recreation for a rebellious physical education class at the Y.M.C.A.'s Springfield College at Springfield, Massachusetts.

It was the winter of 1891. The cutting New England cold had driven into the small brick Springfield gymnasium the eighteen members of the class composed chiefly of Coach Amos Alonzo Stagg's Springfield football team which was still in a fine glow from playing a fourteen-game schedule. They were all being trained to become Y.M.C.A. secretaries. Despite their Christian leanings, they were all red-blooded young fellows who chafed at the boresome routine of their indoor gymnasium classes and longed for some real exercise.

Dr. Luther H. Gulick, head of the college's physical department, listened patiently to their complaints. "We get awfully tired working day after day on the parallel bars and the flying rings," Frank Mahan, their leader, told him. "And if you'll pardon us, Dr. Gulick, the games you suggest for us are even worse. Imagine grown men trying to play such childish sports as 'three deep' and 'tag' and 'drop the handkerchief.' You mean well, Doctor, but we just can't seem to get interested."

Dr. Gulick saw the point. He summoned James Naismith, his assistant, a wiry, thirty-year-old, mustached fellow from Almonte, Canada. Naismith had gone to college at McGill University in Montreal where in 1883 he made the football team at center. As a junior and senior, he had proved his worth by winning the college's all-around gymnasium championships.

"Jim," began Dr. Gulick, "do you remember saying the other day that there was nothing new under the sun? That all the new things in the world were merely combinations of old factors?"

Jim Naismith looked keenly at his superior, wondering, with wild alarm, what he had got himself into now. "That's right." He nodded.

"Well," went on Dr. Gulick, his gray eyes twinkling with amusement, "if what you said is true, you surely wouldn't have any trouble inventing a new game, would you?"

"I guess not," Naismith answered. "Why?"

"Because now is a good time to do it," said Dr. Gulick, with the air of a man dropping a large burden from his shoulders, "and yours is the job, my boy. We need a new indoor game for Mahan and the football crowd, something that will satisfy their restless souls."

Although Dr. Gulick had put the matter in a joking way, Jim Naismith knew it was an assignment. He had always liked hard work and problems, and this was a new kind of problem—a challenge to his ingenuity. He went to work.

It was growing dark. Snow lay on the campus. Through a crimson blur on the western horizon, the December sun was sinking behind the barren branches of the beech and maple trees. But Jim Naismith took no notice of the bleak winter scene. He was hard at work creating a new game. He didn't know it then but it was destined to become a game that would mushroom sensationally among both boy and girl teams in small and large high schools. Today it attracts more spectators than either football or baseball, is played all over the world and has been made an Olympic sport.

Jim sat at his desk, busily figuring his new game out. He wanted a competitive game, one that could be played indoors on the hard floor of the gymnasium and would satisfy the boisterous spirit of the football players in the Springfield gym class.

Gradually it became clear to him that there should be a ball in the game, that there could be no tackling because of the hard floor, that the player in possession of the ball could not be permitted to run with it or injuries might result. But what should the players do with the ball once they got it? And what system of scoring could he devise?

"In football, rugby, soccer—games in which large balls are used—the ball is propelled to the goal by hand or foot as hard as one can send it. But in a small room or gymnasium this might result in injury to one of the competitors. To keep the players from throwing the ball hard, I'll make them throw it at an arc into some receptacle over their heads. That would also solve my problem of how to put scoring into the game," he reasoned. A good thinker, this fellow Jim Naismith.

Thus were born the basic ideas of basketball—(1) no running with the ball and (2) lobbing it into a horizontal goal suspended well over the players' heads.

Naismith's next problem was how to advance the ball to within range of the goal. "If I prohibit running with the ball, I'll have a pretty stationary game," he thought. Then it occurred to him that a good way to advance it would be by throwing or passing it, although this was fifteen years before the forward pass was heard of in football. Later, bouncing the ball down the court, called dribbling, also was introduced.

Just before the Christmas holidays of 1891, Naismith invited several of the football "rebels" to try out the new game he had been thinking over.

They walked through the snow to the Springfield gymnasium, which then had a playing space of only twenty-eight by thirty-four feet, about one-third as long as a regulation court nowadays. Naismith carried a regulation soccer ball. The only question left in his mind was into what kind of receptacle the ball should be thrown. On the way to the gym, he sought the aid of a chap named Stebbins, who was superintendent of buildings and grounds at Springfield.

"Stebbins, have you got a couple of boxes about eighteen inches square that you could let me have?"

"What do you want them for?" asked the superintendent.

"I'm working on a new game," explained Naismith, "and I want to fasten the boxes on poles and let the men throw a ball into them."

Stebbins' forehead puckered reflectively. "Boxes?" he echoed. "No, I haven't got any boxes. But look here, I've got a couple of empty peach baskets down at my house if they'd do you any good."

Naismith's eyes lighted up. The ball was round, so a round target would be ideal. "Just the thing!" he said. "Let's go get 'em."

And that's how basketball got its name. Frank Mahan himself, leader of the restless football faction that quickly liked and adopted the new game, later suggested to Naismith that he call the new sport basketball.

Stebbins' peach baskets were obtained and nailed to the gallery railing at each end of the gymnasium. The players wore long tan gymnasium trousers and full-sleeved blue jerseys and the first game of basketball started.

No printed or written rules existed. Naismith just explained the game and the fun began. Most of the players were members of the Springfield football team, and with whoops of delight they skirmished hotly until finally someone made a lucky goal. Then a new difficulty arose. How could the ball be dislodged from the peach basket? Finally one of the players had to go up into the gallery, climb down the rail and reach into the peach basket for the ball. To meet this difficulty, the janitor and a stepladder were brought into the game.

It was fortunate that the game was promoted by the national Y.M.C.A. college because this assured its widespread adoption. Graduates of Springfield going out all over the world as Y.M.C.A. secretaries took the game with them. Bob Bailey, the old Princeton center, took it to Tientsin, China, in 1894; Duncan Patton to India the same year; Emil Thies to France in 1895; and Ishakawa to Japan in 1900. C. Harek, another "Y" man, introduced it to Persia, now Iran, in 1901. Gradually it was adopted by American high schools and colleges everywhere, and was played principally through the winter months. Now it has a tremendous hold upon the youth of the nation. Requiring only five players and very little equipment, the game can easily be played and financed by even the smallest schools.

Jim Naismith left Springfield in 1895 to become director of the Denver, Colorado, Y.M.C.A. and in 1898 went to the University of Kansas where he headed the physical education school until his retirement from active teaching in 1937. In 1936 Dr. and Mrs. Naismith were sent to the Olympic games at Berlin following a national drive for funds by spectators, officials and players, for basketball had just been adopted as an outdoor sport in the Olympics. There Dr. Naismith addressed the assembled players from all nations before the start of the tourney and saw the powerful American team triumph.

In November of 1939 Dr. Naismith was stricken by a cerebral hemorrhage at his home in Lawrence, Kansas. He made a remarkable recovery and was released from the hospital four days later, only to suffer a relapse. He died at the age of seventy-eight, just as the 1939–1940 basketball season, the fiftieth one since he refereed the first game at Springfield in 1891, was getting under way.

Professional basketball is enjoying great popularity today. It's a wonderful game for spectators with its length of forty-eight minutes, instead of the forty employed by the colleges, and its twenty-four-second rule which requires the offensive team to shoot within that span or give up the ball. Each team scores more than 100 points in many games. The Boston Celtics once scored 173 points in a game against Minneapolis.

It's a sport in which not only big post men but also big backcourt men, like six-six Tom Gola of Philadelphia, are in demand. Most professional offenses are free lance, with the fast break emphasized. Bob Cousey, Boston's six-one ball-handling wizard who formerly played college basketball for the Holy Cross National Collegiate champions, is one comparatively small man whom the giants can't dislodge. He's the sharpest passer and ball-handler in the game. Another good one is little Slater Martin, former University of Texas star who now plays with St. Louis. But most of the headliners in professional and collegiate basketball are tall fellows.

PURPOSE OF THE GAME

Basketball is played by having a team of five players advance the ball down the court by throwing (passing) it or bouncing (dribbling) it until their goal is reached; they then pitch the ball (a process known as shooting) through the top of the goal, which is an orange metal ring, eighteen inches in inside diameter, suspended horizontally ten feet above the floor from a vertical backboard.

However this offensive progress is not easy. The defensive team, which also has five players, will do its best to prevent all this passing, dribbling and shooting. When the defense secures the ball, they will try to advance it by the same means to their goal at the opposite end of the court. The court is a rectangular surface free from obstructions. Its dimensions are ninety-four by fifty feet for college and independent players, eighty-four by fifty for high-school players and seventy-four by forty-two for boys under fifteen years.

Each goal made from scrimmage, called a field goal,

DIAGRAM OF BASKETBALL COURT

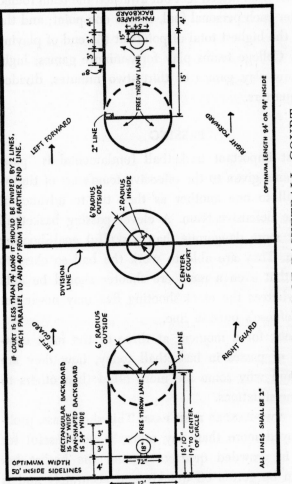

Unobstructed space of at least 3', but preferably 10', should be provided outside the court. If impossible to provide 3', a 1" broken line should be marked inside the court parallel with and 3' inside the boundary. The right backboard is the small one for high school or Y.M.C.A. games. A.A.U. optional. The left backboard is the large one for college games.

counts two points; each foul goal, a point-blank unguarded shot from fifteen feet out awarded the team fouled
against after each personal foul, counts one point; and the
team with the highest total of points at the end of playing
time wins. College teams play forty-minute games; high-
school teams play games of thirty-two minutes, divided
into four quarters.

PASSING

The most important basketball fundamental is "passing," the name given to the offensive team's art of throwing the ball to one another as they try to advance it
through the defensive team. A clever passing basketball
team is far more dangerous than a skillful goal-shooting
aggregation. They are able to work the ball so close to
their goal that even a mediocre shooter should be able
to score, whereas the crack-shooting five may never get
past the defense's outside line.

Let us look for a moment at three of the most common kinds of passes in basketball today, how they are
executed, and why some are more fitted than others to
certain game situations.

TWO-HANDED PUSH PASS: This short pass, probably employed more than any other, is very useful for
fast work in crowded quarters around the basket because it can be gotten off quickly and accurately and is
easy to catch. To execute it, the player brings the ball
with both hands to his chest, keeping the elbows close

to his sides; and then he flips both arms out together. At the same time he releases the ball off the finger tips with a natural snap of the wrists and fingers and a body follow-through. He learns to receive the ball and pass it with one motion. This pass should be of moderate speed and delivered shirt high. To help its deception, the passer should learn to execute it from the same chest plane he shoots goals from instead of dipping his body too low.

TWO-HANDED BOUNCE PASS: Delivered in almost the same fashion as the two-handed push pass, the two-handed bounce pass, which is very hard to guard, is effective all over the court in crowded territory but particularly as a pass into the post man and also from the post man to a cutter. It is also useful when throwing the ball in from out of bounds, or for passing when the player is hemmed in by a fiercely attacking guard, or when penetrating a tight zone defense. A bounce pass should strike the floor about four feet inside the spot where he wants the receiver to catch it. It must not be bounced too closely to him or he may fumble it. Very effective bounce passes may also be delivered with the two-handed side pass, or, for that matter, with one hand.

OVERHAND PASS: This is a one-handed throw, very much like the catcher's peg in baseball, and is used to feed a fast-cutting player who has gotten behind his guard. It is a good pass for a back guard to use when feeding fast-breaking teammates after recovering the ball from the defensive backboard. It is very accurate for long distances. Right-handed players grasp the ball in both hands and, using the left to steady it, bring it back past the right ear. Then the player releases the left hand and throws the ball over-handed, following through with the arm and hand to insure accuracy. He must not twist the wrist as the ball is delivered, or a curve will result. This pass may also be thrown with a side-arm delivery, particularly when the passer is trying to look one way and pass another.

There are several other types of passes, such as the back bounce, the roll, the hook, the two-handed side pass, the underhand pass, and the two-handed overhead pass used by tall players against shorter opponents.

GENERAL HINTS ON PASSING: Try to set up your passes with feints. If you can make your guard show direction first, it will make your pass twice as easy because then he will not have an equal opportunity to cover you. It is much easier to pass when your opponent is playing close to you than if he is playing you loosely and consequently has more time to figure you out, block your pass, or prevent your getting a running start with a dribble. To draw him near you, fake a dribble or a shot at the goal, then pass. Shoot for a teammate's jersey. Passes thrown too high block the receiver's vision and have to be pulled down to the chest before he can pass in turn. Passes thrown too low are hard to handle and if dropped, may hit the receiver's knee and bound over the sideline. Do not pass a ball too hard if a teammate is close to you and do not pass to him if he isn't looking at you. Lead him if he is cutting for the goal. Do not relax after you make a pass, but keep moving and try to draw your defensive man with you away from the play. Above all, always look for the receiver before you pass.

CATCHING THE BALL: As you catch a basketball in your hands, spread the fingers and thumbs, relax the wrists, cup the palms and, above all, keep your eyes on the ball. As in catching a baseball, recoil slightly as the ball strikes your hands. Meet the ball, if possible, by dashing a step or two toward the passer, thus keeping your body between the ball and your guard to forestall interception. Just before catching a ball, learn to bend your knees slightly and to set your body for a prompt return pass, should you want to make one.

All professional teams play with vastly more finesse than the collegians or A.A.U. aggregations. The best passers and greatest crowd-pleasers of them all were the Original Celtics of New York City with Johnny Beckman and Nat Holman at forward, rangy Joe Lapchick at center, and Chris Leonard and Dutch Dehnert, the rugged post player, at guards. Having campaigned together for years, the Celtics knew well each other's playing habits and those who saw this famous team perform in the middle 1920's say its craft was so superb that its opponents appeared hobbled and blindfolded by comparison.

The Celtics didn't try to roll up big scores. Their theory was that there is no benefit in unnecessarily humiliating an opponent. After they had established a safe lead, they would give an exhibition of ball-handling, dribbling, feinting and showmanship that delighted the tremendous audiences that turned out to see them play. Although now and then they purposely dropped a game to establish interest in a re-match, it is said they never lost a series when the chips were down. For instance, during the 1923–1924 season, they won one hundred and thirty-five of one hundred and forty-one games, playing in nineteen states and eighty different cities.

DRIBBLING

Dribbling, the name given to the art of skillfully bouncing a basketball, is the most important complement of passing. It is easily the game's most spectacular fundamental, but many coaches frown upon it because of its frequent misuse by unskilled players who destroy team play by dribbling into congested areas with their heads down. Thus they lose the ball or are fouled for running over opponents, whereas if they had been more intent on team play, they might have seen teammates open under the basket. Other coaches contend it encourages a rough defense.

However, if used wisely and to the full limit of its possibilities, the dribble will give an offensive team a tremendous advantage. Certainly no fair-minded coach will deny its usefulness in carrying an open player quickly to the goal, in extricating a closely guarded player, or freeing a sorely assailed back guard who has just captured a ball off the defensive backboard. A fast team would be lost without the dribble. It is also useful in set plays, particularly when offensive players in the back line of attack bounce the ball laterally back and forth before setting up a screen.

To execute the dribble, a player should not slap the ball but rather push it down with the action of his fingers, wrist and forearm. He should dribble with a high bounce when coming up the floor or when trying for speed in the open. However in crowded territory it is better to use a low bounce with the body bent low from the hips and the ball kept well out in front of the dribbler so it may be better protected.

The best dribblers in the game are those who can bounce by "feel" as they move up the court without having to look for the ball, thus leaving their eyes free to search for a teammate under the goal. The dribbler should learn to dribble with alternate hands and should always go around the side of a defensive man rather than through him, for this will draw a foul on the dribbler for charging.

Deception in dribbling may be practiced both by changing the tempo of the bounce or by employing body feints while dribbling. When a guard approaches, the resourceful dribbler will shift his body between his opponent and the bouncing ball.

The minute a player touches the ball with both hands, or permits it to come to rest in one or both hands, he completes his dribble. Should he then attempt another dribble, he has committed a violation known as double dribble, which the rules punish by requiring officials to award the ball to the opposing team for a pass-in from out of bounds.

Basketball officiating varies all over the nation, owing chiefly to the vastly different rule interpretations in different parts of the country, but booing an unpopular decision by a referee or umpire is universal and despite its obvious want of sportsmanship is usually hard to check.

Bruce Drake, a young Oklahoma official, once stopped a vociferous booer in a novel way while working a game in a small Oklahoma town noted for its critical booing. Every time Drake refereed a game at this place, the champion booer of all, a big fellow who had a deep bass voice that rang like a bell all over the gymnasium, was a particularly troublesome offender. Finally, between halves of a game there, Drake sought out the football coach of the town, whom he knew, and inquired the identity of his booing tormentor. "Oh, that's just old Elmer, the barber down at the DeLuxe," laughed the coach.

Drake walked out into the corridor of the gymnasium and spied the booer getting a drink at a water fountain. He slapped him familiarly on the back and asked pleasantly, "Hello, Elmer, how do you like the game?" The booer spun around and when he saw the official, nearly fainted with surprise. "Why—why—fine game! Fine game!" he stammered, obviously taken aback. All through the second half he was a model spectator! Next day the booing barber accosted the football coach and praised Drake's officiating. "I met that guy five years ago," Elmer told the coach, with pride, "and he still remembers my name."

SHOOTING

Gregg McBride, formerly the University of Nebraska sports publicity director, likes to tell about the time he took his wife to see her first basketball game. It was an early-season contest between the Missouri and Nebraska teams. The ball was thrown up at center but both teams had the jitters and could not score. A Missouri man fired but the ball hit the ring and bounded away. A Nebraska player let loose a long throw that also struck the goal and dropped off. After the first four minutes of the contest the score was still 0 to 0 although each team had shot several times. Suddenly a Missouri player squatted and turned the basket wrong side out with a beautiful goal from mid-court, the first of the game. "Lookie there, honey!" exclaimed Mrs. McBride, leaping to her feet with excitement, "that darned thing's got a hole in it!"

Yes, a basketball goal does have a hole in it but, as Mrs. McBride discovered, it isn't easy to hit. In fact the average high-school basketball team makes only about fifteen to twenty-five per cent of its shots from scrimmage and the average college club does not do much better. The idea, as most good coaches stress, is to develop a team's passing, dribbling and play-making to such a point that the ball can be worked for an unguarded shot closer to the goal where the percentage of hits is much higher than when the player shoots hurriedly from farther out in the court.

The following are some of the most practical shots in basketball today:

ONE-HANDED SHOT: This is used nowadays by nearly all high-school and college players, and is a very good shot from medium range. It originated in the Rocky Mountain area, then spread fast over the whole nation. Players who use it from a jump in crowded territory are much harder to guard than those who employ the two-handed set shot.

It is also a popular free-throw shot.

Place the ball on your right hand, which should be spread. The little finger and the thumb should be spread wide so that the ball will have a good base to rest on. The left hand is used to support the ball, and is kept on the ball during the downward motion and not released until about halfway on the upward delivery of the shot. If you are right-handed, make this shot with the right foot forward and the right knee bent. The throwing arm should be extended fully as the shot is delivered, and the wrist and fingers employed to send the ball, as well as the arm. As you get the ball away, you straighten your right knee and actually leave the floor with both feet. This is the easiest shot to teach beginners, and is very practical because it can be delivered faster than the two-handed shot. One of the mysteries of basketball is why this shot did not come into general use and popularity until nearly fifty years after Jim Naismith invented the game.

ONE-HANDED LAY-UP SHOT: This is the best shot when a player is traveling toward the goal at top speed with no opponent to bar his path. It is made in full stride from the top of a leap. First he sets his left foot firmly and jumps high into the air with the ball grasped in both hands. The jump should be for height and not distance. As he propels his body into the air, he fastens his eye on the goal and keeps it there. At the same time he extends both arms upward with the ball held high. At this point of the shot the player must be completely relaxed. Then comes the shot. As he feels himself starting to fall, he drops the left or inside hand, which has been used to balance the ball against the spread fingers and thumb of the shooting hand. With his eyes still riveted upon the rig, he lays the ball softly and with very little spin against the backboard. Then he alights, with knees bent, and faces the court so he can immediately get back into the scrimmage without having to turn around.

Boys should practice this shot also with the left hand so they will be equipped to score from whatever angle the defense forces them to shoot.

TWO-HANDED PUSH SHOT: This is the shot formerly used by many basketball players for set shots from semi-long or long ranges when the shooter isn't being closely guarded by an opponent. Its form is closely akin to

that of both the two-handed push pass and the two-handed
bounce pass. The player first brings the ball, held in both
hands, to the chest, and keeps his elbows in. In the East
this shot is usually made with the feet close together,
but a world of fine marksmen elsewhere deliver it with
the feet spread and the left foot slightly in advance of the
right. The shooter must be balanced over his feet. The
ball should be held with the finger tips, and the thumbs
serve as a support. Thus the ball is delivered by the fingers and thumbs only. The ball should never touch the
palms during the shot. The knees are slightly bent, the
eyes are fastened on the forward rim of the goal, and
the player delivers the ball by slowly thrusting both arms
forward and upward. The ball is released off the finger
tips just above the eyes. After the ball is released, the
arms and hands are fully extended in a follow-through.
If a player has strong fingers and wrists, he should be able
to do this shot without too much bending of the knees.
He arches the ball but does not forget that a ball arched
too high may rebound far over the heads of his teammates following in, while a ball with no arch has a poor
entrance arc to the basket. However, the one-handed shot
has largely dissipated its usefulness.

FREE GOAL SHOT: Any player fouled in basketball is entitled to one or more unguarded free shots from
the free-throw line, fifteen feet out. The one-handed free
shot has already been described. Another good free-throw
shot is the two-handed underhand swing. Some college teams

have been known to cash as high as seventy per cent of their free throws throughout a season by using this shot. Free goals count only one point, whereas a goal from the field counts two points. However a survey by the rules research committee in 1931 revealed that fifty-five per cent of all games were determined by accuracy at the foul line. Consequently the game's leading coaches emphasize it strongly. Doctor F. C. "Phog" Allen, the former University of Kansas coach who developed twenty-seven championship teams in thirty-four years, made each player on his team shoot one hundred foul shots each day in practice. Most other coaches make their men do fifty.

The first concern of the player about to attempt a free throw by the underhand method should be the position of his feet. They can be uneven, with the forward foot held an inch or so behind the foul line and the rear foot half a step back, or they can be in line. The thrower should stand flat-footed. The ball is held lightly by the fingers and thumbs and the heels of the palms should not touch. As he stands at the line, the thrower should relax and if he is puffing hard, he can breathe deeply to slow his heart action. Then, lifting his eyes to the outer rim of the goal and keeping them there until after the shot is completed, he crouches, rises on the balls of his feet, and snaps his hands up and outward. He releases the ball from the tips of his fingers at about the level of his eyes, and follows through with the arms and hands. He must not move his feet until after the shot is completed.

Ward Lambert, former Purdue University coach, recommended that practice free goal throwing be carried on under game conditions with the shooter thoroughly warmed up or even panting from scrimmage, and making the shots with his sweat shirt off. The shooter should leave the line after each attempt and approach it again for the next shot, as he would in a game.

There are many other shots in basketball: the one-hand over-shoulder hook shot used by players in motion going away from the basket, or by post men in the pivot play; the two-handed shot from over the shoulder with the shooter going toward the sidelines; the pompadour shot or two-handed wrist flip from off the hair.

ADVANCING IN FOR REBOUNDS: Here the player makes an orderly and alert advance in order to be within ten feet of the goal when the ball hits, so it will not bound over his head. Then he drives in hard, gets the ball and, if he can, takes a shot. If the traffic is too thick, he immediately passes the ball back out to a teammate.

TEAM OFFENSE

If the opponents' defense is set under their basket, as it usually will be when the attacking team brings the ball down the floor, it is up to the offense to penetrate this defense with a system of passing and screening that will free a shooter for a clean shot close to the goal.

The method employed by perhaps a majority of the nation's better college teams is the *double post* or 3–2

system, in which the attacking team forms itself in two
parallel lines in the attacking third of the court. The

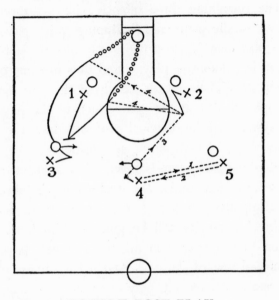

DOUBLE POST PLAY

This is one of the oldest and most effective screens in basketball. It can
be worked to either side. No. 4 passes to No. 5 (this is the key pass that
tells Nos. 1 and 2, the post men, what side the play is going on) and No. 5
passes back to No. 4. Just as the ball leaves the hands of No. 5, No. 1 moves
up to screen for No. 3. As the ball is passed from No. 4 to No. 2 (No. 2
feints in, then comes out to take the ball), No. 3 feints to the inside to set
up his guard for the screen and then, with No. 1 screening for him, cuts
sharply to the outside and in toward the basket to take a bounce pass
from No. 2 and dribble to a lay-up shot. No. 1 must time his screen perfectly or the play will fail. He must not come up too soon and stand
behind No. 3's guard or he will reveal the play. There is a strong option
to this play. If No. 1's guard switches off and covers No. 3 cutting around,
No. 1, who will be inside No. 3's guard, should cut straight for the goal
and No. 2's bounce pass be given to him. All the passes should be bounce
passes.

front line of attack consists of two post men who are planted under the basket on either side of the free throw lane. The remaining three offensive players spread out the width of the court and, whipping quick passes into the two post men, try to drive deeply into the defense to screen off key defensive players and thus free one of their own men for a short return pass from the post man and an unimpeded shot at the goal. Much of the passing in such a system will be diagonal so it will draw the defensive players out of their strong set positions.

The double-post system is strong because it leaves only two defensive men under the goal who can "check off" or trade opponents if the offense screens them out. The other three defenders will be guarding the three offensive men in the back line and usually will have their backs turned toward the goal. And if the offense chooses to pull one post man out, only one defensive man is left in back court.

The system also is sound because with two post men, usually the biggest players on the team, it provides better rebound power with two tall players available to charge in for the ball if the shot is missed. Also, if the defense suddenly obtains the ball, the former offensive team has a strong recovery to defense with the three men in the outside line already back to meet the foe's players.

Some teams use the *single post* offense with only one offensive player placed near the opponents' goal and the remaining four out. This is a system designed for a team possessing a big player who can handle the ball well in crowded quarters, accurately feed teammates cutting by, or, after a fake to feed them, swing back to the opposite direction for a one-handed hook shot at the goal, or for a short dribble and shot.

However, the national rules committee legislated against this play because it encouraged rough congestion under the basket, and also because a clever post man could hold the ball almost indefinitely in spite of everything his guard could do. The rule that checks it somewhat now is the three-second rule that forbids a player to remain in any part of his free-throw area between the free-throw line and the end line, with or without the ball, for more than three seconds while the ball is in play and in possession or control of his team.

POST PLAY: Although post players are ordinarily big men, a little man who can fake one way and drive in the other direction under his guard's arm is an asset. An effective pass into the post man is a roll pass, which is hardest of all to intercept. The bounce pass and the overhand pass are good, also.

The post man should meet the pass by running a step or two toward the passer to make the catch. He should learn to catch the ball in his hands with arms extended so his opponent cannot reach it. He should also protect the ball by holding it away from the guard's reach and by moving it constantly. He should plant his feet evenly so he can go to either side without first having to shift them again. The best passes for a post man to make to cutting teammates are the bounce pass, short two-handed underhand flip and the two-handed flip over the shoulder. Sometimes he merely hands his cutting teammate the ball as the latter

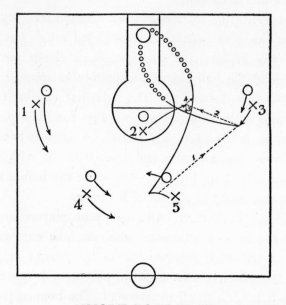

SINGLE POST PLAY

No. 5 fakes to go left, then bounce-passes to No. 3, who comes out to meet the pass. As this first pass is executed, No. 2, the post man, moves outside the free-throw circle to be ready for the next pass, a bounce that comes to him from No. 3. As No. 3 bounce-passes to No. 2, he drives past him very close for a return bounce pass and fast dribble into the basket. Meanwhile No. 5 also drives in fast, very close behind No. 3, hitting off No. 2's hip, ready to take an optional pass from No. 2 and dribble fast into the goal if No. 2 sees that No. 3 is too well covered. No. 3 and No. 5 must time themselves so they almost meet as they drive past No. 2. No. 1 comes out to cover on defense and No. 4 moves over where No. 5 was. This play also can be worked to the opposite side.

speeds past. If his cutting mates are bottled up and he has to pass back out to the back line, the two-handed push pass, the bounce pass and sometimes the hook are good.

After the post man has made a pass to a teammate cutting by, he should immediately whirl in the opposite direction and cut to the goal for a return pass or for a rebound shot. Teammates of a post man should keep the floor around him open by leading the guards off to the sides and corners. However, when a teammate cuts by the post man for a pass, the cutting player should run close enough to the post man almost to brush him. Thus his defensive opponent may be screened off by the post man or the post man's guard. The post play does not work as well against a zone defense as against a man-for-man, since zone defenders will not follow opponents out of the scoring zone as do man-for-man defenders.

Some of the finest post players in basketball were Dutch Dehnert of the original New York Celtics, Jack Mc-Cracken of the Denver Nuggets, Tom Pickrell of the Bartlesville, Oklahoma, Phillips 66 Oilers, Ray Ebling of the University of Kansas, Lloyd Tucker of the Winfield, Kansas, Teachers, Gerald Tucker of Oklahoma, Bob Kurland of Oklahoma A. and M., George Mikan of De Paul and Clyde Lovellette of Kansas.

THE FAST BREAK: By far the most spectacular offensive style in basketball is the fast break, in which the attacking team, suddenly coming into possession of the ball, gets the jump on their opponents and, passing

and dribbling as though their shirt tails were on fire, out-
runs the defense to the opposite goal before the defense
has time to retreat and set itself.

The Phillips 66 Oilers, several times National A.A.U.
champions from Bartlesville, Oklahoma, Rhode Island
State College and the University of Texas team of 1947
were outstanding exponents of this vogue.

Probably the fastest-breaking basketball teams ever developed in the ultra speedy Rocky Mountain loop were
G. O. "Ott" Romney's powerful Montana State aggregations that are still the toast of Mountain fans. In 1929,
the Bobcats from Bozeman not only won thirty-five of
thirty-seven games, but playing their home games on a
regulation ninety by fifty-foot floor, averaged $60^{16}/_{37}$
points per contest to their opponents' $30^{20}/_{37}$ over a
grueling schedule back at the time when the center jump
subtracted five or six minutes' playing time from each contest, too.

Montana State's aggressive man-for-man defense, which
did not wait for the foe to set but covered enemy players
all over the floor the entire forty minutes of each game,
gave her opportunity for countless fast-breaking situations that hurled two men down on one, or three on two.
If the enemy team worked the ball down to the Bobcat
goal and tried a shot, Brick Breeden, Montana State's
great back guard, would come down with the ball and
rifle a long pass to Cat Thompson, crack Bobcat forward
and "safety." He would slip behind the foe defense and,

palming Breeden's passes on a dead run, speed to the distant goal. Like so many notable fast-breaking clubs, Montana State that year was composed of average-sized players. Frank Ward, the six-foot three-inch one hundred and eighty-five-pound center and tip-in specialist, who was also a quarter-miler on the Blue and Gold Track Team, was the biggest man on the team, and could break down the floor almost as fast as Thompson.

Perhaps the fastest-breaking team of the 1930's was Coach Hugh McDermott's University of Oklahoma club of 1938, a colorful sophomoric aggregation known as the Boy Scats, whose deft passing, dribbling, faking and shooting while traveling at blinding speed is a tradition down in the state the late Will Rogers came from.

Oklahoma's fast break was predicated upon deception just as adroit as that practiced by screening teams. Although all her swiftly moving players could dribble, pass and shoot from whatever oblique the defense forced them from, the middle man in the Sooners three-man rushing wave, usually Captain Bill Martin or Jimmy McNatt, handled the ball. He was given full responsibility and it was up to him to select the method for delivering the *coup de grâce* to the startled enemy guard when the Oklahoma rushes reached the goal.

This middle man's assignment was to dribble straight at the nearer enemy guard, forcing him to show direction. If the guard left his man and lunged at the dribbler, the latter slipped a side pass to his open teammate who flitted in from the corner to score. But if the guard didn't fully commit himself, the speeding Oklahoma dribbler would double into the air upon nearing the basket, fake a pass to his mate in the corner to drive the guard back (this is called "jockeying the ball") and float in for a drift shot.

McNatt, the clever Oklahoma forward, had so uncanny a drift shot that he rarely missed. This popular black-haired Oklahoma forward was also a crack petroleum engineering student and, unknown to his teammates, sang in the choir at a Norman church. One Sunday, Marvin Mesch, another member of the Oklahoma team, happened to go to McNatt's church and discovered the forward singing in the choir. After services were over, Mesch, who stuttered, cornered the grinning McNatt in the church vestibule.

"Wh-wh-what are you d-d-doing here?" he wanted to know. "R-r-repenting for all those shots you've been making?"

The fast break is a system demanding speedy ball-handlers, dribblers and shot-makers. It is ideally suited to a squad of small men who lack the height and weight so necessary for a screening game. Fast-breaking teams, used to running, often wear down and exhaust bigger and slower opposing clubs, running off from them in the closing moments of the game.

However since even the fastest clubs won't always be able to beat the defense down the floor, a fast-breaking team must be taught screening and post play, too. The biggest danger in this sytem is failure to recognize a fast-breaking opportunity. In other words, if the attacking five is suddenly unable to outnumber the defense under the goal, it should not try to force the ball in and risk a wild shot, but should allow the defense to form and try to pierce it by post play.

DEFENSE

The old axiom that "the best defense is a strong offense" doesn't hold in basketball. The best teams have a definite system of team defense built upon certain individual skills. Elimination of the center jump after a basket has been scored, which gave the team scored upon the ball just as often as the scoring team, has put more pressure than ever on the defense. It means that every time your team scores, it is going to have to stop the other team from scoring too. Therefore a careful defensive preparedness is absolutely necessary.

Every one of the five players on a basketball team should be an alert defensive player or he will cost his team points. The team whose forwards can defend as well as its guards and center will be a hard team to beat.

Hank Iba, long-time coach at Oklahoma State University of Stillwater, Oklahoma, is everywhere conceded to be the greatest defensive coach in basketball.

INDIVIDUAL DEFENSE: A defensive player must learn to guard cleanly. Since free throwing decides fifty-five per cent of all games in basketball today, it is obvious

that a clean-guarding team has a big advantage. By refusing to commit fouls, it gives its opponents no foul shots.
There is a rule in basketball which requires that a man
must leave the game when he has made four personal
fouls; thus many a good team has been weakened in the
decisive part of a hard-fought game by having its star
waved off the floor after the fourth personal foul. But a
clean-guarding team never worries about this rule. It will
always have its playing strength intact.

A defensive player should always stay between his
guard and the goal. He must never rush his opponent.
Once an offensive player has made his guard show direction, it is easy to pass or dribble around him. That is why
an offensive man makes so many bluffs and feints. Although you will want to play your man closer when the
ball is in scoring territory, you still will not want to hurl
yourself upon him for fear of fouling him or letting him
elude you completely. The faster an opponent is, the
more loosely you should play him. Try to study him and
catalogue his offensive habits.

A defensive player should be shifty, like a boxer. He
should not spread his feet too far but should keep them
closely together so he can be ready to go in any direction.
Because of the popularity of crisscross passing, defensive
men should be able to cover their men diagonally with
short lateral jumps. They guard with one hand high in
the air to disconcert the shooter, and the other extended
at the side to block a possible pass. They yell at the man

they are guarding, stamp the floor with their feet, wave
one hand in front of his face and use any other legal
means their imaginations can dream up to discourage him
from shooting or passing. If he dribbles, they don't try to
knock him off the court but run alongside him, striving
to drive him to a sideline or corner. They take underhand slaps at the ball with the inside arm so they will not
foul him. If he threatens to shoot, they don't leap into
the air to block the shot, but charge him with one hand
held high. They keep alert for a feint.

A guard should learn to face his opponent and also
watch the ball. If he must choose between the two, he
should take the man, but a good guard rarely turns his
back on the ball. Rather he constantly tries to keep it in
view out of the corner of his eye.

A defensive player never leaves his opponent after he
shoots or passes. He sticks closer than ever to him. If the
opponent cuts sharply toward the goal and the player
is obliged to turn his back to the ball while following
him, he waves his arms in the air while running to stop
passes coming through. When wrestling with a foe for a
held ball, he tries to twist it loose by lunging in one direction, then quickly jerking the opposite way, prying downward with the hands and arms. When recovering an
enemy shot off the backboard, the player should not get
too close to the board and let the ball bound entirely over
him. He should leap high into the air in front of the
board, bring the ball to the floor clutched tightly against

his stomach or chest. Then he should crouch over and dribble low to the side of the court where there is the least traffic. Once in the clear, he should turn instantly in order to be ready to pass the ball quickly if his teammates are fast breaking.

MAN-FOR-MAN: This is the most popular basketball defense used today. It works as follows: Before the game starts, the coach, after a careful consideration of the size and ability of each enemy player, assigns each of his own men to one of them. The defensive players pick out their assigned offensive men as the latter cross the center line, and try to stick to them until the ball changes hands or until an emergency arises that necessitates exchanging opponents with a teammate. This exchanging process is called "checking off" or "switching," and all good man-for-man style teams have to learn it if they hope to stop a clever screening aggregation.

For instance, if a defensive player who has his man under control sees a second enemy player break loose from a guard who has been screened out, and drive unchallenged toward the goal, he should leave his own assigned opponent and move quickly to intercept the more threatening offensive player, staying with him until the ball changes hands. After this the original assignments may be resumed. The defensive man who has been screened out then quickly covers the opponent of the defensive man who alertly made the switch. This exchanging of opponents by defensive players is done only when the free offensive player is in a more dangerous scoring position than the offensive player the switcher is patrolling.

The advantages of the man-for-man system are that it puts responsibility on each player to stop a certain opponent and definitely fixes the blame if that opponent scores. It lets a coach plan in advance, when he knows the size and tricks of his opponents, which of his men he will assign to the more dangerous scorers of the enemy.

It gives a team ample training in the art of picking up opponents all over the floor should the latter, ahead in the scoring, try to freeze the ball in their backcourt. Also, it is the only defensive system that permits assigning two men to a dangerous scorer, leaving a poor shooter unguarded far out. To play it successfully, defensive players have to talk to each other constantly. By pointing and talking to one another, they can better manage the exchanging of opponents.

ZONE DEFENSE: In this style of defense, each of the five defensive players is assigned to a certain zone or section of the defensive third of the court and it is each man's duty to stay there and protect his zone until the ball changes hands. Usually the two guards patrol the back sixth of the court, the one in which the basket they defend is located, and divide it between them into two zones. The other three players do sentry duty in the adjacent sixth, which they divide into three zones, each of them taking one.

If the ball is passed into one man's zone, he immediately converges upon the offensive player holding it there until that player moves into another zone, whereupon the custodian of the new zone is responsible. At the same time the other defensive men near him move to the edge of their zones or rush to his assistance, if necessary.

The zone defense has several strengths. It is a difficult system for post play because the defense is permanently set and in excellent position to break up passes into the scoring zones. Also, having a certain fixed zone to protect, the defensive players refuse to be decoyed out of position by the screening machinations of the attackers. The zone defense also is less tiring, since the players do less running around than in the man-for-man defense. Also, because of their position, they have a splendid chance to make a quick-breaking dash as soon as they get the ball.

The biggest drawback of the zone method, and it is apt to be a tremendous one unless the zone team is also schooled in the man-for-man style, is that a zone defense has to be totally abandoned if the offensive team is ahead in the score and chooses, as it should, to freeze or hold the ball in backcourt outside the zone defense. This forces the zone team to come out of its shell and get the ball, or else lose the game. Also a zone team cannot assign a crack guard to a dangerous offensive player, and if the offensive elects to flank a certain zone by sending two men in it, a clean shot at the goal may result, since the zone is weak against shots from the side or the foul line.

CHAPTER 4

BOWLING

THE first known bowling at pins was done indoors in German cathedrals nine centuries ago. In Germany in those days, people had the curious custom of carrying around with them a wooden pin, or *Kiel,* as they called it, shaped very much like our Indian club. This they twirled to exercise their wrists, arms and backs, or they used it in friendly fencing contests, or threw it for distance as does today's javelin thrower.

After spending most of a long day at study and devotion, the German canons, or members of the bishop's council, used to gather for recreation at the open arcade of the cathedral cloister and set up a pin or *kiel.* Then they would hand a stone ball to the parishioners and invite them to roll it at the distant pin, which they playfully called a *Heide* or heathen. The idea was that if the parishioner scored a clean hit he was living an exemplary life, but if he missed he needed to give more time and attention to spiritual things. Afterwards, at dinner, the more accurate parishioners were toasted and the others good-naturedly admonished to get in some extra practice to improve their aim.

Later the custom grew until the canons and the cathedral students regularly opposed each other at *Kegelspiel,* as the sport was called. Every kegler in the game brought a pin. These were then clustered together and the bowler was credited with as many as he could topple over with one cast of the small stone ball.

The sport eventually spread outside the church, and bigger balls were substituted. Each city passed its own rules about scoring and measurement of equipment. But churchmen continued to bowl. Martin Luther, the rough and ready Saxon friar who in 1517 boldly led all North Germany into the revolt against the corrupt Medieval Church that resulted in the Protestant Reformation, was also a reformer of the sport of *Kegelspiel.* Luther was an inveterate bowler, and he is credited with establishing, after lengthy experimentation, the German standard that has stood for centuries of nine pins set in the form of a diamond.

Kegelspiel quickly expanded all over Germany. In 1890 William Pehle, of Berlin, secretary of the German Bowling Society, made a careful research of bowling in his country and found that the game was so thoroughly ingrained in Germany that its nomenclature had been incorporated in ancient German figures of speech that have lived down to the present day. For instance, when it was said of a man that he "had neither child nor ninepin."

it meant he was very poor indeed. A person who died was said to have "bowled out." "He will not hit a ninepin here," meant that a man would not succeed. When it thundered the old Germans were wont to declare, "St. Peter is bowling."

From Germany the sport of ninepins jumped across the lowlands into Holland and it was the Dutch who in 1623 introduced the game to America, when they brought it to Manhattan Island. Records show that Peter Jay, Peter Bayard and John Chambers, for the trifling consideration of a peppercorn, leased for eleven years, starting in 1732, a parade ground fronting the battery fort, now lower Broadway, New York City, and enclosed a bowling green there. Although the lease ran out, the little plot of grass, now surrounded by skyscrapers, is still there under the same name.

Bowling is a sport of such long standing that it has worn a permanent groove in many maps. Eight towns and a New Jersey mountain in the United States today are called Bowling Green, and so are a couple of villages in England and a bay and cape in Australia. Also in America are Bowler's Wharf, Virginia, and Bowlington, Kentucky; in Wales there is a Bowling Bank and in Scotland the town of Bowling.

The present American game is played with ten pins instead of the nine of Martin Luther. In the nineteenth century, ninepins became so much fun in America that several long-faced citizens who could not bear to see peo-

ple enjoying themselves at any kind of sport passed one
of their famous blue laws against it. Of course this merely
encouraged the game. Our astute pin-pelting forefathers
got their heads together, added an extra pin to the game
to escape the ninepin ban, and frightened the killjoys by
threatening to add additional pins every time a blue law
was passed. Thus modern American bowling began its
phenomenal growth. Today there are 26,500,000 active
bowlers in the United States, forty per cent of them women,
according to the survey by the Brunswick-Balke-Collender
company. The sport's devotees claim that makes it the nation's most popular participant sport.

Bowling is a practical game for boys as well as adults.
In 1936 a team of five boy bowlers from the New York
Guild of the Jewish Blind were matched against a team
of sighted lads. The sightless youngsters were permitted
to use a special hand rail to guide their approach and
any pins left standing after the first ball were called out
by number so the blind bowlers could aim their second
ball accordingly. No, the sightless team didn't win but it
lost by the narrow margin of only 16 pins, 654 to 670.

Let us step, for a moment, into a bowling establishment. The long 60-foot stretch of polished flooring to
which the big black balls cling so neatly as they hum
down it is the bowling alley. It was not just thrown together but was expertly fashioned from edge-grained vir-
gin white rock maple and Georgia pine, aged and treated
two years before laying, and cost more than two thousand

dollars. It is 41 to 42 inches wide and has an approach of at least 20 feet behind the foul line.

Noisy place, isn't it? When one of the big balls strikes the cluster of ten sturdy maple pins at the far end of the alley, the clonking crash of the capsizing pins, magnified twofold because it's happening indoors, is startling at first. Maybe Washington Irving was right when he said in "Rip Van Winkle" that the peals of distant thunder in the Catskill Mountains were not thunder at all, but were Henry Hudson and his crew who were bowling.

The idea of this game is to knock down as many pins as possible with each roll of the ball. If all ten are knocked down with the first bowl it is called a strike. To make a strike it is best to roll the ball into the "1–3 pocket" (between the No. 1 and No. 3 pins), hitting just off the right side of the No. 1 or head pin, the one nearest the bowler. This is where every right-handed bowler aims his first ball in each frame. When a strike is made, the player actually hits only four pins with his ball, the 1, 3, 5 and 9 pins, but those four knock down the other six.

The pins are set at regular intervals in a triangle measuring three feet on a side. The bowlers take turns. Each bowler bowls twice. The two bowls comprise a frame and ten frames make a game, one extra ball being allowed for a spare, or two for a strike in the tenth frame. If all the pins are not flattened by the first two balls bowled, one point is scored for each pin down. However if all the pins are leveled by the first ball, a strike is scored. The score made by the next two balls is added to the 10 points awarded for the strike to complete the tally for that frame. Thus the most that can be scored in a single frame is 30 points, the premium for three consecutive strikes.

If the bowler succeeds in knocking down all the pins with the first two balls, he is credited with a spare and gets ten points for that and also credit for the number of pins knocked down by the first ball in the next frame. Thus, if that third ball sweeps over seven pins, his total score for that spare frame would be 17.

There is little danger of beginners overdoing bowling. The friction of the finger grip soon makes the thumb so tender that the newcomer to the game cannot bowl a long stretch even if he wants to. The following hints will aid the beginner:

EQUIPMENT: To protect alleys, expert bowlers use special shoes with a rubber tip or half sole on the toe of the right shoe, which must clutch the floor. The left shoe, which must slide, has a smooth leather sole. Loose garments that particularly have plenty of room in the back and shoulders are essential. Loose-fitting white trousers and shirt are good for this reason. Many people bowl in whatever clothing they happen to be wearing at the time, but perspiration is bound to occur; therefore special clothing is much to be preferred. It is folly for a heated player to walk out of the indoor warmth of a bowling alley into cool air outside without meanwhile having put on sufficient additional clothing.

Beginners should use a light ball. Most bowling alleys carry several balls of different weights and grip-sizes and, like the old-time barber shops that used to keep a fancy individual shaving mug for each regular customer, many alleys reserve special balls for regular league bowlers. A glance along the rail at any bowling alley will show there two types of balls, the rubbery black mineralite ball preferred by "hookers" because it curves well, and the polished mottled ball used by straight-ball bowlers. Most top-notch bowlers roll a hook.

GRIP: Three-hole balls are best for beginners. The holes should be large and smooth enough and also spaced the right distance apart so the fingers won't be cut or cramped. The thumb, second and third fingers are placed in the holes, the first and fourth fingers on the ball.

Keep the thumb on top, pointed squarely at the pins you want to hit. The fingers stay behind the ball throughout delivery unless the ball is to be curved. If the hand perspires, a handkerchief or towel should be used.

POSITION: Face the pins with your shoulders squared toward them, standing erect twelve to fifteen feet back of the foul line. Hold the bowling ball at or slightly above the belt line. Grasp it firmly in the right hand but support its weight in the left hand. Have your right hand slightly under the ball so that the weight of the ball rests in the palm of your hand. Stand naturally and relaxed. Don't squat or tighten up.

FRONT VIEW
OF FOUR-STEP DELIVERY

DELIVERY: Approach the foul line in a straight line. Do not run. Just walk four fast steps. Here's a brief description of what you do on each step: (1) Step forward on the right foot and push the ball forward and down in a smooth motion. Take it easy. Always concentrate on developing a well-delivered, working ball. (2) The second step, slightly longer than the first, is taken with the left foot as the ball swings to the rear. Left arm moves forward for balance. Forward momentum increases. (3) The ball reaches height of backswing on third step, made with the right foot. Left hand is extended forward for balance. Do not raise ball above shoulder level. (4) The fourth step, on the left foot, brings you up to the foul line on a graceful glide. Get the ball well out over the foul line. Then follow through. Good follow-through is important. After delivering the ball, your hand should go forward, following the path of the ball. *Do not jerk your arm back* or you'll kill the action of the ball.

Left-handed bowlers simply reverse this procedure.

Now let's go through it again, adding a few fine points. Remember, you start off with the right foot and deliver with the left foot in front of you, allowing it to slide forward to a point about half a foot behind the foul line. Take even smooth steps, not short jerky ones. Don't crook the bowling arm but let it hang straight. The idle, or left, arm should be extended so the weight of the ball (sixteen pounds is the size used in tournaments) will not over-balance you. Keeping the feet apart also will help the balance.

On the backswing, keep the back straight but bend the left knee and swing the ball back until the arm is parallel with the floor. On the downswing, keep the ball as near to the body as possible and keep it moving in a straight line. When releasing the ball, stoop close to the alley. The ball should never be lofted or thrown but should glide away noiselessly. It should be laid down well in ad-

SIDE VIEW
OF FOUR-STEP DELIVERY

vance of your front foot. As the ball leaves the hand, follow through with the arm.

The best delivery is a well-directed slow ball. Use just enough speed to make the ball go straight to the right side of the head pin. Try for timing and smoothness. A ball bowled with excessive speed may slide instead of roll and scatter the pins unnaturally, causing bad splits. Beginners should set up only the head pin and shoot at it until they have gained some command of delivery.

Sixty feet is a long distance at which to aim, so some champions use the spot method, picking out a spot ten feet down the alley from the foul line and concentrating on making the ball cross that spot. If the roll is correct the first ten feet, it will be correct all the way down the alley. Others keep their eyes on the pins. A third method is to select a spot on the alley on which to release the ball and visualize a straight line from there to the 1–3 pocket. Most bowlers look at the pins when they are shooting at spares.

THE HOOK DELIVERY: The hook is thrown with a twist to the left by the wrist. The thumb comes out of its grip hole first. The fingers apply the spin with a sharp lift. As the ball is released swing the arm to the left across the body and turn the wrist over slightly so that the thumb is to the left and the fingers to the right. This gives the ball an inward spin, similar to the outcurve in baseball, causing it to break sharply just before it reaches the pins. There are many variations of this method. The beginner should learn to roll straight balls at first. Later, if he wishes, he may work out his own form for the hook.

Despite all the form described above, many champions are noted for their unorthodox methods. Don Carter of St. Louis, the 1957 and 1959 champion of the ten-day World's Invitational Match Game tournament that is nationally televised, bends his right elbow instead of holding it straight. Carter creeps slowly down the alley as though stalking the pins and leans sharply so he can release the ball close to the floor. But he makes $40,000 yearly just bowling. Ed Lubanski of Detroit, the 1958 champion, still uses the two-hole grip. Lou Campi of Dumont, New Jersey, finishes his right-hand swing with his right foot forward. Steve Nagy of St. Louis tosses the ball out two feet instead of laying it down on the maple. It is said of him that he makes a strike on the first bounce. While the form described herein is best for beginners, it is sensible to adopt anything unusual that works well for you.

SPARES: Occasionally bowlers knock down all ten pins with their first ball, but in most cases they will get only part of them and a few combinations of pins, called spares, will remain standing. Being able to hit these with the second ball brings out the real skill in bowling. Bowlers always study these remaining combinations of scattered pins carefully before determining where to send the second ball. Every pin in the game is numbered. The head pin is 1 and the remaining pins are numbered from left to right in each successive row. For example, the two pins in the second row are 2 and 3, the three pins in the third row 4, 5 and 6, and the four pins in the back row 7, 8, 9 and 10.

When one pin has been left, hit the pin as squarely as possible with the ball. When shooting at single pins on the left or in the center, such as the 2, 4, 5, 7, or 8, release the ball for both straight-arm and hook delivery from the right side of the foul line, the same as when bowling for a strike.

However, for pins on the bowler's right, such as the 3, 6, 9 or 10, move more toward the center of the foul line if you bowl a straight ball or slightly to the left of the center of the foul line if you bowl a hook. When bowling for the 10 pin, a wide hook is impossible but even a slight spin will make it hug the alley and prevent its tumbling into the gutter.

BABY SPLITS: When one or more pins have been knocked down between two or more pins left standing, that "leave" is called a "split." The 2–7 and 3–10 combinations are called baby splits because they are easy to make. On each of these simple splits, the bowler should direct the ball between the two pins, making the ball knock down both.

OTHER TWO-PIN SPLITS: Some two-pin splits, such as the 4–6, 7–9 and 8–10, are usually impossible and the bowler should content himself with only one pin. The 5–7 and 5–10 splits are difficult but can be made by hitting the 5 pin thin on the right when trying for the

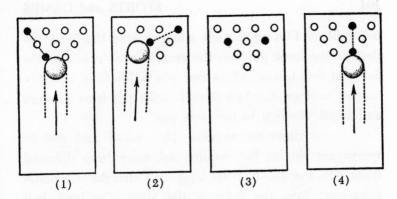

1. 2-7 split; strike 2 pin on its right side or direct ball between the two pins.
2. 5-10 split; hit 5 pin on its left side.
3. 4-6 split; go after one pin only.
4. 3-9 spare; strike front pin full.

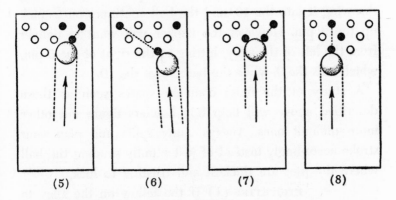

5. 6-9-10 spare; strike 6 pin on its left side.
6. 3-7-10 split; strike 3 pin thin on its right side.
7. 5-6-10 spare; roll straight for the 5-6 pocket.
8. 2-5-8 spare; strike front pin full.

A FEW COMMON SPLITS AND SPARES
AND HOW TO PLAY THEM

5–7 split, or thin on the left when seeking the 5–10, deflecting the front pin into the rear in each case. On the 2–8 and 3–9 leaves, where one pin is lined up squarely behind another, the ball should strike the front pin full and smash through to the back pin.

THREE-PIN SPARES: The 4–7–8 and 6–9–10 spares are similar but require deliveries from different spots. On the 4–7–8, both hook and straight-ball deliveries start from the right of the alley. The hook ball strikes the 4 pin on its right side, the straight ball on the left side. On the 6–9–10, the straight ball, bowled from the right of the alley, strikes the 6 pin on its left side, throwing it into the 10, and the ball continues on to pick up the 9 pin. However the hooker will want to deliver from the left of the alley, hitting to the right of the 6 pin, which kills the 9, while the ball erases the 10.

A study of the more common spares such as those described above will help boy bowlers figure out other more difficult ones. Always study splits and plan your stroke accordingly instead of just blindly sending the ball where the pins are thickest and trusting to luck.

ETIQUETTE: (1) If the fellow on the alley to your right has begun his approach, allow him to finish before beginning yours. (2) Don't double-ball the pin boys. Any manager will tell you pin boys are much harder to get than customers. (3) Try not to laugh at the mistakes of beginners. People will think you have a short memory. (4) Although body English is part of the game, confine it to your own lane. (5) Don't offer advice to other bowlers unless they ask for it.

(6) Check your temper and your language with your coat. You can't frighten pins. (7) Be prompt for league matches of any kind. (8) If you're losing, don't alibi. (9) If you're winning, don't boast. (10) Get set before making your approach but remember the fellow behind you. Meaningless motions like shuffling your feet or juggling the ball too long will only make you more tense. (11) Before getting on the approach, be sure there's nothing on your shoes that will mar the wood. (12) Stay on the bench until your turn to bowl. (13) Stay back of the foul lines at all times, even if nobody is calling them. (14) If you're a beginner, get to know the ball you're using.

(15) Keep the game moving. After your ball hits the the pins, walk directly to the back of the approach. (16) When a bowler on the adjoining lane is addressing his pins, respect his priority. Don't step in front of him to pick your ball off the rack. (17) Splits, misses and taps are just as much a part of the game as strikes and spares. Don't blame the equipment. Correct your own faults.

Before 1895, bowling was in bad repute because of its association with gambling and its want of uniformity in rules and specifications. To give the sport a good reputation and standardize rules, dimensions, weights and sizes, the American Bowling Congress was organized in 1895 in New York City and has operated efficiently ever since. It conducted its first national championship, now called the A.B.C., in Chicago in 1901. These championship meets have been continued annually ever since. Like baseball's world series, they are attended from all over the nation.

The financial set-up of bowling makes it unique among most American sports. Bowling tolerates no hypocritical distinction between professionals and amateurs since almost every bowler professionalizes himself by competing for cash prizes in the American Bowling Congress. Another of bowling's peculiar features is that it is not dependent for its existence upon huge gate receipts. In fact it collects far more money from its contestants than from its spectators. For instance, approximately thirty thousand bowlers from all over the country compete in the A.B.C. championships each year and pay a ten-dollar entry fee for each event they enter. When you compare bowling's thirty thousand contestants with the total of fifty-five hundred men and women athletes who compete every four years in the Olympic Games, you begin to see why bowling has the world's largest and most enthusiastic national championship meet, rated strictly from the angle of the contestant.

In duck pins, bowling has spawned an off-shoot that should greatly interest boys still too small to heft heavy bowling balls. Duck pins is almost exactly like bowling except that it has pins only about half as big and is played with a small light ball only five inches in diameter and three pounds twelve ounces in weight. The finger holes have been omitted from this ball. The bowling distance in duck pins is only fifty feet and players are required to bowl three balls in a frame and two frames at a time. Otherwise, its rules are like those of American ten-pins.

There's another bowling game called lawn bowls, a gentler, quieter and much older sport than bowling at pins, that enjoys great popularity in Scotland and is played sporadically in America. In lawn bowls, no pins are used and the game is always played outdoors. The purpose is to leisurely roll the large black biased (not entirely round) balls across a velvetlike green, stopping them as close as possible to a small white ball called a jack. In this respect, the sport is similar to horseshoes.

George Washington used to play lawn bowls on his own green at Mount Vernon and legend has it that this was the sport Sir Francis Drake was amusing himself with at Plymouth Hoe in 1588 when he was told that the formidable Spanish Armada was approaching off the coast of Cornwall. "Let us finish the game and then we'll finish the Spaniards," Sir Francis is said to have exclaimed, and calmly bowled out his end before directing the vigorous English naval action that destroyed the Spanish ships.

However neither duck pins nor lawn bowls are nearly as popular in the United States today as American ten-pins, or "just plain bowling," as the average American calls it. High-school boys and girls are bowling a great deal in physical education programs that seek to teach them a game they can play through life. Today bowling ranks with fly-fishing as the only American sport that brings cheers, not jeers, for three strikes.

CHAPTER 5

BOXING

B OXING teaches grit and courage at the formative period of life when every young man ought to learn it. Bob Fitzsimmons, world's heavyweight boxing champion from 1897 to 1899, said that the boy who boxed was "never in a hurry to seek a quarrel, because the knowledge that he can take care of himself renders him good-natured at affronts that would wound his pride were he unable to resent them." Likewise, a boy who is not afraid to risk a licking with the boxing gloves will very likely grow into a man with nerve enough to tackle any crisis in his business, professional or personal life. Pluck, therefore, is the most important quality which is derived from boxing. The following incident, taken from Robert H. Davis' fascinating little book, *Ruby Robert*, illustrates the difference between boxing courage and boxing skill. "Ruby Robert" was Bob Fitzsimmons, the old champion. He had a son Bobby, who not only grew up into a youth of magnificent physical proportions, but was a born boxer, fast as chain lightning and a hard hitter.

One day while visiting the elder Fitzsimmons, then over fifty years of age, on the Fitzsimmons estate at Dunellen, New Jersey, Davis asked the old fighter how good a boxer he considered his son Bobby, who was then grown to young manhood. Fitz answered:

" 'E's fast. 'E can 'it 'ard. There's no man living can put a glove on 'im when 'e's at 'is best."

"How is he in the ring?"

Bob shook his head. "I don't know. 'E's never been in the ring. I don't even know it 'e can take a punch. There's a difference between boxing and actual fighting. I don't think I'm a good boxer, but when the gong sounds and the fight begins, I'm at 'ome. I 'ate to train, but I likes to fight. Come out in the barn and I'll put the gloves on with Bobby."

It was a marvelous exhibition. The younger at that time was six feet in height and weighed about one hundred and sixty-five pounds. Bob was one hundred and seventy-five. They used eight-ounce gloves.

Bobby walked up to the old man, feinted him into a knot and stabbed him twice on the nose. Bob countered and missed. Bobby leaned back like a sunflower in a light zephyr. Without changing the position of his feet and moving only from the upper part of his body forward, back, right and left, he hit Robert Fitzsimmons, senior, ten times before the Antipodean finally got under cover. The son blocked, sidestepped, ducked and pulled every trick known in the ring. . . .

Bob tried every maneuver he knew on his own shadow, but without success. The boy laughed and played with his father. Emboldened by the presence of a spectator who had seen the great master win the championship of the world, Bobby began to get gay. All art has a frontier, a precise definition beyond which the artist encounters jeopardy. Bobby stepped across this barrier and received a wallop on the chin that enabled him to look down his own back. Before he had completely recovered, Fitzsimmons *père* slammed him on the ear with a left hook.

The boy threw up both hands in an effort to block what was coming, but failed to protect his mouth, upon which he was bashed twice with accuracy and fervor. Before he could get his hands down, papa hit him a swat in the wind, whereupon the boy's entire ambition blew out of his nostrils. He stepped out of range, still holding both hands in front of his face, and peered at the old man between the gloves.

In spite of the expression of wonderment on his face, a bright idea suddenly came to him; at least I thought it was a bright idea: He put the wrist of his right-hand glove to his teeth, untied the bowknot, performed the same office on the left glove, threw both mitts on the floor, and left the barn at once, striding into the house and slamming the kitchen door loudly enough to knock most of the cooking utensils off the pantry shelves.

Father Fitzsimmons looked at me with an air of bewilderment, as though he had never seen the younger Fitzsimmons before, and let out a long sigh.

"Well, what do you know about that? 'E don't like it! 'E can't take it! I just barely tapped 'im. Too bad, ain't it? 'E'll 'ave to get over that—or *goodbye!*"

Maybe the incident is not entirely fair to the younger Fitzsimmons. Surely it takes a good deal of nerve to lace on the gloves against a former world's champion, even if he is your father. Nevertheless, boxing should breed the courage all boys own but have little chance to develop.

In 1932 a National Collegiate boxing tournament was established and has been held ever since, although many schools have abandoned the sport lately. Collegiate boxing gained its original impetus during World War I when American college men were required to box in the army training camps, and upon their return in large numbers to colleges and universities after the war ended in 1919, they transferred the sport to their schools.

Safety is its keynote. Large twelve-ounce gloves are required; the bulk of the padding is centered over the striking surface, the ring floor must be extended at least two feet beyond the lower ropes, the floor, ring posts and turn-buckles must be padded, no adhesive tape or other heavy material may be used in bandaging the hands, contests are limited to three rounds of two minutes each with a one-minute rest between rounds, rigid weight reducing is prohibited and no boxer may compete in any class unless his weight is specified within the limits of that class. Perhaps the best precaution is the insistence of the rules committee that a medical officer, who gives each boxer a careful checking over four hours before actual competition, shall always attend every meet and have absolute power to order the withdrawal of one of the contestants in case of injury. When either of the boxers is cut or hurt in any way the bout is stopped, the medical adviser goes into the ring to check the injury carefully and his decision is not subject to appeal by either coaches or officials. After the meet, contestants are re-examined by the doctor.

Boxing is a sport for both young and old. Anyone doubting that it is an old man's sport has only to go to the records of the professional prize ring. For instance, Jack Broughton, the old English champion, was forty-six years old before he lost the title in 1750 to Jack Slack; Mike Donovan was forty-four when he defeated twenty-seven-year-old world's champion Jack Dempsey the Non-Pareil; Jack Johnson, Negro heavyweight champion from 1908 to 1915, came back in 1926 at the age of forty-eight to whip Pat Lester, a twenty-four-year-old fighter, in fifteen rounds under a blazing sun in the bull ring at Nogales, Sonora, Mexico. Bob Fitzsimmons fought at the age of fifty-two; Bill Richmond, a fifty-six-year-old American Negro, thrashed young Jack Carter in England in 1818; Edward C. Rollins, a Negro known as "Starlight," fought at the age of fifty-seven; and Gypsy Jem Mace, champion of England in 1862, boxed at the age of sixty.

Fighters of a later day who still punched sharply and craftily at an advanced age were Joe Walcott, Archie Moore and "Sugar Ray" Robinson.

That boxing is a healthy sport is reflected in the longevity of some of the old champions. Among the old bare-knuckle kings of England: Broughton lived to be eighty-five, John Gully eighty, Daniel Mendoza seventy-three, Tom Belcher seventy-one, Tom Cribb sixty-seven, and Mace seventy-nine. Of our own American world's champions, John L. Sullivan lived to sixty in spite of a life of dissipation, Jim Corbett died at the age of sixty-six, Jim Jeffries died in his seventies. Jess Willard, Jack Dempsey, Gene Tunney and Joe Louis, later champions, are still going strong.

FOOTWORK

Footwork is the first fundamental of boxing. A boxer who is nimble of foot can keep away from a sharp-punching foe, particularly the bruising body punchers, and Jim Jeffries said body blows win fights. He can also avoid having to block blows with his arms; thus he has both hands available when he suddenly chooses to jump in and shell his opponent.

Jim Corbett, the one-hundred-and-seventy-eight-pound Californian who was heavyweight champion of the world from 1892 to 1897, probably had the fastest and cleverest footwork of any man ever to fight for the world's heavyweight championship. Thanks to it, Corbett didn't carry a single mark on his handsome Irish face upon his retirement from the ring. Corbett excelled in footwork. He always said it was half of boxing. In a four-round exhibition bout with John L. Sullivan, several months prior to the Sullivan-Corbett championship affair, Corbett took special care not to reveal his fast and baffling footwork to the world's champion. It was the part of his armament he was most anxious to conceal. He wanted it to be a complete surprise to Sullivan when they met for the world's title, and it was.

"I ran every day," Corbett said later, "doing sprints for speed and distance for endurance. I skipped rope lots, too, and soon I could move about on tip-toe for hours without fatigue. In my matches, I always knew, on every step, exactly the angle at which I moved and how far each step took me. Finally I got so I could always step within a fraction of an inch of the spot I wanted. You might say I learned to think with my feet."

The fundamental position of the feet in boxing is as follows: Put the left foot forward in a straight line, bend the knee slightly and place a little of the weight on the toes. However most of your "heft" should be on the right foot, which is held nearly flat; the toe is held a little outward. Your feet should be just far enough apart to assure good balance and should never be crossed or kept side by side. If they are too close together, a light blow will easily upset you. If they are spread too widely, you will not be able to generate speed enough to move within range of your foe.

When you are attacking, the left foot takes the lead. Take a short step forward with it, pushing off the ball of the right foot. Then quickly bring up the right foot the same distance. Practice this maneuver in short, fast steps all about the ring, first in slow motion, then speeded up. Notice how it puts you on top of an opponent and still lets you maintain balance.

The retreat is similarly executed, but here the right foot takes the lead. Pushing off the left foot, step back a few inches with the right, then bring the left foot back the same distance. Practice this retreating maneuver at both slow and fast tempo in a series of short steps all about the ring.

As in traffic, stay to the right when side-stepping, to keep yourself away from an opponent's dangerous right hand. Always start this side step by stepping with the right foot first, pushing off your left. The initial step with your right foot should be from twelve to eighteen inches right oblique. This is stepping about as far forward as you can to the right. The side step is very useful in dodging under an opponent's left hand lead to the head, as will be discussed later.

Practice the advance, retreat and side step described above, mixing them together. The purpose of the short fast steps is speed and balance. Try to stay on the balls of your feet as you work.

HOW THE BOXER STANDS

In his *Tale of James Carabine*, that fine story of the early American prize ring, Donn Byrne talks about "the hunched left shoulder, the eye that moves while the head does not." This describes quite well the *upright stance* in boxing.

Of course there is more to it than just that. With the body leaning a little forward from the hips, put your left side forward. This allows more body and shoulder swing for your blows, lengthens the reach of your left arm and presents a smaller hitting target to your opponent. Hold your chin cupped low on your chest. Boxing authorities differ on the position of the shoulder. Many favor hunching it slightly so it will help protect the jaw.

However Bob Fitzsimmons always contended that "a boxer with his shoulders about his ears and his body held rigid cannot move quickly," and recommended holding the shoulder naturally to get ease of arm movement and more reach. However, there is more than one school of thought on the matter and the boxer should adopt the stance that seems to suit him best.

The left arm is extended at almost full length and held a few inches below the perpendicular so it will not become heavy. The right arm is held across the body, the elbow is kept in to protect the short ribs. The hand is held just below the left breast, the knuckles face outward and the thumb down and held against the clenched second and third fingers.

Left-handers will find this orthodox stance of the right-handers a good one for them, too, rather than the stance of the right foot and right arm extended. Jim Jeffries, two-hundred-and-thirty-pound world heavyweight champion from 1899 until he ran out of opponents, was a natural left-hander, yet he adopted the orthodox stance of right-handers. Blessed with an abnormally powerful left hand, he used it with murderous effect as a lead. Jeffries' left jab was so powerful that he knocked opponents flat on their backs with it. He also had the habit of starting for the body, then hooking it up to the chin; or he jabbed a left lead to the jaw, then followed in almost the same motion with a left hook delivered by merely hooking his left wrist upward with his weight behind it. He also owned a heavy right-hand punch.

Another stance is the *crouch,* usually employed by short stocky boxers who can't get into taller opponents from the upright stance, since they haven't so much reach. Tommy Burns, a small man who lost the world's championship to Jack Johnson, the Negro, liked the crouch. Burns said the crouch was more natural, "forced the foe to hit down at you, thus enabling you to take his blows on top of your head where they don't hurt much, while you will be in a favorable position to get well into him with his body open to your attack. By stooping in this fashion," Burns went on, "you are also well placed to cover yourself from wild attacks with your arms. Also your body is withdrawn as far as possible from the scene of operations and you don't want any more punches in the stomach than you can help. Also, you will find that your own blows are even more effective when they shoot up from below, and also more difficult to parry as their direction is hard to judge."

Jeffries is usually given credit for introducing the crouch. He hit upon it accidentally as a means of preventing his opponents from striking his one vulnerable spot, his liver. Hit there by John Brink during a friendly practice match, Jeffries was in such pain that he doubled over and could not straighten up, and was forced to fight from the crouch. He then discovered, much to his surprise, that he could deliver much harder punches from the crouch than he could standing up, and used the crouch in his fights thereafter.

TRAINING AND CONDITIONING

The best way to learn to box is to do lots of it. "You can't make omelettes without breaking eggs," is the way the English middleweight Ted Lewis put it. One of the finest fighters of all time, the little American Negro, George Dixon, who held the world's flyweight, bantamweight and featherweight championships at one time or another from 1890 to 1900, developed his marvelous ring craft through fighting two or three times a week. At the end of his long career he had fought eight hundred ring battles, an all-time record for pugilists of any weight or time.

However, a boy who always boxes the same companion will not learn much. If he wishes to improve his art he should box with several different opponents—tall, short, fast, slow—and box often. The only caution is to box with somebody approximately the same age and weight as himself, and if possible, someone a little better than he is.

While a boy is learning something of the science of boxing, he should also gradually be acquiring physical condition. Next to boxing, running is the best conditioner for a boxer. However this type of training should not be too strenuous. A three- or four-mile outing into the country, during most of which the young boxer briskly walks (although occasionally he should break into short sprints of from twenty to thirty yards or slow striding for two hundred or three hundred yards), is very beneficial. If possible, he should cover hilly ground during these training rambles to deepen his chest and develop his stamina and leg muscles.

If you are going to box, first of all see a qualified physician and take a thorough physical examination. Don't start your training with a physic, as many foolishly do. Remember Addison's definition of it: "Physic, for the most part, is nothing else but the substitute of exercise and temperance."

Avoid all rope climbing, parallel bars and the use of heavy weights, dumbbells and medicine balls. Speed, suppleness and agility are what you want—not tight, bunchy muscles. It is wise to train and box outdoors as much as possible. Tobacco smoke, dust and floating threads are apt to enter your lungs when you breathe heavily during exercise in a closed room.

Remember that sleep is very important. Gene Tunney, the fighter who dethroned the modern Jack Dempsey for the world's title in 1927, always slept ten hours daily during training. Don't sleep in a draft but have plenty of fresh air.

Don't starve yourself. Eat about anything you want provided your menu includes plenty of meats, fruits and fresh vegetables. You will know what food agrees with you, and you will be surprised at the wide variety of foods a boxer or any other athlete can train on. For instance,

Tommy Burns was fond of rhubarb, Fitzsimmons liked calves'-foot jelly. Sullivan had a predilection for celery and Jack Johnson would argue for hours about the caloric value of the banana, which he ate in generous quantities while he trained. Don't eat or drink too much at the last meal prior to actual boxing itself or right after competition, but don't totally deny yourself, either.

Don't guzzle cold water after exercise. Jim Corbett had a splendid system for this. After a hard workout during his training for the Sullivan fight, the thirsty Corbett would go to a spring, take a dipper of water, rinse his mouth out half a dozen times and gargle his throat. When he felt cooler he would repeat the process. Thus it took several minutes for him to empty that first dipper, after which he found his appetite for the evening meal was good. "I simply adopted the principle of treating my machinery as one does an automobile," Corbett afterward said. "You don't pour a lot of cold water into a heated engine, but let it dribble in gradually." Corbett also varied his training menu for Sullivan by eating a couple of plates of ice cream at night, which should be convincing to those who advocate too strict a training diet.

If possible, every boy boxer should have access to a punching bag and also a heavy dummy bag. Set the punching bag at shoulder level or a shade higher, and, to keep from scuffing your knuckles, wear light gloves or an old pair of kid gloves with the fingers cut out. Practice your straight punches first. Dance around the ball and hit it hard, as though it were your foe's head. Avoid fancy bag-punching. Good bag-punching requires a world of practice but it will pay you in the long run because it will teach you to nail a moving target, develops hitting accuracy and footwork and strengthens the muscles of shoulder and arm. Use the dummy bag to develop punching power; try your in-fighting and body punches on it. Rope skipping is fine for footwork and stamina but it must not be overdone. Fifteen minutes a day is plenty for a boy.

Although you can train as steadily and as busily as you like, don't work so hard that you will go stale. When you feel tired, can't perspire and have little relish for boxing, it is time to lay off a couple or three days and forget all about the sport. Keep the feet and body warmly covered during training and after exertion. Bob Fitzsimmons always went around overweighted with clothing. He believed, and sensibly, too, that a continuous mild warmth was preferable to a single chill.

Learn to protect your hands. No boy's hands are very strong. Georges Carpentier, the French heavyweight, points out that any injury sustained to hands is usually felt throughout a boxer's lifetime. "A small mishap, a false movement, and the pain will immediately reappear, the place of injury being forever tender," Carpentier says. Although the modern twelve-ounce intercollegiate glove is padded so heavily that bandages aren't necessary,

Carpentier recommends that if bandages are used, they should be wound firmly enough to avoid slipping but never tight enough to retard the circulation, because a fighter's hands may swell during a bout. Carpentier further warns against the use of safety pins or straight pins to fasten bandages. Instead, he advises tearing the ends of the bandages in two lengthwise strips a foot long, tying them to prevent further tearing, then winding the loose strips in opposite directions. Intercollegiate rules permit the use of adhesive tape about the wrist to fasten the bandage.

Philadelphia Jack O'Brien, who won the world's light-heavyweight championship from Bob Fitzsimmons in 1904, gives good advice regarding equipment in his and Doctor Bilik's splendid treatise, *Boxing*. Obviously speaking to older boys who have embraced the sport seriously, O'Brien says:

"Get good equipment, gloves, trunks, etc. Cheap equipment doesn't last, gets misshapen, and is apt to bring injuries. An attractive suit gives you confidence and pride. Leather-soled high shoes are best. There are clever inexpensive headguards to protect your forehead and ears. The odonto-guard is a teeth protector which has just been made legitimate by the New York State Boxing Commission. There are thumb, knuckle and wrist protectors. Tape your hands in order to protect your knuckles. I believe the woven elastic bandages, such as the Ace, are far better for the purpose than the felt binders which are popular at present."

The best way to assure the protection of your hands is to learn how to punch correctly. Never land a blow that will hurt your hands. Always hold your hands open when boxing, never closing your fist until in the act of landing a punch. Constant clenching of the fist strains the muscles of the forearm. Keep everything loose and relaxed. Never hit with the thumb.

In landing a straight punch, turn the palm of your hand inward and downward so the top of the knuckles will strike. When you swing, turn the fist and forearm inward and downward in order to land with the knuckles up. Blows are usually landed with the first two knuckles of the hitting hand.

Shadow boxing before a mirror so that errors may be detected and corrected is good. Jim Corbett used a mirror in his youth while perfecting his puzzling feints and footwork. Carefully go through all the maneuvers of attack and defense before the glass. Don't waste a step. Get the footwork and punching stance down pat for both leads and counters as you face your imaginary opponent.

In conclusion, remember to warm up carefully each day prior to actual training and lay off all heavy work a couple of days before an important bout.

If you can patronize a good instructor, do so.

PUNCHES

STRAIGHT LEFT LEAD: The fastest punch in boxing, and the one most frequently employed in the ring, is the straight left lead to the head. It is used to annoy or confuse a foe, or as a counter to one of his swings, to stop him if he rushes you, or to set him up for a more damaging blow to follow.

It is an easy punch to land because the left arm is carried in such an advanced position that it is always knocking at the door of a foe's jaw before the blow starts.

A good time to deliver it is when your opponent has his guard a little low, to which indiscretion you can encourage him by constant feinting. Suddenly take a short step toward him with the left foot and, swinging your left shoulder from the hip, lash out straight with your slightly cocked left arm for his face, following through with the body.

Aim to make each punch sting. Don't draw back your left glove, but shoot it from where it is at the moment. As you release the blow, shut the fist. Remember to turn your arm inward and hit with the knuckles up.

Don't forget the possibility of a counter punch by your opponent. Keep your right up to block his counter. Recover quickly. As soon as your punch is snapped, hurry the left arm back to its former position. Keep dancing after the punch, working to your right, away from his dangerous right.

STRAIGHT RIGHT: This is a good punch to use as a quick follow for the left lead; the two of them together are known as the "one-two." As you land your straight left lead to the head, the right shoulder, the

right side of your body, and the right fist will naturally
pivot back to your right. In delivering your right as a
quick follow-up, throw your body and right shoulder to
the left again without changing the position of your feet.
Then twist your right arm inward and, hitting with the
knuckles up, land on his jaw or body. The terrific follow-
through of this punch, accomplished by the long shift
of the body from right to left, makes it a teeth-rattling
blow. If you shoot the punch without the straight left
lead buildup, take a short quick step forward with your
left foot to put you on top of your opponent. Then let
your right go, following through with your body and
right shoulder and transferring most of your weight onto
your left foot. Watch for your foe's right. Keep your left
glove up to block it as you shoot your punch. After you
land, spring off your right foot back into position, watching keenly for a chance to let drive with your left.

Delivering a straight right is more risky than shooting
a left-hand lead because the right has to go a longer distance and therefore your opponent has more time to spoil
it and nail you with a counter. Also, as a boxer throws this
punch, he exposes his whole body and therefore presents
a wide target for a counter punch to the body.

HOOKS: In his memorable fight with Joe
Choinyski on the barge in San Francisco Bay in 1890,
Jim Corbett fought with the knuckles of his third and
fourth fingers on his left hand painfully smashed. He
discovered he could save the two damaged knuckles by

swinging his left sideways and upward, a sort of round-house blow, instead of punching straight. This punch let him absorb the impact on the side of his hand and on the first knuckle, and thus the left hook was born by accident. After the Choinyski fight, the knuckles on Corbett's left hand were so flattened that he couldn't even hit the punching bag with a straight left without wincing, and so was obliged to perfect his newly found hook instead.

Soon the punch, which was a cross between a straight blow and a swing, began to be adopted by American fighters everywhere. They discovered it could be shot from any angle which a sudden opening permitted, was short, fast, accurate, difficult to guard and had the kick of a mule in it. Jeffries probably owned the deadliest left hook the prize ring has ever known; the modern Jack Dempsey ran him a close second.

To deliver the left hook, bend the left arm slightly, tense it, and, taking a short step forward and to the left with your left foot, swing the left glove, held slightly away from the left side, sideways and upwards. Then hook it down on the jaw, following through with the shoulder and body and rising on the toes of the left foot. Twist the fist downward in order to hit with the knuckles up. Be careful not to telegraph the punch. Start it from the place where your left fist is held at the time the opening presents itself.

Hooks may also be delivered with the right, and sent to the body. The boxer who doesn't practice the hook to the body is passing up one of the ring's most destructive punches.

For a fine short story about a fight between a hooker and a straight puncher, read Ernest Hemingway's "Fifty Grand."

Swings are risky because they have such a long way to go and therefore may be easily avoided or stopped. Then too, they leave the swinger wide open to counter blows. Also they may do more damage to the swinger's hands than to the opponent. The best punches are shorter ones, with more speed of fist or glove.

The right-hand swing to the head is the heaviest blow in boxing. Bob Fitzsimmons described its technique as follows: "Wait until you get your opponent's guard low before trying this punch. You can do this by making believe to hit him in the body. Then, when you think you have the opening, drop your right hand down and back, with the elbow bent so the forearm and upper arm are almost at right angles. From this position throw your arm in a half-circle up and over to the side of your opponent's head. Close your fist while the blow is traveling. As the blow starts, swing the right leg and all the right side of the body with it. Just as it is landing, stiffen the arm and push the shoulder forward, turning the body at the hips. A blow to have force must have the send of the legs and the swing of the body with it."

The left swing is made in the same manner, except the position of the legs is not changed. It does not carry as much dynamite as the right swing because it does not get as much body follow-through. However, being shorter, it is more accurate.

It is easy to break the thumb with this blow unless the knuckles are up and the thumb down when contact is made.

The *uppercut* is a good punch to use occasionally on an opponent who persists in clinching or "covering up" or who likes to lead a right-hand punch for your head, thus precipitating himself within reach of your guns. The blow gets its name because you hit upward at your opponent. It is dangerous because you are apt to bash your wrist against his elbow. Also it leaves your own stomach un-protected for his counter.

However it is a handy punch in any boxer's repertoire. To land it, whip your arm upward, with the elbow bent, to your foe's chin. At the same time rise on your front foot and follow through with the right shoulder and right side of the body.

FEINTING

Feinting is the art of luring or tricking your opponent into a defensive maneuver that will yield an opening for a telling blow. You accomplish it by bluff movements of your hands, feet, shoulders or eyes. A good boxer sets up his punches with continual feinting. An opponent with any defensive knowledge at all can stop the average punch if he is sure with which hand his foe will try to land it, or for what part of his own anatomy it is destined.

For example, if you want to create an opening for a left-hand lead, you might pull down your opponent's guard by dropping your eyes to his stomach, feinting to drive your left to his body. Then when he has pulled his guard down, suddenly snap the left to his unguarded jaw. Or you can feint to go into him, thus luring him into making a lead himself which you can avoid and follow up with a vicious counter of your own. There are scores of feints in boxing. Every boxer should know several and learn to mix them up.

DEFENSE

Although offensive boxing is more spectacular and easier to learn, defense is equally important. Perhaps the reason it is so neglected nowadays is because of the great emphasis placed upon aggressiveness. Jim Corbett, who knew a great deal about defense, contended as late as 1927 that the men who control boxing today do everything they can to cultivate the out-and-out slugging fighter and hinder the clever boxer.

"If the bout is fairly even, they nearly always give it to the aggressor," Gentleman Jim protested, and with considerable logic, too. "Now who is going to be the aggressor but the big slugger? Naturally the clever boxer is using his feet, keeping out of the way of the wallops. But the decision goes to the aggressor. That is a very bad thing. The decision should be given on points, on style, on generalship. If a man is being rushed but can't be hit, he deserves credit for not being hit."

The best method, but hardest to learn, of getting away from a punch is to avoid it entirely by side-stepping, ducking, bending the body back from the waist, or dodging with the head alone, from the neck. The purpose in this form of defense is not to duck entirely out of range, but to make your foe miss by inches so he will still be in range for your counter blows. This is the ideal defense because you will have both hands free to counter with.

The second best method is parrying or delivering the blow by suddenly interposing the glove or forearm. Don't reach out with your guarding arm to parry a punch and thus unguard yourself. Wait until the blow is almost on top of you. Learn to catch a punch, when it has to be done, with the palm of your glove outward and your hand open, as this presents a larger defensive surface. Never close your fist when guarding with your glove. Jack Johnson, the famous heavyweight, was as accomplished at catching punches as an outfielder is at catching a baseball.

Parry from the inside, if possible, so you will have your foe more open for counters. As a general rule, use your right to parry his left, and your left to parry his right. Parrying isn't as effective as avoiding the blow entirely because you are left only one arm with which to counter, the arm that is not being used to ward off the blow.

The third method is blocking, which means deliberately taking the punch on your arm, shoulder, elbow or some portion of your body other than a vital part.

There is also the knack of riding a blow which Jim Corbett said is simply the act of swinging your head and shoulders to the right with your opponent's right, to the left with his left, thus dissipating the force of his attack.

Clinching, or tying up a foe's arms at close quarters so he cannot punish you, is often a sensible way of avoiding terrific punishment, of gaining a short rest when you are fagged or hurt, or of stopping an opponent's vicious infighting. Jim Corbett said the real skill in clinching was knowing just when to grab an opponent and when to let him go. "All one can do to weather a rocky round is, first grab for an opponent's arms, catch him wherever you can (at wrist or shoulder or elbow), putting your head on the other fellow's left shoulder, and then stay as close to him as possible," he declared.

Philadelphia Jack O'Brien says the method depends upon your foe's physique. If he is short and stocky and you are tall, O'Brien advises passing your left glove under his right arm and carrying it on upward toward the right shoulder to impede the movement of his right arm, leaning heavily against his shoulder and right side. At the same time move your open right glove down his left arm, which can readily be controlled.

If you are shorter, O'Brien recommends placing both gloves on the foe's shoulders and quickly sliding them downward until you are able to grasp his biceps. At the same time try to imprison one or both his gloves by trapping them between the side of your body and your elbow.

If the two boxers are about the same height, O'Brien advises getting your arms inside and under the opponent's, and, by forcing your arms under his armpits, lifting his arms upward and sideways. Never neglect to tie up your opponent's arms, not his body, and in breaking from a clinch, never drop your hands until you get completely away.

Briefly, the following defensive measures against certain punches are best for beginners:

Against straight left leads, catch the punch with your open right glove which is held close to your chin, palm turned outward. Or parry the punch to the outside with your right arm. Or avoid it entirely by dodging and sidestepping to the right so the left side of his body will be exposed to your counter.

Against straight rights to the head, catch the punch in your right palm, or parry it with your left forearm. Also you can side-step to the right, leaning low and avoiding his blow entirely.

Hooks are hard to guard because of their circuitous route but parrying and blocking in the same manner you parry and block straight-arm blows is a good method of guarding, while a straight well-timed counter is even better.

Swings are the easiest punches to fend off. You can duck under them, or counter them with straights, or parry them with the open palm, forearm or elbow. Experienced boxers sometimes check them by leaping in and punching at a swinger's hitting shoulder or upper arm just as he cocks his arm to throw the punch.

Uppercuts are best avoided by swaying or side-stepping to the right or catching the blow in the open glove.

Against a *right-hand body punch,* hold the left arm across the body, turn the body to the right, suck in your stomach and tighten your stomach muscles. Against a *left-hand body punch* guard with the right arm and turn the body to the left. If a right-hand body punch comes in under your left-hand lead to the head, throw your right arm across your body and turn to the right, away from the punch. Don't forget to counter fast.

The best defense against a *right cross* is to sink your chin well behind the buttress of your left shoulder when you shoot the left-hand lead to the head. You may also cover the left side of your jaw with your right glove, which should be open with the palm out and the fingers up.

COUNTERING

A boxer who can't counter, or who will not try to, may just as well give away his gloves and start rolling a hoop. Every time an opponent leads, he leaves himself open to some kind of return blow which must be sent in fast and sharp and usually will arrive so soon after the lead as to appear almost simultaneous with the lead punch. A counter should hurt far more than the lead punch that made it possible since its force is doubled by the fact that your opponent is coming forward to meet it. Since the target for a counter is gone in a flash, counter punches have to be shot quickly and instinctively.

Many of the best fighters in the ring, Jack Johnson among them, rarely shot lead punches. They did all their hitting with counter blows. In fact, there is a bout on record between Joe Coburn, the old-time American champion, and Jem Mace, the clever English gypsy, staged in Canada in 1871, in which the two stood in the ring with their hands up for an hour and seventeen minutes without striking a blow. Eventually the fight was called off. Coburn had been warned that Mace always made his foes lead, then cut them to ribbons with counters, so he resolved not to fall prey to those tactics.

A few of the simplest and best counters follow:

When your opponent leads straight left to your head, keep your eye on the oncoming punch and step forward to your right with your right foot. Duck under the blow so that it will slide harmlessly over your left shoulder. His whole left side is then exposed to your attack if you work fast. You can hit him with a straight right to either jaw or body, or with a left hook to stomach or jaw. Another effective counter is your deadly right cross to his jaw, the best knockout punch of them all. Sway your body and head to the left, inside his left lead, and at the same time crash your right to his jaw, over his extended left arm, putting plenty of shoulder behind the punch and hooking your knuckles downward on his jaw. Also you may parry his left lead outward with your right forearm and with the same motion shoot your right to his jaw.

When your opponent leads straight right to your head, your straight left jab should beat him to the punch every time. Shoot it as you step forward and duck to the right, away from his right. Or parry the blow outward with your left and drive a straight right to his body or jaw.

When your opponent tries a hook or swing, remember that they are round blows and can be countered effectively with straight well-timed punches. All the counters described above for the straight left- and right-hand leads will work against hooks and swings.

When your opponent tries a right uppercut, if you catch the blow in your open right glove, counter with a left hook to his head. If you avoid his right uppercut by swaying or side-stepping to the right, hook your left to his stomach or shoot your right to his head. You will face few left uppercuts, but if one does come, catch it in your left glove or avoid it by swaying to the right, and drive your right to his body or head.

INFIGHTING

Infighting is fighting at close range. The purpose of it is to get in close to an opponent by ducking under or blocking his left lead. Then with your arms between his, stay close to him, raining short heavy blows with alternate hands to his body with the shift of your shoulder and body behind each punch.

This vicious body-smashing is done with the feet flat, knees slightly bent, elbows at hip level and chin glued to your chest. Stay on top of your man and comb him with punches as fast as you can send them in. Uppercut his jaw, too. About all your foe can do is hammer at your flanks or at the back of your head, and this flank attack can be scotched by sticking out your elbows.

Pretend that you are facing an infighter: Try to keep away from him with fast footwork and a multitude of left-hand leads to the head. However, once he does get in, bend over, pull in your stomach, contract your stomach muscles, cover your body with your elbows and try to give him as good as he sends. If you wish, try to tie him up in a clinch.

Infighting is usually the resort of the short stocky boxer who, because of lack of reach, cannot afford to stand back and box at long range against a taller foe.

RING TACTICS

"Keep cool, don't get rattled, don't lose your temper," was Bob Fitzsimmons' sage advice.

Before a bout you should scout your opponent, if possible. Watch him box somebody else and try to learn his best punches and decide how you would stop them. Look for weaknesses and formulate a plan for capitalizing them, too. Does he crouch or stand up straight? Is he tall or short, fast or slow? Does he start fast, can he take punishment, does he have stamina? Gene Tunney beat Jack

Dempsey chiefly because he bought moving picture films of one of Dempsey's other battles. He studied them carefully and discovered that Dempsey always turned his head momentarily toward his right shoulder before plunging in to attack. Corbett learned through watching Sullivan box that the champion always slapped himself on the thigh with his left glove before unloosing a terrific right swing. Little points like these are often vastly important.

Study your foe's style carefully in the first round. Jimmy Wilde, the British flyweight, once said, "In the first round I am thinking hard, and after that punching hard." Sometimes the first blow decides a fight, so watch for your chance to land it. Tunney says the punch that won him the world's championship from Dempsey was a straight right-hand counter to the cheek bone inside Dempsey's left hook in the first round.

The reckless rushing opponent should be an easy mark for you, barring accidents. Keep cool, and stand firm before him and meet him with straight punches. If he reaches you with a heavy blow and you feel groggy, clinch at once until your head clears. Above all, do not let him know you are hurt. If you are knocked down, never jump up immediately and renew the bout, but get slowly on one knee, face your opponent and wait until the referee has counted nine before arising. Any punch heavy enough to knock you down is bound to make you slightly dizzy, so take all the rest allowed.

Learn to pace yourself in each round, saving your most

SPORTS *and* GAMES
138

aggressive tactics until the last thirty seconds, when your second can signal you. Of course, if you are far behind on points you have to start your sprint sooner. If you are tall, avoid infighting unless you have natural skill for it. Use your reach to keep your opponent off with your straight left and shoot your right when the opening occurs. If you are short and rugged, bore in close and punch viciously at his body. One good body punch is worth three to the head, as a rule. Then, too, when you land a body blow, you are shooting at a wide, soft, stationary target at which you can strike without injuring your hands.

Always save a little of your strength for one final spurt. Jim Corbett liked to relax between rounds and also at every possible moment during the fight to store up energy for his climax effort. He never poured himself out completely, or risked his brittle hands with terrific punching, until he had gradually weakened his foe and had him ready for the polishing off.

SECONDING A FIGHTER

Today, seconding a boxer is sensible and humane. It consists of both caring for the fighter's physical ills and giving him wise ring counsel. A good second can give his boxer a world of good advice because he is in a better position to judge the effect of certain punches, the condition of both his man and the opponent and weigh all he sees against the point tally and the time left in the bout. Of all the handlers in your corner, he alone should

advise you. He should apprise you, during the action, of
how much time is left in each round in a way that will
conceal that information from your opponent. He and
his implements should stay outside the ropes.

A second's implements should include a chair (on which
the boxer can sit between rounds), a bottle of cold water
(so he can gargle to keep his throat moist), two towels
(one can be used to wipe perspiration off his face, shoulders
and legs, and the other, wetted in cold water, to wipe his
face), smelling salts (to be used if he is groggy or tired),
and a small first-aid kit (to be handy in case of cuts or
injuries).

Between rounds, the second should have his boxer's
chair waiting for him, seat him with his back supported
against the ropes and make him relax, holding the front
elastic band of his boxing trunks away from his stomach
so he can breathe deeply. Nothing should interfere with
the boxer's breathing.

Eddie Kane, manager of Mike Gibbons, well-known
St. Paul middleweight of 1915–1916, always had small pa-
tience with too officious seconding. "The minute interval
is for the boxer's rest and reflection," Kane contended.
"How can he rest if he is being pulled all over the place
by men whose 'rubbing' is mostly done in the wrong way?
As to fanning a man when he has gone to his corner, it is
ridiculous. A boxer who has been fighting for three minutes has got his blood up and is heated. It is most absurd
to start waving a towel at him directly as he sits down, or

to throw cold icy water on him, for fear of chilling him instead of refreshing him. It may take him half a moment to get warmed up and back in stride the next round because his seconds have foolishly taken his edge off."

Tommy Burns always liked to have his seconds raise him gently by the arms and lift him bodily, but without any jerk, to his feet at the call of time. "It is but a slight exertion they have spared me, but even the slightest exertion is a very big point," Burns said.

After a bout, a second should carefully attend to the boxer's injuries. In intercollegiate bouts, the medical advisor is compelled to do this.

HISTORY

The ancient Greeks were the first known boxers. They required their youth to practice it with their bare hands to strengthen their bodies, dissipate all fear and teach them manly courage. However, with the rise of the great national games of Greece, boxers were equipped with the cestus, a long length of oxhide which was wrapped about the hands and forearms. Sometimes they used the dreadful gauntlet that Denis Diderot's *Encyclopedia* tells us was a "length of leather, studded with knobs of lead or iron, which encircled the hand in criss-cross fashion, and even covered the wrist and a part of the arm to prevent them from being broken or dislocated, and moreover, to add greater force to the blows."

The aim of the sport in Greece was to develop skill,

courage and strength, and if a boxer killed his antagonist he was severely punished unless it could be proved death was accidental. But during the Roman period the cestus became a crueler instrument and boxing a more terrible sport. Its object was to kill your opponent as soon as possible. The Emperor Honorius finally abolished the bloody gladiatorial shows in A.D. 404 because of the objection of the Christian Fathers.

Boxing was suppressed during the Middle Ages chiefly because it was a sport of the common people and therefore not regarded as fashionable by the new feudal aristocracy. As Alexander Johnston tells us, "The medieval mind rather ran to poison and poniard than to knuckles or gloves."

But with the coming to England of the Renaissance in the sixteenth century and the rise to national consciousness of the English middle class, prize fighting and the subsequent heavy wagering upon it began to occupy the bloods of the town and the gentlemen of the country in spite of its prohibition by statute. Those were roistering days in which the spectators themselves, sleeping in their carriages in open weather or fifteen in a room on the floor of some inn, willingly suffered hardships as they followed the fighters around. The fighters and their retinues were busy dodging the fussy magistrates. It was the day of the old London Prize Ring rules, which called for bare knuckles, wrestling and a finish fight. The anxious relatives of the boxers, many miles away, had no way of learning the result save by the ancient radio of carrier pigeons, pretty sure messengers at that unless they happened to meet a hawk, as Thomas More observed in his diary.

The sport drifted to America, as did everything else British, and was just as quickly outlawed here, chiefly because of the unsavory reputation of some of the early American champions. One of them, Yankee Sullivan, had escaped from a British penal settlement in Australia. Also, swarms of pickpockets always infested the fight crowds. In fact boxing was held in such bad repute in America that when John L. Sullivan and Jake Kilrain defied the laws of Mississippi and fought with bare knuckles at Richburg, July 8, 1889, Sullivan, who won the fight after seventy-five rounds, later was extradited from New York, returned to Mississippi and fined eighteen thousand dollars. What angered the proud Sullivan still more was the fact that Kilrain, who had been knocked down fifteen times, was convicted of "assault and battery," a charge that Sullivan bitterly declared showed the ignorance and partiality of the court in the affair.

The thing that saved boxing everywhere was the adoption of padded boxing gloves. Gloves did away with the brutalities of a fight with bare knuckles without detracting from the sport's quality or thrill. The sport was also helped by the new Queensberry rules, which forbade wrestling, demanded five-ounce gloves and three-minute rounds, and stipulated that a boxer who was knocked down had to get up without assistance in ten seconds and continue fighting or lose. Leading athletic clubs all over the nation began to hire instructors, many of them from England, to teach the sport. Harvard University adopted boxing as an intramural sport as early as 1880.

The Corbett-Sullivan fight at New Orleans in 1892, first world's championship bout ever settled with gloves, and Corbett's own quiet behavior thereafter did a great deal to popularize boxing and establish it as a clean and gentlemanly sport. Theodore Roosevelt, when he was governor of New York in the late 1890's boxed twice a week with Mike Donovan, the old middleweight champion, at the New York Athletic Club. Late in the afternoon of the day before his inauguration as president, he stepped ten fast rounds with Donovan.

The sport was given further respectability when the American government made boxing a required training routine in its army camps during World War I. This move introduced boxing to the nation's colleges and universities. The carefully supervised Golden Gloves contests started all over America in the early 1930's. To these, any amateur, whether he attends high school, college or no school at all, is eligible; they have given the sport a wonderful boost and have done much toward restoring it to the old Grecian ideal that boxing should be a part of every youth's education, not only to strengthen his body but to teach him qualities of courage and aggressiveness, as well.

CHAPTER 6

FOOTBALL

AMERICAN football is an autumnal game played principally by college, high-school and grade-school teams in the United States. The game also thrives here as a professional sport. It is played upon a rectangular field of thick grass, 120 yards long and 53⅓ yards wide. The field is usually laid out north-south so neither team will have to look into the sun, and is partly or entirely surrounded by a stand or stadium where up to 110,000 spectators may sit and see the game.

Goal posts twenty feet or more high, twenty-five feet apart in college and high school games, and connected by a horizontal crossbar the top of which is ten feet from the ground, are placed in the middle of each end line. Field goals and points after touchdown are kicked between the posts and over the crossbar.

The game is played with an elliptical ball of pebble-grained leather approximately eleven inches long and weighing at least fourteen ounces. This ball is easy to kick and throw but hard to hold onto during rough action.

144

The object of the game is for one team of eleven men to score more points than the opposing eleven.

There are four ways in which a team may score: *touchdowns* (six points) are scored by rushing (carrying) the ball across the opponent's goal line, or by completing a forward pass (one player throws the spiraling ball to a teammate) in the field of play or in the opponent's end zone. When a team scores a touchdown, it gets the opportunity to score one or two extra points on a play executed from the three-yard line, a place or drop kick between the goal posts and over the crossbar which counts one point, or a rush or forward pass which if successful counts two points. A *field goal* (three points) is made by kicking the ball from the field of play over the crossbar of the opponent's goal by a place kick or a drop kick. A *safety* (two points) is scored when a ball legally in possession and control of a player guarding his own goal becomes dead on or behind the goal line, provided the impetus which sent it there came from the team defending that goal.

The length of the college game is sixty minutes, divided into four quarters of fifteen minutes each. However, due to frequent periods when the ball isn't in play and to the various intervals of rest between periods (fifteen minutes between halves, one minute after each first and third quarter), college games average two and one-half to three hours in length. Teams exchange goals after the first and third quarters. Most big American college games are played on Saturday afternoons. Most American high-school

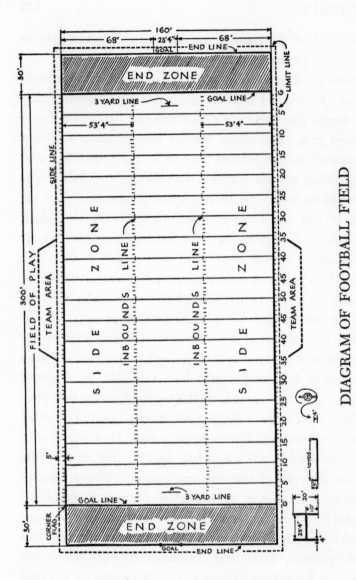

DIAGRAM OF FOOTBALL FIELD

Depth of team area box is optional. Yard lines extending from sidelines are optional.

games fall on Friday nights with the field brilliantly illuminated by electric floodlights suspended on tall poles
outside the field. High schools play twelve-minute quarters
or games of forty-eight minutes' total time.

American football is fast, rough and so thrillingly attractive to spectators that they buy season tickets months
in advance of the season, drive as many as 600 miles
roundtrip in one day to see a game and enthusiastically
discuss the sport and all its aspects the year round. In
America baseball is king in summer, basketball in winter,
but football holds sway in the crisp, windy days of September, October and November.

Unlike soccer, American football is not a game of continuous running. Rather it consists of a succession of individual plays starting from wherever the scrimmage line
happens to be on the field after the preceding play.
Speed and a fast start are of the greatest importance, all
eleven men on a side sprinting through their assignments
as they block and tackle with purposeful savagery. After
the ball is dead on one play, there is a brief truce during
which contestants of both teams pick themselves off the
turf and line up for the next play. The offensive team
retreats in a huddle several yards behind the scrimmage
line, where their quarterback tells them, out of hearing
of the defense, what the next play is going to be. All such
plays have been so carefully rehearsed in advance that
each of the eleven men on the team in possession of the
ball instantly knows his assignment on them.

The nature of each play varies. Rushing is usually employed to advance the ball, although forward passing and occasionally a kick are also resorted to. Each college game averages a total of from 140 to 185 individual plays.

The measure of ball advancement is the *first down.* The 100-yard field of play is chalked at intervals of five yards with long white lines that extend from sideline to sideline, parallel to the goal lines. When a team comes into possession of the ball, it has four downs in which to advance ten yards. If it does gain those ten yards within the series of four downs (sometimes it makes them on first or second down), it has won a first down, which entitles it to four more chances to gain another ten yards. If a team's offense is strong enough, it may steadily drive the length of the field until a touchdown is scored. Or if, after the first three downs, it has not made ten yards and does not wish to risk the possibility of not making it on a fourth trial, it can punt the ball downfield to the opponents, whose safety, or rearmost man, will catch it and come back as far as possible before he is tackled to the turf. Then the opponents try to make ten yards before their four downs are up and thus the game progresses with the rival teams alternating on offense and defense.

Each team consists of eleven men. The offensive team has a wall of seven players called a *line,* massed along the scrimmage front. Behind it crouches a *backfield* of four players. Chief duty of the offensive line is to charge roughly into opponents and, using the shoulder, drive them out of the area to which the ball carrier will eventually run. This is called *blocking*. One of the seven linesmen, the center, starts each play by bending over the ball and passing it back between his legs to one of the four backs, usually the quarterback, who not only selects the play to be attempted but does the major share of the forward passing and handles the ball on each play from center, feeding it (handing or tossing it) to one of the other backs.

The defensive team lines up differently, usually posting from five to seven linesmen along the scrimmage front directly opposite the offensive team's line, and stationing two or three additional men close up to act as line backers. Their job is to stop the offense's rushing attack by *tackling* the ball carrier to the ground. Blocking and tackling are the game's roughest and most important fundamentals. Still farther behind the line backers are two defensive halfbacks and the safety, who on fourth down may retreat farthest of all. It is the safety's job to come up and tackle the foe ball-carrier, defend against forward passes, field and return opposition punts.

So much for a general description of American football. Now let's dig more deeply into the technical phase of the game as it is played in the United States, taking as an illustration the Split-T offensive system used by Coach Bud Wilkinson's University of Oklahoma Sooners, who won national collegiate championships in 1950, 1955 and 1956 and seven of eight major bowl games from 1947 through 1959. This formation was devised by Don Faurot, veteran Missouri coach, who first introduced it to football as long ago as 1941.

In the Split-T the offensive line is spaced more widely than in the other formations, providing a broader area over which the fast-hitting offensive can strike. Thus the defense must spread too, providing the offense a bigger hole to hit, or if the defense stays tight, the offense gains a decisive blocking angle on it. Speed and deception are the essence of attack in the Split-T. Oklahoma concentrates on a quick start by every man on its team. A team that starts fast is hard to defeat.

PURPOSE OF THE SPLIT-T

The Oklahoma Split-T formation employs a slightly different offensive technique from that of any other formation. In order to understand the type of blocks and the type of ball handling it uses, it is necessary to know what the formation is trying to accomplish.

On nearly every play, the Split-T quarterback works *down the line of scrimmage* with the ball. He gives it on the hand-off; fakes the hand-off, fakes a lateral and keeps it himself; or fakes a hand-off, fakes keeping the ball and then laterals to the other halfback, who goes wide. It is essential on all these plays that the quarterback work down the line of scrimmage. By doing this, two very important things are accomplished:

(1) The quarterback rarely takes the ball behind the line of scrimmage; consequently no yardage is lost even if the play is a total failure.

(2) By the time the defense knows who has the ball, the offense is already making yardage beyond the line of scrimmage.

If the quarterback is to work freely down the line of scrimmage, it is essential that the offensive line move with the starting count, every man charging forward like a dash man in track, so that the quarterback has room to fake and run. On every running play the offensive line must know this, remember this and block with this thought constantly in mind.

Blocking is the most important thing in any offense, and also the hardest to teach. The two most important technical points in blocking are good stance and quick starting. A fierce determination to drive your opponent out of the play is also of terrific importance. Let's imagine you are a player on a Split-T team and you want to learn the various blocks, (1) against opposition linesmen, (2) against opposition line backers, and (3) against opposition defensive halfbacks and safety. Let's carefully consider each of these important blocks.

BLOCKING AGAINST LINESMEN

(1) Charge out at the defensive man with short digging steps, as if you were starting a sprint. Move your feet fast.

If you don't, your quarterback will have to give ground to move around you.

(2) Drive your head directly at the stomach of the defensive man. Never step for position.

(3) Just before making contact, slide your head past your opponent on the opposite side from which you wish to drive him, hit sharply with your shoulder and rise up, working around the defensive man so that he cannot retreat away from the line of scrimmage or reach across you and get his hands on the ball carrier.

(4) Keep your feet *driving* until the play is over.

To execute this block successfully, you must:

a) Start fast with the snap signal.

b) Move off the line of scrimmage with short, driving steps.

c) Get contact with the proper shoulder.

d) Turn the defensive man away from the play and back toward the line of scrimmage.

BLOCKING AGAINST LINE BACKERS

Downfield blocking on the Split-T is primarily a matter of good position against the defensive man. When starting down the field, always go to the point to which the defensive man must move to stop the ball carrier, not to the point where he is when the play starts. You must anticipate his movement and lead him in the same way a forward passer leads a receiver when he throws. When you have moved to the proper spot, and are ready to take your opponent out of play, block as follows:

a) Drive your shoulder at the defensive man's chest.

b) Hit sharply and turn him back toward the line of scrimmage.

c) Make your primary effort to block at the man and beyond him, getting your head well past him so that he cannot slide off.

d) Never hesitate. Take your shot full speed and let the ball carrier decide on which side to cut around you.

BLOCKING AGAINST DEFENSIVE HALFBACKS AND SAFETY

The approach is the same as when blocking against a line backer. You've got to lead your opponent to the spot on the field where he will make contact with the ball carrier. Contact should be made in the same way, except that you should slide your arm and shoulder past the man so that you definitely cut him one way or the other and the ball carrier can make his break to the proper side. *Never hesitate.* Go in and take your shot at him full speed. The ball carrier will decide which way to cut. If you hesitate, you will slow him down, which is fatal to the play. Never dive at an opponent and lose your feet. You should *never leave your feet* until the force of the contact knocks you off them. Ninety-nine per cent of all missed blocks downfield occur simply because the blocker leaves his feet and dives at his opponent. Block *high,* block at and beyond the defensive man, and *stay on your feet* as long as possible.

THEORY OF BALL-HANDLING

Responsibility in Split-T ball-handling is different from that in any other formation in American football. The ball-carrying back *does not look for the ball* when the quarterback slips it to him as they crisscross full speed at right angles. Instead, the ball carrier keeps his eye on the hole opening in front of him. Charging like a sprinter, he watches the blocking so he will know which way to cut. He's got to decide this in a fraction of a second because the play is developing very fast; consequently he must give all his attention to it. While moving at top speed, he won't have time to glance down at the ball, then raise his eyes again and try to find the hole.

It's the quarterback's job to hand the ball to the speeding halfback, and moreover feed it to him so accurately that the halfback will feel it on his hip without looking for it, and will grasp it securely and maintain possession of it during his rapid progress forward.

Here are some Split-T hand-off tips:

  a) The quarterback will reach out as far as possible to get the ball to the halfback as quickly as possible.

  b) The quarterback will keep his eye on the halfback

at all times and will *place the ball on the halfback's far hip.*

c) Halfbacks will keep their eyes straight ahead and watch the blocks. *They must never look at the quarterback or the ball when accepting a hand-off.*

d) Halfbacks will have their inside arm up and their outside hand along their hip.

e) As they feel the ball placed on their hip, they will grasp it by dropping their inside arm over the ball and controlling it with their outside hand.

f) Halfbacks never look at the ball. They must watch the blocking in the line ahead of them and be prepared to take advantage of the movements of the defense.

BALL-CARRYING

Most of the actual advance of the ball in any game will come from carrying it (rushing). Many other factors are involved, but all are topped by the actual ball-carrying. In forward passing and kick runbacks, as well as in rushing, a lot depends upon the skill of the ball carrier.

Most of this skill involves the backs and, next in order, the ends. However, at any time, in any game, any player may suddenly find himself in the role of a ball carrier by intercepting a pass, for example.

All ball carriers have special talents and characteristics. One may have a lot of speed, one may be very shifty, while another may be solid on his feet and have a lot of power. But every player should attempt to improve all his characteristics and become versatile.

There are many axioms, rules and tips that apply to all. Here are some of them:

(1) You must *retain possession* of the ball. A fumble will cancel all other good work. Hang onto the ball. That is what you are playing with.

(2) Always move straight toward the opponent's goal unless there is a very definite reason for doing otherwise. Reasons: (a) to get to the hole, (b) to outflank opponents, (c) to make better use of certain blockers, (d) to dodge an opponent.

(3) *Always move with maximum speed* unless there is a definite reason for doing otherwise. Reasons: (a) to preserve the timing of the play, (b) to utilize your blocking while it is effective.

(4) *Take full advantage of your blockers by proper maneuvering.* Your blockers are there to help you. If you make them look good, you help yourself.

(5) Keep the tackler guessing. Do not tip off whether you are going to run around him, run over him or dodge him. Don't try to dodge him until you are near him.

(6) *Keep fighting for ground* after you are hit. Never admit defeat until you are actually down or the whistle has blown.

(7) Know where you are and what to do to be successful. Ordinarily the objective is to score a touchdown each

time you carry the ball, but judgment must be used in this. For example: You may have third down and two yards to go on your own 40-yard line. Make the supreme effort to get the two yards. After you have made that, you can then gamble on trying to go the whole way.

But if this situation occurs on first down, take the gambling chance and try to score, because the two yards are of little value on first down. You must always be aware of the tactical situation if you expect to carry the ball intelligently.

Use everything you have to keep advancing the ball, including: (a) your speed, (b) your dodging ability, (c) your stiff arm, (d) your drive. Don't ever admit defeat. When you have possession of the ball, you have the game in your hands.

STRATEGY OF SPLIT-T OFFENSE

The major objectives of football offense are (a) to score, (b) to make first downs, (c) to move the ball into a more favorable position to score from, (d) to keep the ball away from the opponents, (e) to leave the opponents deep in their own territory so they can't unleash their best plays, and (f) to consume time with your offense so the opponents will have as little as possible of that precious substance for their own offense.

Anybody can understand the strategy of Split-T offense as employed by Coach Wilkinson's Oklahoma teams. There are four main faking areas, all of them in a moving zone on one side of the scrimmage line, and the play is gaining ground while the fakes are being made. Let's look, for a moment, at these four faking areas. If the defensive linesman strays from his position in any of them, he leaves his area open for a long gain by the offense.

Wilkinson says the quarterback sneak is the Split-T's best play. If the defensive guard slides to the outside to stop the hand-off to the right half, the quarterback sneaks or the fullback counters inside him to keep him "honest." This is the first area of faking.

The second area of faking is at the defensive tackle. If he stays in to stop the hand-off, the right end blocks him in, the right tackle swings for the line backer and the play goes outside him. If he flares out, the quarterback hands off to the right halfback inside him.

The third area of faking is at the defensive end. If he plays the sliding quarterback, the quarterback laterals out to the left half, who runs around him. If the end flares out to cover the left half, the quarterback fakes the lateral and, retaining possession of the ball, runs the quarterback keeper inside the end.

The fourth and final area of faking is at the defensive halfback. The left half has taken a lateral from the quarterback and is loose around end. If the defensive half sucks in to stop the wide run, the left half passes over him to (a) the right end, who breaks into the territory vacated by the defensive half, or to (b) the right halfback, who runs straight down the middle to hold the safety in. If the

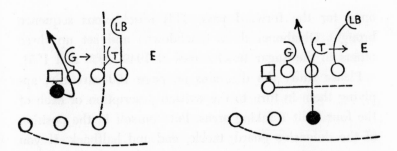

1. PRESSURE ON THE DEFENSIVE GUARD. Quarterback sneak holds him inside.
2. PRESSURE ON THE DEFENSIVE TACKLE. Hand-off, quarterback to right half, holds him inside.

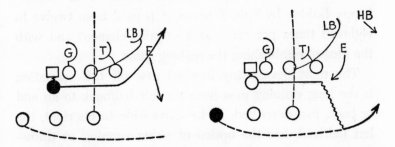

3. PRESSURE ON THE DEFENSIVE END. If he flares out, quarterback keeps ball.
4. PRESSURE ON THE DEFENSIVE HALFBACK. If he comes in to tackle, left half will throw over him.

FOUR SPLIT-T FAKING AREAS

safety ignores him and covers the right end, the left halfback forward passes to the right halfback down the middle. If the safety stays put, covering the right half going straight down the field, then the right end should be wide open for the forward pass. This mischievous sequence brought Oklahoma three touchdowns and set up three others in the Sugar Bowl games of 1949, 1950 and 1951.

Please study the diagrams on page 159 carefully, applying them in turn to the written description of each of the four Split-T faking areas. Put yourself in the position of the defensive guard, tackle, end and halfback. If you were in each one's shoes, what would you do?

SPLIT-T FORWARD PASSING

While the forward pass is not employed in trigger-happy fashion by Split-T teams, it is used from twelve to eighteen times per game as a surprise element and with the idea of establishing the rushing game.

The most devastating forward pass off this formation is the long running pass from the left halfback to an end or back, just described. As he starts wide to his right, the left halfback has the option of either running or throwing. If the enemy line-backers come up fast to stop his running, the halfback quickly scans the field for receivers —one, two and three, in that order. He throws the ball to whichever one is the most open and usually this man will be safely behind the defense. To become proficient at this play, halfbacks have to practice it for hours.

Most forward passing off the Split-T is done by the quarterback, who usually draws the defense in by faking a hand-off, after which he hides the ball, retreats and throws. Screen passes are also effective. The formation has so much rushing threat that the defense frequently masses on or near the scrimmage line to stop the rushing, thereby making itself vulnerable to a passing attack.

KICK RUNBACKS

The easiest way to make yardage in football is on organized kick runbacks. In 1948 Oklahoma set a new national collegiate record by averaging 22.4 net yards for each punt runback. This far surpassed the average of the same team's rushing game, 5.8 yards per play, and its forward passing average for each pass thrown, 8.4 yards. Although all opponents tried to punt away from Oklahoma's deadly double-safety combination of Jack Mitchell and Darrell Royal, the Sooners that season made more yards returning punts (963) than they did forward passing (838), although they originated more than twice as many forward passes as punt runbacks.

The organized punt runback occurs on sure kicking down (fourth down, long yardage to go, ball in opponent's territory). A double safety is played and if possible they crisscross on every punt, the punt-receiver either handing the ball to his teammate, or faking a hand-off and concealing it on his hip. In either instance, the man who ends up with the ball races to the sideline, where his teammates, waiting and acting as a wall of blockers, escort him to the goal line. The better the deception practiced by the two safeties during and immediately after they pass each other on the crisscross, the more successful the play will be.

Kickoff runbacking may also be organized so that the

runback starts in one direction to draw the defense, then strikes back fast to the opposite side, where the entire team has gathered and becomes a blocking shield. All the blocks are timed so that the whole team is blocking together. This is the most important factor in the play.

PUNT PROTECTION

Most punts are blocked because of a mechanical error by the center or the kicker. Occasionally a punt will be blocked because some player on the kicking team loafed. Protecting the kicker is relatively simple, yet a single mistake on the part of one man can completely nullify a perfect effort by the other ten men. Each player must know his job thoroughly. There must be complete team coördination.

Basically, protecting the kicker means defending the area in which the ball will be kicked. The kicking team forms a blocking shield for this area. Never move out to block but get in position quickly and make the defense come to you, striving to hold your ground.

If the kicker is right-footed, the backs will protect with two men on the right.

DEFENSE

The major objective in football defense is to obtain possession of the ball as near the opponents' goal as is possible. This is done by (a) stealing the ball or taking it away from an opponent, (b) recovering opponents' fumbles, (c) intercepting opponents' forward passes, and (d) stopping their advance so that they fail to make first downs.

American football rules give one important advantage to both the offense and the defense. The offense knows *what* the play is and *when* it will start. But the defense is granted an almost unlimited use of the hands and arms.

Speaking generally, there are two basic differences in how the defensive line and the defensive secondary reacts to the offense. Defensive linesmen have to act, then diagnose. But the defensive secondary players have time first to diagnose, then act.

Different defensive positions have different fundamental reactions. Defensive guards and tackles have opponents playing so closely to them that they don't have time to wait and see. They must act instantly as follows: (a) charge hard enough to control the man or men blocking them, (b) keep their legs free and move to the most favorable spot from which to protect their territory, and (c) approach the ball carrier and make the tackle.

Defensive end play is different in only one respect. With opponents playing farther away, defensive ends have more time to move quickly to the most favorable spot from which to protect their territory.

The defensive secondary (line backers, defensive halfbacks and safety) must concentrate on these four points: (a) no opponent is close to them at the start of the play, (b) before the ball is snapped, they must be lined up in the best possible position from which to defend their territory, (c) before moving they *must* diagnose the play, and then (d) they must move fast and play in the manner outlined above for guards and tackles.

Don't try to guess what the offense will do. They can do too many things and while you may win if you guess correctly, the odds are about six to one that you will guess wrong. That means you would get the advantage once out of six times while the offense would get it five out of six times. Obviously, this is a poor gamble. Protect your territory and diagnose. Don't guess.

Speaking generally, when a small gain will not hurt you seriously, you should play loosely and conservatively. But when a small gain will hurt you, you must play more tightly and recklessly. To illustrate, let's take two cases:

(1) Your team is leading 7–6. There are twenty seconds left to play. The opponents have the ball on your one-yard line and it is fourth down, goal to go. Here you should play them very tightly, concentrating everything to stop them short of one yard. If you do prevent them from scoring, you are completely sucessful. If you don't, you have completely failed.

(2) Your team is leading 7–6. There are forty seconds left to play. The opponents have the ball on their own thirty-yard line (seventy yards from your goal) and it is fourth down and seven yards to go. Here you would take strength from your defensive line and clog your defensive secondary. Even if they make seven yards you have lost

very little. But if you played very tight to stop them cold, as in situation one above, they might throw a long forward pass over you for a touchdown and you would have lost everything.

To summarize, it follows that the only way the offense can gain is to whip the defense physically. Football is a fighting game. Despite the intricate team machinations, an American football game consists largely of several individual battles between rival players. The team that wins the majority of these has the best chance of winning the game.

FORWARD PASS DEFENSE

All football coaches have a mortal dread of being beaten by football's home run, the long forward pass to a touchdown. No matter how strong your defensive line, if your pass defense is weak you may yield several easy touchdowns to enemy aerial play and be decisively beaten.

Forward-pass defense falls into two phases: (a) rushing the passer, and (b) covering the receivers and playing the ball.

Since you never know when a pass will be thrown or where it will be thrown, alertness and quick reactions are major factors in success. As is always the case in football, pass defense requires fine individual play plus complete team coördination.

Three pass-defense axioms must always be remembered:

(1) If the passer is rushed hard and hit hard, his timing

and accuracy will not be good. Besides, you may throw him for a long loss behind the line of scrimmage.

(2) An intercepted pass (other than a fourth-down long pass) is far more valuable than one knocked down. *Try for interceptions* above all else.

(3) An enemy pass caught *behind* your defense is an almost certain touchdown. Don't ever let a receiver get behind you.

RUSHING THE PASSER

Regardless of the defensive alignment, you rush the passer the same way. Your initial charge is the same as on a running play. You must be aggressive and fight through the blocks. Never go around resistance.

The men on the flanks (usually the ends) must approach from an outside position, keeping *outside leverage* and angle on the passer so he cannot run around them. Your secondary has usually dropped back to cover, and they are in no position to support you if the passer gets to your outside.

Inside men must rush hard and direct by lowering their shoulders and arms, and fighting up and through the blockers. All inside men should be alert for a passer retreating more quickly than is normal. This usually tips off a screen pass. If no one tries to block you and you get through too easily, be alert for a "mouse-trap" play through your position, usually a fake pass and run.

Hard, low, aggressive driving is needed to rush the passer. If you get to him while he still has the ball, hit him fairly high with a hard tackle. Never let yourself think for a moment you won't reach the passer before he throws. Get him before the ball is in the air.

COVERING THE RECEIVER
AND PLAYING THE BALL

As the ball is being snapped from center, you must keep your eye on it and also on the eligible receivers. Remember that on a forward pass, nobody but eligible receivers can cross the line of scrimmage, while on a running play, linesmen nearly always come across the line of scrimmage to block. This constitutes your best tip-off on whether the play is a run or forward pass.

Good footwork is the most important fundamental in covering the receiver. It is essential that you be always in a position to go with the receiver without getting your feet crossed.

Always maneuver so you can see both your man and the ball. Try to watch the ball through the man. The most ideal position is to have the receiver on a straight line between you and the ball. Of course, when the receiver gets too close to the sideline, you should play him from the inside. Once the ball is thrown, go for it. Remember these points:

(1) Do not close in on the receiver until the ball is thrown.

(2) If the receiver stops, don't rush toward him until the ball is thrown. He may buttonhook and go past you.

(3) Smooth, accurate moving on your part is essential. Jerky, panicky movements get you out of position.

(4) Keep a comfortable distance away from the receiver. If you don't, he can lose you with a quick turn or change of pace.

(5) Do not look too intently at the receiver. If you do, he may fool you with a fake. Watch his stomach, not his feet, shoulders, arms or head. He can't fake you with his stomach.

(6) Never turn your back to the ball to cover a receiver.

(7) Once the ball is in the air, *play it*. It is a free ball.

In order to have good team play against opposition forward passes, it is essential that all defensive men talk to each other and call the enemy receivers as they start downfield.

The following basic principles must always be kept in mind: (a) as soon as a pass shows, start dropping back, (b) always keep your eye on the passer, (c) line backers always try to knock down any receiver close enough for them to hit, (d) halfbacks and safety never let a receiver get past them, (e) halfbacks and safety are alert to switch men as receivers cross, (f) when time to play is short, drop back fast and play it deep, (g) as soon as the ball is in the air, go for it *hard*. You have as much right to it as the receivers. Try for an interception.

FOOTBALL PRINCIPLES

Coach Bud Wilkinson of the Oklahoma team believes that spirit is still the most important thing in football. He says that every play of every football game consists of eleven individual battles. "Against opponents of our caliber we will seldom win all eleven contests. However, we must win at least six on every play if we are to defeat the opponent. We must win the individual contests before we win the team fight.

"All of our opponents will be in condition. All of them will have the spirit and desire to win. Thus if we expect to beat them, we must lick them physically by being in better shape and by hitting harder. We must lick them mentally by understanding the game and by playing it better and more intelligently than they do. But there is no easy road to success in football. It's a battle all the way. We won't win unless each man is willing to pay the full price for victory."

Wilkinson says that football is a demanding game that requires players to go full speed even when they are tired. Every game starts with a sixty-yard dash, then the men have to keep going, play after play. "The mark of a great football team is to be able to drive hard with increased courage and competitive spirit when it grows tired;

to disregard fatigue and go out and whip down an opponent," declares the Oklahoma coach.

"Watch the average team in a football game. On one play, six of the players may go at full speed, but the other five, tired from the preceding play, go at only half speed. On the next play the five who coasted go all out but the six who tried hard on the preceding play now loaf. Obviously, this type of team will never be great. The problem is to build a team where most of the men are going all out on most of the plays. The two things most needed are condition and desire."

So every good football player must learn to go hard on every play. How do you learn this? By driving yourself every minute in practice. All football is habit. In practice you must cultivate the habit of doing everything well and with the maximum of effort. Desire is terrifically important in football. This means every player must hustle and strive for improvement in practice. There is no place in football for a loafer, or for a player who rests on every other play. You must learn to do everything full speed.

Wilkinson says that when a player keeps looking for something else to do after he has already thrown two blocks on one play, he has desire. "There's a way to check up on whether a team has desire," says the Oklahoma coach. "After each play, when the whistle blows and the ball is dead, count how many of your players are inside an eight-yard circle of the ball. If nine or ten of them are there, good. But if your men are scattered all over the field, watch out."

Always close in on the ball or ball carrier unless there is a definite reason to do otherwise, such as moving away from the ball on a fake, or when you are a pass receiver, or a decoy who moves away from the ball until it is thrown.

Always stay on your feet. About the only times you don't do this are (a) when you are diving to catch a forward pass, (b) when it is necessary to dive over a man to make a tackle, and (c) when linesmen leave their feet temporarily on a submarine charge.

Aim to cut down on errors. Football is a team game and frequently an error by one man on a team will cancel brilliant play by the remaining ten. For example, a team blocks, runs and fakes perfectly for a thirty-yard gain, but the left end is offsides. The play is ruined. Everything that spoils a play comes under one of the following headings: (a) lack of knowledge, (b) carelessness, (c) going to sleep, and (d) physical loafing. Many games are won not through superior playing by the better team but by errors by the poorer team. Usually the team making the fewer mistakes wins.

Mental attitude means everything, says Wilkinson. "A team has got to be ready mentally as well as physically to control a game. Not only must it hustle terrifically against a dangerous opponent, but it must also have the quality of being able to win in stride from opponents whose record is not outstanding. Like a great gloves fighter, a great football team is one that can soundly defeat an opponent, once it dazes him. Unless a football team is afraid it may be beaten in every game, and plays savagely and alertly to prevent what it fears, it won't play very well and may, at any time, be defeated."

PROFESSIONAL FOOTBALL

Professional football, which employs the best college players and develops them into a state of near perfection, is tremendously popular today. It began in Pennsylvania, in 1895, where the Latrobe, Pennsylvania, team, managed and sponsored by the Y.M.C.A., met a rival club from Jeanette, Pennsylvania. Other early professional teams were the Pittsburgh, Pennsylvania, Duquesnes (1896), the Mc-Keesport, Pennsylvania, Olympics (1896), the Orange Athletic Club of Newark, New Jersey (1897), and teams from Canton and Massillion, Ohio (1902 and 1903).

Surviving tremendous handicaps, professional football is big business and, because of intelligent promotion of the game through national television, liberal rules that make for high scoring, and scheduling of games on Sunday, when everybody can attend, it is steadily outstripping the college sport in popular appeal in the large city areas. Back in 1933 it began seeking for a more exciting style when it returned goal posts to the goal line and legalized forward passes thrown anywhere back of the line of scrimmage. It is primarily an aerial game. While its rushing attacks are dull, it has brilliantly exploited forward passing and field-goal kicking. Unlike professional baseball, it refuses to sign college players until after their normal four-year graduation date.

FOOTBALL INJURIES

Football injuries can best be prevented if the thorough examination of each squadman by a reputable physician before the season starts includes a detailed medical history, with old injuries and past illnesses being ascertained and card indexed on each boy. The examination also should include besides routine tests, chest X-ray, heart plate, blood count, urine analysis and examination of the teeth and eyes.

Too much scrimmage takes energy out of the players and is harmful. Ankles should be wrapped, and pads and helmets worn for each practice session. Especially pernicious is the habit of throwing off a helmet and playing bareheaded. Practice should be held on turfed fields combed for glass and nails, and from whose sidelines all benches and water carts have been removed. A maximum schedule of nine games, a three-months season of practice and play and no matching of 150-pound teams against 175-pound ones are other precautions that will cut down the number of injuries.

Injured players should never scrimmage or play. They should have the courage to inform the coach, trainer or team physician instantly when they are hurt. Players should warm up well immediately preceding practice or play, gradually increasing the heart beat until they sweat a little. Tired players are easily hurt, so frequent substitutions not only will prevent injury, but will build up the squad's reserve playing strength, too. Boys from twelve to seventeen years of age need at least ten hours' sleep daily and boys over seventeen can well use nine hours.

Dr. Mal Stevens, New York University coach, has made a fine study of football-equipment precautions.[1] He advises the use of well-ventilated locker rooms that are thoroughly cleaned and scrubbed daily, and with pegs suspended around the wall so the players' togs always may be hung up and aired. He also recommends plenty of toilets and urinals so players won't have to stand in line and hence put off regular elimination, and plenty of indoor space for both teams to lie down between halves so they won't have to take their rest on wet straw, cold ground or benches beneath the grandstand. To prevent the spread of athlete's foot, Doctor Stevens counsels a solution of one-half per cent sodium hypophosphite in foot baths before and after showers, and also a careful drying between the toes after the daily splash. Fresh laundered jock straps, undershirts, half socks and towels should be issued daily and there should be no mixing of any item of equipment.

Colds can be prevented by requiring each player **to**

[1] From *The Control of Football Injuries* by Stevens and Phelps. Copyright 1933 by A. S. Barnes and Company, Inc.

drink one-half teaspoon of soda in a paper cup of warm water daily at the stadium before each practice and gargling with a one per cent solution of salt water. Some trainers restrict this to periods of threatening weather or to players who habitually have colds.

HISTORY OF FOOTBALL

The game of football is very old. The Greeks played it with a stuffed goatskin under the name *sphennida* and later taught it to the Romans who dubbed the game *harpastum* or "stealing" because some of their roughest players sometimes found it necessary to take the ball away from opponents prior to giving it a lusty kick. That the Chinese played long before the coming of Christ has been proven. The following inscription for a celestial football ground in A.D. 50 by the poet Li Yu indicates he had a surprisingly sensible conception of the sport:

> The teams take their places according to the venerable rules.
> The ball goes flying across like the moon.
> No allowances are made for feelings;
> There must be no partialities.
> But there must be determination and coolness;
> Without the slightest irritation at failure.
> If all this be necessary for football,
> How much more so for the business of life!

During the Middle Ages, the game flourished among the common people of England. It was probably intro-

duced there sometime between the coming of the Greek
Pytheus in 330 B.C. and the departure of the Romans in
A.D. 410. The sport was generally frowned upon by the
nobility and no wonder! In 1314 so many shop fronts
were smashed by football players jousting in the narrow
streets of old London and so much business was ruined
that Edward II forbade it by royal decree. Edward III re-
newed the ban in 1365 because his yeomen played football instead of practicing the archery that was so vital to
the national defense.

But Henry VIII, the Tudor monarch who was an all-
around athlete, excelled at tennis, wrestling, hunting and
staff play. He endorsed football for his soldiers. The story
goes that when he needed an army to invade France,
Henry was informed by the Earl of Buckinghamshire that
the latter's husky yeomen preferred playing football to
fighting the French. The King had never seen football
but was curious to view any game that could divert
soldiers from war. He rode to the protesting district, be-
held the entire male population lined up in two teams
ready to play football, climbed off his horse and kicked
the ball that started the game. He played until the contest
was over and then, sporting a purpled eye and with his
royal raiment badly torn although his countenance shone
with enjoyment, stayed to enlist both sides for the war.

The first royal parent to bar his son from playing football was James I, king after Elizabeth. Passing a football
game one day on Clapham Common, James was horrified

to behold bloody shins and broken noses and asked a courier to go see what the war was about. Upon being informed that it was football, James immediately issued a decree that the Prince of Wales, later the hapless Charles I, could not "kicke ye balle," and it is said the order still stands.

However in other parts of Europe, particularly in Florence, Italy, the sport was held in high repute, and rich costumes were worn by players and spectators and a painstaking ritual was observed that smacked something of modern polo. In fact the rules of the Florentine football game, called *calcio*, prohibited its being played by "any kind of low persons; or artisans or servants, ignoble men or infamous; but by honest soldiers, men of noble birth, gentlemen and princes."

The game was quickly introduced into America by the English. However it did not bloom luxuriously at first. As late as 1857 we have this unique protest by a writer in *Harper's Weekly*, who indignantly declared:

It is really an indictment of our system of college education that faculties have given students so little opportunity for physical expression, but have permitted them to over-indulge their craving for scholastic achievement. We see halls crowded for oratorical contests, standing room only when a work of Sophocles is performed by the dramatic club and feverish competition for the honor of delivering a Latin salutatory. . . . The winner of the "math" prize is carried to Prexy's house on the shoulders of his cheering classmates. Straight A men are absurdly lionized at banquets.

. . . Is not this a one-sided view to take of education? Is it fair . . . never to say a word of praise of the Yale halfback who scored on Princeton? If football received a little more notice, it might take a firm hold on college life. Give the players a smooth field and a few benches and the game would soon attract spectators.

The first intercollegiate game in America was played November 6, 1869, at New Brunswick, New Jersey, when Rutgers defeated Princeton at soccer, 6 goals to 4. In 1873 Cornell and Michigan scheduled a game at Cleveland, with thirty players on each side, but this contest fell through when the university president at Cornell refused his student players permission to make the long trip, declaring sternly, "I will not permit thirty men to travel four hundred miles merely to agitate a bag of wind."

McGill University of Montreal, Canada, introduced the running game to American football when its football club came to Cambridge, Massachusetts, in 1874 to meet Harvard. Harvard noticed that the McGill players, while practicing, not only kicked the ball but tucked it under one arm and ran with it, too. This was new to the Harvard players but it promised such tempting action that they sportingly agreed to play the game under the McGill rules and held the Canadians to a 0–0 tie. After that bracing taste of the running game the American colleges always continued to use it.

And so developed American football, until by 1905 it had

become an exceedingly speedy but rough game (eighteen were killed and one hundred and fifty-nine seriously injured that year) with eleven players on a side and an elliptical ball used instead of a round one. Each team was given three downs to make five yards. However, this style was dangerous to players and unattractive to spectators, who seldom saw the ball except when it burst beneath the weight of the players and a new one had to be kicked out. Therefore President Theodore Roosevelt called the rules committee to the White House in the middle of the 1905 season and by a series of sweeping rule changes, the game was opened up to make it safer for players. The forward pass was introduced, teams were required to make ten yards instead of five in three downs, players of the kicking team were judged onside as soon as a punt touched the ground, hurdling was forbidden, halves shortened to thirty minutes each, six offensive players were compelled to toe the scrimmage line and the referee was instructed to blow his whistle when any portion of the ball carrier's body, except his hands and feet, touched the ground while he was in the grasp of an opponent.

Out of these radical alterations, and others added since, has grown modern American football, unrecognizable, perhaps, to the players of antiquity but still demanding that "determination and coolness and no allowances made for feelings" about which the clear-sighted Chinese poet Li Yu wrote back in A.D. 50.

CHAPTER 7

GOLF

THE object of golf is to hit a small white ball into a hole only four and one-half inches in diameter in the fewest number of strokes; this ball is played from the teeing ground into the submerged can by successive licks of different clubs.

The sport is played upon what is known as a golf course or links. The distance between the holes of the links is rarely shorter than 100 or longer than 600 yards. Although Bob Davis once defined a golf course as "an outdoor insane asylum peopled with madmen suffering from the delusion that they will finally master the game," it is actually an expansive sweep of well-groomed grass. It is usually located at the edge of a city or town, and built and maintained at considerable expense.

Since golf is an outdoor sport, it is usually conceded to be a healthy one, although some of its opponents have mischievously asserted that most people who derive health from its pursuit would be equally benefited by long walks.

180

This statement leads golf lovers to retort that only a few of us are strong-minded enough to take long walks regularly for health. A third point of view was once advanced by a well-known author who said he knew "but three men who took long walks on principle and two of them were 'cracked.'"

Golf found an outstanding ambassador in Dwight D. Eisenhower, president of the United States, who began playing in 1927. Slowed by arthritis and a knee lamed by football, the president wasn't an enthusiastic or a regular golfer until after World War II when he grew to love it. Four days after he took the oath of office, he was hitting golf balls on the White House lawn and, later, when shooting well, he toured the rugged Augusta, Georgia, National Golf Club course in the 80's.

Even after President Eisenhower had his heart attack and an operation for ileitis, his physicians prescribed golf for him. Thus the president dramatized the benefits of exercise for older people even after heart attacks and operations, demonstrating a new trend in medicine. Physicians advised Ike to play golf whenever he could, three times weekly if he felt like it. Major General Howard McSnyder, the president's personal physician, said then, "Golf is good for his nerves and good for his muscle tone. It takes his mind off the scores of anxieties that confront him daily."

Few other games so put a boy on his own as does this one, for in golf it is never against the adversary that a player wars so much as against himself. Of all games, golf is the least adapted to the spectator, who cannot sit still and watch it but must move around with the golfers. And yet it is a sociable game for the players themselves, for the longish intervals between strokes permit conversation, which is usually impossible in other sports. Golf probably permits of a higher percentage of luck than any other sport. Jerry Travers, a former American champion, once estimated that the four ingredients most needed for tournament success in golf, in the order of their respective proportions were, skill fifty per cent, temperament twenty per cent, experience fifteen per cent and luck fifteen per cent, which is probably one important reason golf champions repeat less often than those in most other sports.

And yet it is possible to practice so painstakingly that you can reduce that percentage of luck. Ben Hogan, the solemn little professional from Fort Worth, Texas, proved this. Hogan always strove unceasingly for perfection. Jimmy Demaret, his golfing partner, once said of Hogan, "No matter how far he is ahead, he's grimly determined to get still farther ahead." Once when Hogan and Demaret were five strokes up in a match, Hogan told Demaret, "We're only five up. If we concentrate and fight hard, we may win by eight or ten."

Hogan had as complete an approach to golf as Bill Tilden had to tennis. Although he took a long time to choose his club and line up his shot, he hit the ball quickly once he had decided what he wanted to do. He was a great hand to study carefully and think out the courses he played. He wanted to know what a ball would do on each type of grass.

Most tournament players don't like to practice, including two of the greatest moderns, Byron Nelson and Sammy Sneed. Practice for Hogan meant five or six hours of work, during which he might hit as many as one thousand balls. His methods paid off. In 1953 he won five of six major tournaments, the British Open, the United States Open, the Masters, the Pan-American, and the Colonial National. He tied for third at Greenbrier.

A boy can hardly start playing golf too young. It is a good thing for boys to imitate good adult players. Boys are the greatest imitators in the world. They copy by instinct. For example, Bobby Jones, the young American from Georgia who, at the age of twenty-five, grand-slammed all four major golf titles, once said: "The biggest piece of golfing luck I ever had was when the Atlanta Athletic Club got Stewart Maiden for its professional. I was five years old then and lived opposite the gate of the East Lake Golf Course. I had taken up golf in a small way with a sawed-off cleek which one of the East Lake players had given me. Stewart never gave me any lessons. I just followed him around and watched him. I imitated his style like a monkey . . . and Stewart had the finest and soundest style I have ever seen. I grew up swinging like him."

Boys should not play golf to the exclusion of other games, but should tackle them all in season. When a boy

begins golf, he should start with the irons, then try the
woods and later the putter. If he can practice under a
good professional so much the better, but for the vast
majority who cannot, these hints might help:

GRIP: If he is less than ten years old, or has
small hands, or is not husky for his age, a boy should grip
the club with all his fingers on the shaft, keeping the
thumb of his left hand in the palm of his right. If his
hands are big and strong, he should use the overlapping
grip employed by three-fourths of the top American
professional golfers today, keeping the little finger of the
right hand overlapping the first finger of the left. This
grip was devised by Harry Vardon, the great English
golfer of an earlier generation, so that the two hands
could work as one.

Without squeezing, get a good tight hold of the club
with the left hand. Keep the wrist supple and exert the
main pressure with the third and little fingers. This will
prevent the club's turning in the hand during the stroke.
The palm of the left hand should be down, and the
thumb should encircle the shaft so that when you look
down the shaft, only the top of the left hand and three
knuckles are visible.

Without disarranging the position of the left hand,
grasp the club gently with the fingers of the right hand,
the palm of which should be facing upward. Remember
to place the thumb of the left hand in the palm of the
right, or, if Vardon's overlapping grip is used, overlap

the little finger of the right hand with the first finger of
the left. The main pressure of the right hand should be
applied by the first finger and thumb. There should also
be a slight pressure between the connecting link of the
two hands, the heel of the right and the thumb of the
left.

Checking up on the grip, the thumbs should ride the
sides of the shaft, not the top, and should never protrude
beyond the first finger of either hand. The fingers should
cover the downshaft laterally, instead of straight around
it. In hitting with the iron clubs, where the turf must be
taken to put a backspin on the ball, there is always a jar
at impact that often loosens the grip and will be fatal to
the stroke unless the grip of the left hand is firm.

STANCE: Relaxation and comfort are im-
portant here. Gripping the club as described, stand erect,
then bend forward from the waist just enough to reach
the ball with the club head. Keep the arms hanging almost straight down from the shoulders. The knees are
bent a little to relieve leg tension, the body weight is
distributed evenly on both feet, which are not spread
too much, and the toes are turned slightly outward. Both
feet should be parallel to the ball's line of flight. For wood
play, spread the feet about as far apart as the shoulders.
However for iron play, the feet should come closer together until the heels almost touch on short shots. On
wood shots, line the ball up on the heel of the left foot.
Fix the eyes and point the chin just back of the ball and

hold them there. Never move the head either laterally or up and down during the swing.

GOLF SWING: Most professional teachers emphasize that the force moving a golf club should originate near the center of the body, not in the hands and arms. They also say that the main propelling force comes from the twisting of the body, not from the arms. The golf swing should be quiet and smooth. The action resembles a rock suspended from the end of a swinging cord. Good golfers think in terms of the feel of the club head, like the rock on the end of a string, quietly and smoothly swung round and round.

Adults find it difficult to grasp this idea. Possessed of more strength than boys, the average adult tries to swing the club all the way as though it were a baseball bat. He depends on sheer power, particularly of the right arm, to drive the golf ball far. This is wrong.

Boys have an advantage over grownups here, says Bruce Drake, former coach of the University of Oklahoma golf team. Luckily, the average boy does not have the strength to swing a golf club hard. When a boy swings a club, he has to let the club head drop largely of its own weight and volition. That is fortunate, because it means he will not develop the bad free-swinging habits of his elders. That is one reason why almost all great American golfers of today were formerly boy caddies. As boys they had a better chance to learn the game properly.

The true golf swing is so difficult to learn because the

left arm must be the dominant one, and the muscles most used are those on the left side of the body, which are not as strong or as well-trained as those on the right side, unless the person is left-handed. In the correct golf swing, the left hand has to control the club and can do so only when the right arm is held in a comparative state of rest. And to the average person, who uses that right arm and hand at the expense of his left in nearly everything he does, whether it's throwing a baseball, swinging a tennis racket or eating with his fork, it is hard suddenly to start stressing that untrained left.

It is best not to try to slug the ball. George Bayer, a gigantic young pro from San Gabriel, California, who stands six-five and weighs 240, has walloped a golf ball 420 yards or more with his secret of perfect timing, great strength, and his uncocking of the wrists at the moment of contact.[1] But he is a prodigious exception.

Dr. Cary Middlecoff, the dentist who in the 1950's became an outstanding professional golfer in the United States, advises against hitting the ball too hard. Middlecoff says a favorite place to lose control of both one's game and one's temper is on the first tee where the average player, without warming up, tries to knock the cover off the ball to impress the many club members and spectators who are always assembled there.

"Your only thought," says Middlecoff, "is to whack one long and true to bring a groan of approval from the assem-

[1] See *Look* magazine, 21:117, March 19, 1957.

bly. It is much better to forget the crowd and think about that little dimpled white fellow on the tee in front of you. My advice is just to try and hit a nice, comfortable one down the fairway—the straighter the better."

Middlecoff says that as a man gets along in years the strength of his golf game lies in (1) the straightness of his shots, and (2) the mastery of his short game. The same thing holds true for boy players.

BACKSWING: The club is started back slowly with the *left hand,* and the right hand rides lightly. As the club goes back, the weight shifts to the right foot and the hips turn toward the right. The left heel leaves the ground slightly and the left knee should bend naturally to aid the body pivot. As the club is brought back, the wrists start cocking so that when the top of the swing is reached and the club is approximately parallel to the ground, the wrists are fully cocked and held somewhere near the right ear.

The top of the swing is most important. Then the left arm should be straight but not stiff, the wrists should be cocked, the weight on the right foot and the head remaining in the same motionless position as when the swing began. The eyes should be fixed on the ball.

DOWNSWING: The club is also started down with the *left hand,* and the weight gradually shifts to the left side. Halfway down the swing, the right hand starts helping the left to whip the club through. However this assisting force from the right hand must not be applied too soon or the club will be detoured from its true arc and cause one to hit from the outside in instead of from the more desirable inside out. At the impact of clubhead and ball, the left hand is still firm, and the left arm still straight. The weight is on the left foot and the chin is still pointed back of the ball; the eyes are glued to the ball. In other words, you must have something to hit against and the left side of the body serves this purpose.

Don't stop the club after hitting the ball. Let its momentum carry hands, arm and body into the follow-through; keep the club head following the ball toward the target as far as both arms will permit. At this point the elbows will have to break slightly, and the club comes to a stop over the left shoulder. The wrists then will be held near the left ear. The weight is now held firmly on the left foot, the right heel is slightly off the ground and the right knee is bent to prevent any locking of the hips. Thus you can freely perform the body pivot so essential to a golf swing.

Looking up too anxiously spoils more golf shots than any other fault, so beginners will do well to keep their heads down after the ball is hit until they count three. After they get the correct habit, they can raise the head a little sooner to pick up the flight of the ball.

GOLF CLUBS: The United States Golf Association forbids a golfer to use more than fourteen clubs in tournament play. The average tournament player will carry four woods and ten irons.

The wood clubs are longer and therefore capable of more leverage. They are built chiefly for distance and crack golfers sometimes hit a ball almost 400 yards with them. The most common wood clubs are the No. 1, which is used to hit the ball long and low off the tee; the No. 2, which has a brass plate on the sole, is lofted more than a No. 1 and is used to hit a ball high off the fairway or off the tee with the wind so the breeze can ride it out; and the No. 3, which has still more loft than the No. 2, and therefore hits still a higher and shorter ball. It is used principally off the fairway or off the tee on a short par three hole. The No. 4 wood has a smaller, thinner and more lofted face. It gets the ball up into the air quickly. The iron clubs are shorter with faces inclined as much as thirty degrees so the ball may be lofted over traps. They are constructed for accuracy, such as shooting at the target of a nearby green after the wooden club has propelled the ball within the range of the green. In golf, the shorter the club, the more accurate. The shortest club in the bag is the *putter*, used for the stroke that demands the most painstaking accuracy of all, the close-up shot into the cup.

Iron clubs nowadays are identified by numbers one through nine, inscribed on the sole of the club. The number one club is usually not carried along. In the old days each iron club had a name. For instance, what is known today as the two iron was formerly called a midiron, the five was formerly the mashie and the nine a niblick. Simplification, and also mass buying of the new numbered clubs, was the purpose of the sporting goods companies when they banished names and substituted numbers.

Starting with the number one, which is the longest iron in a set and is lofted only ten degrees, the irons gradually grade shorter in length and higher in loft. The number nine iron is the shortest in the bag and is lofted approximately thirty degrees. Extra iron clubs are the *wedge*, used for a lofted shot over the apron or heavy grass (from constant watering) around the green, and the *sand wedge*, which has a wide flange on its sole to prevent its digging too deeply into the ground and is capable of imparting more loft and backspin to the ball than any other club in the bag.

The longer the iron, and consequently the lower its identifying number, the more distance and less height it will yield. For instance, a boy who can drive 150 yards with a number two iron could roughly estimate his distance at ten yards less as he goes through the set, realizing 140 yards with a three iron, 130 with a four, 120 with a five. No two players get the same distance with the same club.

Distance from the green largely determines the selection of a club to be used. For example, if you come up to your ball and it looks as though it were about 125 yards distance from your lie to the pin and there is no intervening trap or troublesome wind, you would select the iron club in your bag that consistently nets a distance of 125 yards. Each golfer will know, from long usage and experience, how much distance he can realize with each club. He also will learn to estimate how far he is from each green, which is also important.

IRON PLAY: The general idea in all iron play is to hit the ball high with backspin so it will drop onto the green and stop with very little roll, thus obviating the risk of the ball's bounding over uncertain fairway surfaces. But this is hard to do when the wind is blowing with the golfer. No matter how much the ball is cut, the wind takes so much spin out of it that it won't "set" immediately upon dropping to the green, but will bound and roll beyond.

The rule for playing irons with the wind is to use a more lofted club than ordinary and hit higher; also the player should pitch well in front of the hole, thus allowing for the run.

When hitting dead into the wind, stopping the ball is no problem. However there is danger of the shot's climbing so high against the breeze that it drops short. For this reason, choose a club of slightly less loft and try for a more boring shot. Almost any well-hit ball against the wind will stop where it drops, but unless more power than usual is tried for, it may drop short.

Beginning players should shoot for the left of the green in a crosswind blowing from the left, or to the right of the green when the crosswind comes from the right, and allow for the drift of the ball.

HOW TO SWING AN IRON CLUB: We have already seen that when using a wood, the player must hit the ball with a sweep at the bottom of a swing. However, with iron clubs, there is less backswing. At its top, the iron club forms an angle at about twenty degrees with the ground instead of being parallel to it, as the wood club is. In iron play, the ball is hit on the downstroke and turf taken (hit the ball first, then take turf) so backspin may be imparted, causing the ball to "set" when it drops on the green.

Remember that the feet are held closer together for iron play. The right foot should be a bit closer to the ball's line of flight than the left. As a general practice, start hitting the longer irons close to the left heel. However, when shorter irons, that is, the ones with higher numbers and increased loft, are used, move the ball back toward the right. For example, in playing the number one iron, hit the ball about two inches inside the left heel. The two and three irons should be played a little more toward the center, the four, five, six and seven irons in the middle of the stance, and the eight and nine to the right of the center of the stance, or closer to the right foot.

PUTTING: Gene Sarazen, the American professional, said any dub can learn to putt. His theory is somewhat strengthened by the fact that several years ago on a prominent course in the East, a scoffing spectator, after watching several holes of putting, remarked that he could hole a ten-foot putt with his umbrella, and did.

However it is just as easy to miss putts, too, as Tommy Armour, who has won both the American and British

Open championships, can tell you. Tommy once required three putts to get down from one foot away, a mistake that cost him the Canadian Open championship.

Unbounded confidence in your ability to lay the ball dead or run it down from several yards away is the secret of good putting, says Walter J. Travis, the early American champion. "The simpler the means to get the ball into the hole, the better," Travis advised. "Don't unduly hang over the ball and don't be too keen to notice any fancied irregularities of surface between it and the hole. In respect to both the correct line and the necessary strength, be governed by your first impressions and act without further ado."

Alex Smith, one of the best putters among American professionals, never believed in "fooling around" with a putter. "Miss 'em quick!" was his motto, but he rarely did. The average American "pro" stands up to the ball and hits it boldly and freely, a putting practice that can safely be recommended to anybody.

Putting stance, even among the American professionals, varies ridiculously. Perhaps the best advice that can be given is as follows: try for a smooth, comfortable stance, relax every muscle in the body, don't worry about holding the head still, be sure to swing the club back far enough on the backswing, concentrate on making the blade travel close to the ground on both sides of the ball, and don't tighten or stop the left forearm but let the left arm swing on through after the ball is hit.

Some putters, after taking a preliminary glance back of the ball toward the hole, trace an imaginary line over which the ball must pass, noting for guidance a particular blade of grass somewhere along this line. Then letting their eye run quickly over this imaginary line, they estimate the force to be applied and make the stroke.

Always go for the hole. It is better to roll a little beyond and cash your proportion of long putts than to be short and never hit any.

Everyone who plays golf should buy the tiny booklet of rules printed by the A. G. Spalding and Brothers Company. This book costs only twenty-five cents and readily fits into any pocket. A glance inside it reveals that ninety-eight per cent of the rules used everywhere in America today are those approved by the Royal and Ancient Club of St. Andrews. This should excite the curiosity of any boy. What and where is St. Andrews? How did golf start?

HISTORY OF GOLF

The origin of golf, like that of so many sports, is lost in obscurity. Holland and Scotland are the countries generally given credit for its birth although the Romans had a pastime called *paganicia* which was played with a crooked stick and a leather ball stuffed with feathers.

Holland's claims, and they seem sounder than those of any other nation, are based chiefly upon a picture in an old Flemish manuscript of 1500–1520 at the British Museum which shows two men putting at the hole while a third addresses his ball at the nearby tee. The claim is also upon the origin of the name of the game itself which is derived from the German *kolbe,* meaning club. In low Dutch this was *kolf,* the guttural pronunciation of which is *golf.*

However it is in Scotland that the sport has been most carefully nurtured the past four hundred years; its record is richly woven into Scottish history, legislation and literature. With football, golf was forbidden to the common people of Scotland in 1457 because archery, the chief weapon of national defense, languished in competition with it. By a stern order of Parliament "the fut ball and golf be utterly cryit down and nocht usit."

But the monarchs themselves apparently were exempt from their own ukases because King James played golf with the ruffian border noble Bothwell, and French-schooled Mary Queen of Scots, the first known woman golfer, not only played the game a few days after the murder of her husband Darnley, but was the first to call the boy who sighted her golf balls a *cadet,* which is French for student. The Scots later adopted her pronunciation but spelled it caddy or caddie.

Sunday golf is so common in the United States that Bobby Jones once innocently asked, "Dad, what do people who don't play golf do on Sunday?" But it was barred in Scotland until James VI finally granted the petition of his people that they be allowed to play on the Sabbath,

since they were busy earning their bread and butter every
other day. Thereafter, "having first done their deutie
to God," they hied themselves to the links, armed with
their crooked-shaped clubs with horn faces and leaded
backs, and with their little hard balls imported from
Holland.

The Marquis of Montrose played golf at St. Andrews
and Leith and always insisted on the best golf balls, clubs
and caddies obtainable. The news of the Irish Rebellion
came to King Charles I while playing a golf match at
Leith. James II, the Catholic Duke of York, once won a
foursome with an Edinburgh shoemaker as a partner.
James VI of Scotland not only laid a heavy tariff on golf
balls from Holland, but when he left the North country
in 1603 to rule England upon Elizabeth's death, golf
followed him south across the Grampian Mountains and
made its home at Blackheath where, under the care of
Scottish Londoners, it throve in a small way until the
establishment of the famous clubs of Banbury, Westward
Ho, Wimbledon and Hoylake, after which it spread all
over England.

However the shrine of golf continued to be Scotland,
and in the small and ancient city of St. Andrews, a quiet
place of ten thousand souls located on the east coast, the
sport has been hallowed for centuries. Although the
oldest university in Scotland was founded there in 1411,
St. Andrews is much better known for its golf. The
taverns there greet you in its name, the streets are even

called for the game and upon many of the tombstones are inscribed the golfing feats of the Scottish dead who made history on the links.

The St. Andrews course, played so often by golfing royalty down through the centuries, is a links of wild desolate beauty located on the North Sea, where the cool salt air is always in one's nostrils and the fairways are so thickly carpeted with daisies that often it is difficult to find one's ball. The bunkers are sunken and do not always show from the tee, yet they are well-distributed, and the shifting winds will try the skill of any golfer.

Two of the most famous bunkers there are suggestively named "Hell" and "Walkinshaw's Grave," and golfing veterans like to tell an incident occurring at the former bunker that illustrates the golfing spirit of St. Andrews. Andra Kirkaldy, a Scottish professional, was one day playing with the Bishop of London, a very great personage. The bishop got his ball in the terrible sand pit of "Hell" bunker but by a masterly stroke of his niblick, extricated himself.

"Andrew!" the bishop called elatedly to Kirkaldy, "Did you see me get out of 'Hell' with my niblick?"

"Yes, my lord," promptly replied the professional, "and I'd advise ye to tak that niblick wi' ye when ye dee."

Of all the old-time golfing champions developed at St. Andrews, perhaps the three most famous were Allan Robertson, Old Tom Morris and Young Tom Morris. In 1834 Robertson set a record of 79 at St. Andrews. Young Tom Morris cut it to 77 right after the Civil War and so the record-shattering continued decade after decade, reaching something of a climax in 1927 when Bobby Jones, twenty-five-year-old American phenomenon, shot four consecutive rounds of 68, 72, 73 and 72 that totaled seven strokes under the par of 73 for the course and cut the British Open record by six strokes.

No wonder the veteran Andra Kirkaldy exclaimed after witnessing young Jones's feat, "Mon, he's nae gowfer at all! He's juist a machine! In all my sixty-seven years I hae never-r-r seen such gowf!"

And yet the St. Andrews course when Jones triumphed was far less difficult than in the old days when Robertson and the Dunns, Piries, Morrises, Straths, Parks and Kirks played. The chopping of iron clubs had cut down the heather that formerly encroached upon the fairways, and the tramping of millions of feet wore down the long bent grass. Also, modern golfers have a tremendous advantage in their clubs. The old iron clubs were heavier and clumsier than modern ones, and the old wooden clubs were lighter, with slimmer shafts and shallower faces.

Nor did the old-timers have modern streamlined balls that permit the terrific drives of today. Until 1860 golf balls were seamed in leather and stuffed with boiled feathers and rarely could be driven more than 175 or 200 yards. Later, gutta-percha balls came in. In 1898 an American inventor, Colburn Haskell of Cleveland, Ohio, brought out a ball with a rubber center wound under mechanical pressure with thin rubber thread and covered with a thin layer of gutta-percha, which was the pro-

genitor of the modern golf ball. As a result, the old
champions were celebrated more for skillful placing than
for long driving, and their scores naturally were higher.

For instance, Allan Robertson, who was born at St.
Andrews in 1815, was a short thick-set Scot. He played
long spoon shots as close to the hole as though the ball
had been pitched with an iron. He was a master of the
short game and liked to do his approaching with a cleek,
which was something of an innovation since the crack
Scottish golfers of his time did not approach with irons
or iron lofters, but with the harmless "baffey spoon." All
were known for their extreme steadiness in the face of
hazards, bad lies, rains, cold, winds and snow. They have
been known to play as many as ninety consecutive holes
without making one bad shot or one stroke other than the
one that was intended.

Much of the tradition of Scottish golf centers about
the memory of Old Tom Morris, famous greenkeeper at
St. Andrews, who was born in 1821 and lived to be
eighty-six. Morris started playing golf under the tutelage
of Robertson at the age of twelve. When he was forty he
won the open championship at Prestwick in 1861. At
St. Andrews, Old Tom was also an elder in the Presby-
terian Church and as greenkeeper of the Royal and Ancient
Club he presided over his golf course with all the in-
tegrity and much of the reverence he showed in the kirk.

In 1904, at the age of eighty-three, Old Tom played
the old course at St. Andrews in 94, scoring a 46 out and

a 48 in. He died May 24, 1908, as the result of an accidental fall down a flight of steps in the St. Andrews clubhouse within a few weeks of his eighty-seventh birthday.

Perhaps the most picturesque figure of Scottish golf,
and the finest player of all was Young Tom Morris, "poor
young Tommy" as he was affectionately called by the
Scots. His play was so incomparable that, although he
died at the age of twenty-four, he was the most formidable golfer of his time. He was the son of Old Tom, the
St. Andrews greenkeeper, who taught the boy all the
golfing guile he knew. Young Tommy, at the age of
twenty, had three times in succession swept the championship from the top veterans in the Isles. In 1868 he
won the championship at Prestwick with 154, six strokes
under the record, and in 1869 did 157, eleven strokes
better than his nearest opponent. In 1870 he shot a blazing 149 to take outright possession of the championship
belt, still held by the family as an heirloom. This was
top golf, considering the handicaps of that day.

Any sort of a putt was easy for Young Tommy, the Scots
tell us. He had a queer, painstaking way of standing with
his right foot so near the ball that it seemed his putting
blade would not have room to clear it. He was also a
slashing driver, reveled in bad lies and was a master of all
manner of forcing shots. Legend has it that Young Tommy's wrists were so powerful that when he waggled a club
with the flamboyancy that characterized the Scottish style,
the slender shaft sometimes snapped in his hands. On

Christmas day, 1875, he died of complications brought on
by grief over the death of his young wife and newborn
son. He lies buried in the Cathedral golfing grounds at
St. Andrews.

His father, Old Tom, who outlived the boy thirty-three
years, always said, "I could cope wi' Allan [Allan Robert-
son] masel' but never wi' Tommy."

HOW TO CADDIE

Since so many boys learn their golf while caddying for
older players, perhaps it is almost as important for them
to learn the correct rules for caddie conduct as it is for
them to learn to play golf properly. Probably the best
caddie code ever devised is that of Tom O'Hara, veteran
caddie-master of the Denver, Colorado, Country Club
who has been training boys for caddie duty for more than
thirty years.

Here is O'Hara's code:

1. It is not easy to be a good caddie and a bad one is
   worse than none at all, so read the rules.
2. Do not forget that they are made to be always carried
   out, whether you are with a good player or a beginner.
3. Replace any turf cut out by player.
4. Do not talk with other boys while on duty.
5. Remember you are responsible for finding the ball;
   you must mark it down very closely and keep your
   eye on the ball until you walk to it. If you watch
   others drive you will forget your line.

6. Keep right with your player, never let him have to call you to come on.

7. When he is going to play, stand well to the side of him, never behind the stroke.

8. Keep clubs in bag, never take them out and swing them; you are paid to work, not to play.

9. Never hand a player a club unless he asks you to. Learn the clubs so that you make no mistakes.

10. Caddies should keep ball clean, and if it goes in rough it will be easy to find.

11. Never touch a ball or move anything within a club's length of it without orders from the player.

12. Wait until players have holed out before walking to the next tee.

13. When a player is about to play, keep perfectly still.

14. Give the player the putter and walk to the flag; do not stand with you feet close to the hole nor rest the iron on the putting green; never walk across the line of a putt.

15. Do whatever you have to do promptly and cheerfully.

16. Caddies must stay around the caddie house; caddies not allowed in locker room.

17. Caddies not engaged must keep still while players are putting on greens near caddie house.

18. Caddies must only caddie for members to whom they are assigned.

19. Caddies must keep quiet while waiting for members at the first tee.

20. When waiting at the tee do not sit on the benches so that the players have no room to sit down. You cannot see the ball when sitting down.

21. Any caddie interfering with any tree or bush or any buildings on club grounds will be discharged.

22. Caddies should not go in bunkers or on top of mounds in bunkers.

23. Your most important duty as a caddie is to know where the ball is every time, and beat the player to it.

24. Caddies should not enter club grounds before 8 A.M. unless asked to do so by caddie-master, and caddies should be off club grounds by dark.

25. No caddie will be assigned to any player nor reserved for him until player has entered club grounds, and has applied in person to caddie-master for a caddie.

26. No attention will be paid to request for caddies over telephone.

27. These rules must be obeyed.

CHAPTER 8

HANDBALL

HANDBALL is a deceiving game. At first sight it looks easy. But after the novice has tried it a few minutes, he will discover that he is drenched with perspiration, that he is exercising muscles not even listed in the average physiology textbook and that he is covering more ground than a rural mail carrier.

Also, there is an erroneous impression that slapping a tiny black rubber ball against a wall with the palm is a dull pastime. Perhaps the best refutation of this was written more than one hundred years ago by William Hazlitt, British critic and essayist, in his essay condoling the death of John Cavanagh of Cork, an old-time Irish fives champion (fives was the old English name for handball).

"It may be said," wrote Hazlitt, "that there are things of more importance than striking a ball against a wall—there are things indeed which make more noise and do as little good, such as making war and peace, making speeches and answering them, making verses and blotting them; making money and throwing it away. But the game of fives is what no one despises who has ever played it. It is the finest exercise for the body, and the best relaxation for the mind."

There are two main kinds of handball played today: *four-wall,* the original Irish game that can be traced back a thousand years to the Firbolgs, an ancient Irish race, and *one-wall,* its more popular American offshoot, which is said to have originated about 1900 in eastern United States, although Hazlitt's essay intimates that the Irish played a single-wall game in Cavanagh's time. Of the two games, one-wall is faster and because no back or side walls are used, requires more speed and stamina to cover court. Four-wall is more scientific.

The growth of one-wall handball has been aided by the fact that it is a far better spectator sport since it may be watched from three sides of the court, and also because a one-wall court is less costly to build than a four-wall court. Four-wall handball has been cruelly handicapped by the peculiar construction of its playing arena, which leaves no room for spectators except in a small gallery above the lowered back wall, although it has been suggested lately that glass courts might be the answer to this criticism.

SINGLE-WALL

In one-wall handball a sixteen-foot high front wall and a floor 34 by 20 feet comprise the two playing surfaces. The contestants stand near one another and play the ball in turn off the wall. If two people play, the match is called singles. If four play, it becomes doubles. Victory in a game goes to the first side scoring twenty-one points, and only the serving side can score. Matches are usually awarded to the first side winning two games.

The sport gets its name from the striking implement, which is the hand. The use of the foot, or of any portion of the body excepting one hand, is barred.

After a coin toss to determine the server, the latter stands anywhere he desires in the serving zone and begins the game by dropping the ball to the floor between the short line and the service line. He strikes it with the hand on the first bounce in such a manner that it will first hit the front wall and then rebound on the floor back of the front line and within or on the two sidelines and rear line. The serve may not be volleyed.

Then the receiver goes into action. He returns the ball to the wall by striking it either on the fly or the first bounce so that his stroke, too, will hit the front wall before rebounding to the floor. However he does not have to strike the ball with sufficient force to propel it off the wall back of the short line, as did the server. If he wishes he may softly drop it low off the front wall so that it scarcely bounces at all, forcing his opponent to sprint almost to the wall if he is to reach the ball before it rebounds off the floor twice, and costs him the point or hand-out.

After the serve, players on both sides pay no attention

to any lines except the outside ones that bound the court, for the idea is to hit the ball off the wall so hard that it cannot be handled, or so low that it cannot be reached in time, or at so clever an angle the opponent cannot touch it, or in such a manner that the opponent is forced into error when trying to return it. The chief requirements are that the ball must be hit with one hand, must strike the front wall, and upon flying back off the front

DIAGRAM OF STANDARD
SINGLE-WALL COURT

wall must land somewhere inside the playing rectangle.

Play continues until either the server or receiver is unable to return the ball legally, in which case a point is scored for the server or a hand-out against him, and the serve passes to his adversary.

The server loses the right to serve if he steps over the short line or outside the sidelines while serving, or bounces the ball in the serving zone more than three times prior to serving. As in tennis, he is given a second chance to put the ball in play if his first serve goes out, falls short or is illegal. He loses the service if he hits two such short balls in succession, or two long balls in succession, or a short and a long ball one after another, or his ball strikes the ceiling, floor or any other part of the room before it strikes the front wall.

In doubles, one partner serves until his hand is out, whereupon the other partner serves until he too loses, after which service passes to the other team. While one player is serving in doubles, his teammate must stand outside the sidelines between the service line, and rear line and cannot enter the court until the service ball has passed beyond him. Violation of this rule counts a short ball.

Frequently in handball a player will be struck by a ball delivered by his opponent. If such a ball hits an adversary before striking the floor or the front wall, the ball is dead and the point must be played over. However, if the ball on its way back from the front wall strikes a player, it is charged against the player touched. Hitting a partner with a ball in doubles is charged against that side.

Most of the disputes in handball center around what is called blocking or hindering. If a one-wall player, after striking the ball, immediately moves into a new position to anticipate the return, and by so doing crosses in front of the rebound off the wall, thereby obstructing his opponent's view or causing him to miss the ball, he causes a hinder and the referee declares the ball dead and the point must be played over. However, if a player, after striking the ball, remains perfectly still and by so doing momentarily hides the ball from his adversary's view or prevents him from securing a clear return, the play is legitimate and not a block or hinder.

EQUIPMENT: White shirts and pants are worn in tournament games. Correct shoes are important, preferably high ones of crepe or suction soles, laced firmly to support the ankles, which are easily sprained in handball. Heavy white woolen socks that absorb perspiration and lessen shock are best. Watch your hands. They receive much wear and tear in handball and frequently bruise and swell, especially in cold weather. Soaking the hands in hot water a few minutes before playing helps them. Regulation handball gloves securely tightened at the wrist are worn by most players.

SERVICE: A strong service is far more important in one-wall handball than in four-wall where the receiver has the assistance of the side and back walls. The underhand or low sidearm services are most popular among the champions, although occasionally the speedier overhand or high sidearm stance is very effective. Some experts have perfected the hook service, executed by drawing the hand sharply underneath or across the top of the ball while serving, causing it to spin and break to right or left upon striking the floor so that the receiver cannot get set for it. However this is a difficult maneuver.

Learn to hit with either hand. Players who run far to their left to play a ball right-handed are badly out of position for the opponent's return shot. You can develop a good left hand by playing games where there is a mutual agreement between you and your adversary that only the left hand will be used. Concentrate on the development of either an underhand, sidearm or overhand drive. Volley the ball whenever possible. Do not play too much. Two fast games of either singles or doubles are plenty for the average boy or adult.

FOUR-WALL

Although there is great similarity in four-wall and one-wall handball, beginning four-wall players will do well to examine the chief essentials of the latter sport:

ANGLES: In four-wall it is necessary to master the various angles the ball will assume off the walls. A good way to study them is to go onto a four-wall court alone, hit ball after ball to the side and back walls and try to anticipate the angle at which the ball will return to you so you will be ready for the second shot.

UNDERHAND DRIVE: Practice the underhand stroke constantly. It is used far more in four-wall than in single-wall. Execute it with the left foot advanced, using plenty of backswing and keeping the eyes on the ball until after it has been hit.

PLAYING THE BACK WALL: Back-wall play is all-important and beginners should practice it unceasingly, taking plenty of time, keeping the eye on the ball until after it has been hit and following through with a full extension of the arm. Timing is important and a wrist snap in the midst of the underhand hitting stroke will add power to it.

FIGHTING THE BALL: Don't fight the ball or run to meet it. Let it come back to you.

LEFT HAND: Work hard to improve your weak hand. Like the backhand in tennis, a good left hand is absolutely necessary in four-wall. Play left-handed games to develop it.

SERVICE: Probably the best service for four-wall beginners is the high toss that hugs the left side wall. Standing about a yard from the left side wall, the server lifts a slow ball high to the front wall. The ball clings to the left side wall all the way back on the rebound, striking the floor just behind the short line and bouncing high to the back wall corner where it is too spent to be played off the back wall. If the receiver is able to play this ball at all, he must do so with his left hand. Never direct a serve straight back to the back wall.

SHORT BALL OPTION: In four-wall handball the receiver may play a served short ball if he elects, so the server must be alert.

SERVICE RULES: Two types of service are permitted in four-wall; one that hits the front wall, then strikes the floor back of the short line; and one that hits the front wall, strikes one side wall, and then strikes the floor back of the short line. If the receiver wishes, he may volley this latter type of serve after it comes off the side wall and before it strikes the floor.

HINDERS: Unlike one-wall, a four-wall player, after striking the ball, cannot root himself to the spot and thus obstruct his opponent's view or prevent him from making a clear return. Such a play is a hinder. It is the duty of the side playing the ball to get out of the way of the opponent, moving to one side or the other so the adversary will have ample opportunity to see and play the return stroke.

SIZE OF COURT: A four-wall court is larger than a one-wall court, for it is twelve feet longer and three feet wider. Moreover its front wall is seven feet higher and its service zone is two feet farther from the front wall. If there

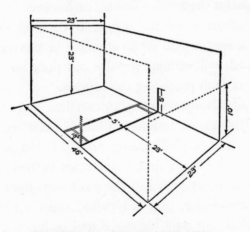

DIAGRAM OF STANDARD
FOUR-WALL COURT

is a gallery, the rear wall must be at least ten feet high.

CROTCH BALL: A crotch ball is one that hits at the juncture of the service wall and the ceiling, floor, side wall or in the corners. An out is scored against the server who hits one.

A ball coming from the front wall on fly or bounce, that goes into the gallery or through an opening in the side wall, shall be a hinder; but if it goes into the gallery or opening referred to after a player has touched it (ball caroming off hand or glove) it shall be a point against the player attempting the return.

SERVER'S PARTNER: In four-wall doubles, the server's partner must stand within the service box (located eighteen inches from each side wall at each extremity of service zone) with his back against the wall until the ball passes the service line on each serve. Two consecutive violations retire the server. If the server's partner is hit by a service ball while standing in the service box, it is a dead ball without penalty but does not eliminate any short or fault preceding this service.

Handball has always been an excellent sport for conditioning athletes in training. Boxers, wrestlers, runners, ice hockey and baseball players all like it and so do musicians, billiard players and business executives. Irish Jim Corbett, the boxer who had the most marvelous footwork of all heavyweights, played handball daily while training for his fights, not only for speed and endurance, but also to coördinate his eyes and hands so he could hit more accurately in the ring. In fact, Corbett burned up so much energy playing handball while training for his match with Fitzsimmons that Billy Delaney, his worried manager, considered burning down the handball court at the Corbett training headquarters.

Handball is Irish in origin and nearly all the old professional champions of the past one hundred years were Irish. Among them were William Baggs of Tipperary, David Browning, John Lawlor, Michael Eagan of Galway, James Kelly of County Mayo, Tim Twohill, Jim Fitzgerald, Tom Jones of County Kerry and the immortal Phil Casey who was born in Mountrath, Ireland in 1845, but played most of his handball in Brooklyn.

As a lad of sixteen Casey came to America in 1861 and, discovering that handball was a stranger sport, set about introducing and establishing it. This popular Irishman was never defeated in a matched game, and held the American championship twenty-nine years, to retire unbeaten in 1900. So well did he advertise the sport with his tours all over North America that he lived to see it played in nearly every police and fire yard and in most of the parishes and schools of the East. He well deserved his designation as the Father of American Handball.

It was Casey who in 1887 signed to play the famous international series of twenty-one games for the world's title against John Lawlor, the Irish champion. The first ten games were to be played at Cork in Ireland and the remaining eleven, if the full eleven were necessary, at

Brooklyn. The purse of one thousand dollars and the championship was to go to the first man who won eleven games. On the large Irish court at Cork, Lawlor won six games to Casey's four. However on the smaller court at Brooklyn four months later before crowds that were far too large to squeeze into the tiny gallery, Casey was at his unbeatable peak and swept seven straight games to close out the series, eleven games to six.

Old-timers assert that Casey was the greatest handball player of all time, but the sport is so old that of course there is no accurate way of telling. One person who would probably dispute that claim were he alive today was the British essayist, Hazlitt. He would undoubtedly vote for the long-dead Cavanagh, great Irish champion of the 1820's and '30's, who must indeed have been superb if we may believe Hazlitt's brilliant description of him which was written more than a century ago:

> It is not likely that anyone will now see the game of fives played in its perfection for many years to come—for Cavanagh is dead, and has not left his peer behind him. . . .
>
> His eye was certain, his hand fatal, his presence of mind complete. . . . He recovered balls as if by a miracle and from sudden thought, that everyone gave for lost. . . . He could either outwit his antagonist by finesse or beat him by main strength. Sometimes, when he seemed preparing to send the ball with the full swing of his arm, he would by a slight turn of his wrist drop it within an inch of the line. In general, the ball came from his hand, as if from a racket, in a straight horizontal line; so that it was vain to attempt to overtake or stop it.

He was the best *up-hill* player in the world; even when his adversary was fourteen, he would play on the same or better. . . . The only peculiarity of his play was that he never *volleyed*, but let the balls hop; but if they rose an inch from the ground he never missed having them. There was not only nobody equal, but nobody second to him. . . . He could give any other player half the game or beat him with his left hand.

His service was tremendous. He once played Woodward and Meredith together (two of the best players in England) in the Fivescourt, St. Martin's Street, and made seven and twenty aces following by service alone—a thing unheard of. . . . He used frequently to play matches at Copenhagen House for wagers and dinners. The wall against which they play is the same that supports the kitchen chimney, and when the wall resounded louder than usual, the cooks exclaimed, "Those are the Irishman's balls," and the joints trembled on the spit!

And yet how do we know that Cavanagh, or Casey either for that matter, could have beaten the long line of older Irish champions who played in the day of the Norman Conquest, the Ulster Uprisings, the Act of Union, and have been sleeping for centuries in nameless dust?

CHAPTER 9

ICE HOCKEY

ICE HOCKEY is advertised as the "fastest game on earth" and in many ways it deserves to be billed as the roughest as well. It has become the nation's foremost winter outdoor sports diversion and probably ranks next to basketball and boxing as America's top indoor sport.

It started in snowy Canada, where the world's finest players revel in it from boyhood, and has spread southward all along the northern border of the United States. Thanks to the invention of the indoor rink with artificial ice, it expanded down through the American midlands as far south as Houston, Texas, where a seven-team high-school league annually contended for the city championship before large crowds in semi-tropic temperature.

Ice hockey is a particularly thrilling sport for spectators who, seated almost on top of the playing rink and therefore enjoying an unusually clear view of the action, are thrown into frequent pandemonium by the long passing sallies down the length of the rink or the jolting body clashes at high speed, punctuated by the musical ringing

218

of protesting steel blades suddenly braked on ice, or the whack of the busy sticks. It is a game of graceful, fluent movement too; the players, who sometimes travel as fast as thirty feet per second, sweep in great curves like hawks sailing in the blue or trout streaking in a mountain stream.

There is no questioning Canada's grip on the game. The Canadians have won the ice hockey championship at five of the last eight Olympiads. More than ninety per cent of the players on the powerful professional clubs in America and Canada are Canadians. The Canadian boy grows up pushing an old sardine can across a barnyard rink and when he is thirteen years old he signs up with one of the many midget clubs controlled by the Canadian Amateur Hockey Association. By easy stages he advances from that into juvenile, junior, senior and eventually the professional strata, where salaries are lucrative.

Canadian players acquire quickly the skill which Americans plug years to achieve. They shoot quickly and accurately and know how to use their weight so that when they collide with an opponent, he falls while they remain upright. They know all about passing, dribbling, feinting and controlling the puck and are as thoroughly at home on ice skates as the average American is in his favorite pair of lounging slippers. However, the Americans have improved so greatly that they were upset winners of Olympic hockey in 1960.

The game is played on a rectangular-shaped rink of ice.

The players wear ice skates. Intercollegiate rules recommend a rink two hundred by eighty-five feet with rounded corners of fifteen-foot radii, but the length may fluctuate from one hundred and sixty-five to two hundred and fifty feet and the width from sixty to one hundred and ten feet. Sideboards and endboards entirely enclose the rink. They must be at least three feet high, free from all projections and preferably painted a light cream.

At opposite ends of the rink are the goal cages, located at least ten feet from the ends so skaters may deploy behind them. These cages consist of two upright posts (preferably of metal) four feet high placed six feet apart with a net, supported by a frame, enclosing the backs and sides so that the puck may enter only from the front.

The puck is a vulcanized black rubber disk, uniformly one inch in thickness and three inches in diameter, weighing from five and one-half to six ounces and free from all cuts and indentations. It is recommended that it be slightly round on the edges and that it be chilled before being used in a game.

The rink is divided into three zones (see diagram) called defensive, neutral and offensive, and marked off with ultramarine blue water paint lines. The primary purpose of these zones is to determine whether a player is offside or onside. The six-foot long goal line, which is the front boundary of the goal cage, is painted red. So are the lines bounding the small rectangular area in front of each goal called the goal crease, in which no player of

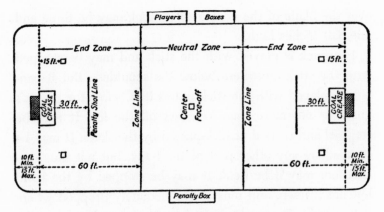

DIAGRAM OF HOCKEY RINK

an attacking team may stand or stay (1) when the puck is in possession of a teammate outside the crease, or (2) when a goal is scored by a teammate outside the crease. Penalty-shot lines, face-off marks, etc., are also located about the rink and may be found on the diagram above.

There are six players on each team: center, right and left wings, right and left defense, and goal-keeper. The goal-keeper stands directly in front of his goal cage. A little in front of and flanking him are the two defenses. All three stand in the defensive zone at the start of a game. The two forwards range in the neutral zone near their center, who faces-off in the center of the rink.

The striking implement of the game is a wooden hockey stick that must not be more than fifty-three inches long. Its blade or striking surface may not be more than fourteen and three-quarter inches long nor three inches high. However the blade of the goal-keeper's stick may be three and one-half inches high.

The puck is played with the stick and may be stopped with the stick anywhere below the shoulders. But it cannot be played with the stick unless it is below the player's knees or not more than two feet off the ice. It may be stopped and carried or kick-passed by the skate. It may be stopped by any other part of the body, but not thus carried, nor may it be held. It may be stopped by the hand but not thrown, and must be immediately dropped where it is caught. It may be batted by the open hand but the player, except the goal-keeper, who batted it must be the first to recover it for his team.

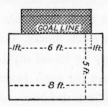

CLOSE-UP OF GOAL CREASE

The object of the game is to score the greatest number of goals. A goal is scored by a team that knocks the puck across the goal line, between goal posts and below the top of the net.

Three periods of twenty minutes each, separated by rest periods of ten minutes, comprise the playing time. Overtime periods are played in case of a tie score at the

end of regular playing time. Intercollegiate rules call for
one overtime period of ten minutes after a ten-minute
rest, and after it, if the score is still tied, the match is declared a draw.

The game is started by the puck's being placed on the
center spot. The two center players face each other, their
sticks six inches from the puck. Then the official blows
his whistle and the game is on, the two centers trying to
gain possession of the puck and flip it back out to their
wings.

The team which gains the puck immediately speeds
to the attack. This is usually led by the three-man forward line of the center and two wings, with the center
handling the puck in the middle rushing lane. Passing
and dribbling, this swift attacking trio tries to advance
the puck through the defense and score a goal.

This, however, is not easy. The defense is led by two
aggressive, strapping defense men with the goal-keeper
behind them as a competent last-hope back guard. If the
defense steals, intercepts or otherwise comes into possession of the puck, the defense sextet suddenly becomes the
attacking team. Body-checking with the hip or shoulders
above an opponent's knees is allowed if done from the
front or side, in the defensive zone against an adversary
who is playing the puck. However, the body-checker is not
allowed to take more than two steps prior to bumping his
opponent. Blocking, or screening the opponent away from
his objective by thrusting the body into his path also is

permitted. Players may harass an adversary who is playing the puck by hooking his stick with theirs.

EQUIPMENT: A good hockey skate should be strong, light and well-sharpened. High skates strain the ankle more than do low ones; therefore skates should be just high enough to prevent the sole of the boot from touching ice when the player turns or cuts a corner. Intercollegiate rules stipulate that a blade shall not extend more than three-quarters of an inch beyond the shoe at either toe or heel, and that both ends shall be rounded and blunt so there will be no points which might cause injury to a player.

Hockey sticks should be light, straight-grained and stiff. When the player finds one he likes, he should select several more of the same kind at the beginning of a season so that he will not have to contend with a strange size in case of breakage. Ash is a good wood since it combines strength with lightness and does not absorb the water that often appears on ice. Since weight varies, it is well to use light sticks on dry ice and heavier ones on slushy ice. Tape binding is permitted and boys should use shorter sticks to acquire skill in stick-handling.

Hockey gloves should be worn to keep the hands from injury. The backs should be padded but the palms thin so they will not interfere with securing a firm grip. Clothing should be light but warm, with trousers padded at hips and heavy stockings used. It is well to cover the head with a knit cap when playing outdoors.

Skating is probably hockey's most important fundamental. A hockey player must learn to skate with his feet wider apart than the average skater so he will be set for bumps. He must learn to start fast from a dead stop and thus gain the jump on his foes; change pace; turn well and stop himself within four feet from a mad sprint, turning the skate to an abrupt angle with the line of advance, and throwing the body well back of the perpendicular and grinding the skate into the ice. The ice hockey skating stride is shorter, quicker and moves in a straighter line.

If the beginner is puzzled about which hand to place down on the shaft of the hockey stick, let him grasp a broom and sweep with it. The lower hand, which will be placed naturally on the broom, should also be the lower hand on the hockey stick.

PASSING: Ice hockey passes usually are short and quick. The puck is slid or pushed, not batted. It should be kept flat on the ice, not lifted. This can be done by making the puck leave the blade of the stick before the blade is at a right angle to the front of the body. Too much follow-through will cause the player to lift the puck.

When passing, lead the receiver. Many of the passes are caroms against the sideboards in which, as in billiards, the passer must carefully reckon the angle although, unlike the billiard player, he has far less time to do it.

With both hands on the stick, the receiver should keep

it on the ice as a target for the passer. He should not accelerate his speed but should skate at a steady pace. After the puck is passed it is up to the receiver. As the puck makes contact with his stick, the receiver withdraws his stick slightly to "catch" the puck. Sticks held too rigidly will repel the puck at such a long rebound that it may be lost.

DRIBBLING: Hockey players should learn to carry a puck nestled against their firmly held stick without looking at it. Thus the defense may better be scrutinized for an opening. Feints and deception are valuable here. After playing a puck to one side to pull a defense man over, the player should not change back unless the defender moves to parry the player's thrust. If he doesn't move, then the player should keep on going in the direction of his feint. As Albert I. Prettyman, the Hamilton College coach, points out: "Mind-set is fatal to a good dribbler. He must be open-minded and govern himself according to the movement of the opposition."

SHOOTING: Although there are several different kinds of goal shots, lifting shots are the most popular, as the puck is then more difficult for the goal-keeper to stop. About half a foot above the ice is ideal, but occasionally when the swamped goal-keeper is off his feet, the puck may be flipped to the upper corner of the cage over his prone body.

Another of the best shots is a short accurate one that is chiefly a wrist snap with very little "telegraphing."

The puck is flipped off the center of the blade. Shooting backhanded is just as important as shooting forehanded.

The speed shot is a good one to use from about thirty feet out. It is executed so quickly that the goal-keeper has very little time to get set for it. Draw the stick in, get a slight run on the puck and suddenly snap the blade toward the opening in the goal cage. Roll the hands with the shot, whipping the blade forward with the lower hand and twisting the upper hand backward and outward.

HISTORY

Ice hockey is a northern offshoot of the much older game of field hockey, dubbed hurley by the Irish, shinty by the Scotch and bandy by the English. It was played before them by the Greeks and Romans. In fact, the oldest evidence of the game is a Grecian pedestal unearthed near Athens in 1922. It shows two boys with crooked sticks bending over a ball, ready for the bully or face-off, while four other boys are standing ready to receive it.

Although founded in fair play, the game has always been a rough one, and is very hard on the shins of the players. The ancient Irish could hit terrifically, as we see in the tale of the Destruction of Dinnree: Labrad Loingsech, afterward King of Ireland before the Christian Era, was dumb when he was a boy. But one day when he was playing *inmán* or hurley on the play-green, he received a blow of a hurley on his shin which gave him such a paroxysm of agony that he shouted out and spoke for the first time. Ever after that he retained his speech!

The modern name of the game is derived from an old French word *hoquet* which means shepherd's crook. In an old prayer book that belonged to the Duchess of Burgundy there is an illustration depicting the shepherds before the Nativity playing hockey to warm themselves.

It is not known who first transferred the game to ice. A detachment of Royal Canadian Rifles stationed at Tete-du-pont Barracks near Kingston Harbor is said to have tried the ice sport as early as 1876, but most authorities credit its origin and development to R. F. Smith and W. J. Robertson, two students in McGill University in Montreal. In 1879 they drew up the first known set of rules and organized the first game which took place on river ice. At that game the enthusiastic Canadian players used walking sticks, lacrosse clubs, broom handles and tree branches for clubs.

Americans, who live farther south than Canadians and consequently are not as used to frosty temperatures, could never become enthusiastic about ice hockey until George C. Flunk, a noted ice engineer, began building indoor rinks of artificial ice. This cozy invention quickly made the game tremendously popular in the United States. The late Tom Duggan persuaded William V. Dwyer to install an ice-making machine in Madison Square Garden in New York City in 1925 and when the first game was played there in December of that year, it drew a capacity throng of seventeen thousand persons. Ice hockey on artificial indoor rinks was here to stay. Now it is played in America from November to April.

At Madison Square Garden, because the floor space may have to be used a few hours later for six-day bicycle races, horse shows, wrestling or basketball, speed and efficiency in manufacturing ice are vital.

When the ice rink there was first built, it took approximately fourteen hours to freeze it. The floor was usually covered with terrazzo, a synthetic stone composition, at a depth of three-fourths of an inch. Under the terrazzo were thirteen miles of coiled iron pipe imbedded in concrete. Because of expansion and contraction, the entire plant, one hundred and eighty-six feet long, eighty-six feet wide and five inches deep, floated on cork. Eight hundred tons of refrigeration machinery pumped seventeen thousand gallons of brine into the pipes at fifteen degrees below zero. Workmen then sprayed the surface about twenty times to get a half-inch playing surface. After the tenth spraying, the lines were painted in with red and blue cold water paint.

People who viewed for the first time this magic of refrigeration could not believe the ice was real, and wondered what became of it after the game was over. Disposing of it was easy. Engineers merely raised the temperature to almost seventy degrees; as the ice softened, plows chopped it up and pushed it down manholes to a basement melting chamber.

A crowded rink gives off so much heat that the temperature is often raised twenty degrees and engineers have to be on their guard. Tobacco smoke, especially in small arenas, is also a problem. Some of the larger American plants are air-conditioned, which of course helps. The new Harringay indoor stadium in England has an oxygen room into which players are hurried between periods to recover from the effects of the incessant smoke.

POSITION TECHNIQUE

The *center* on a hockey team should be the playmaker, the coolest stick-handler and the quickest thinker. He must be a good dodger and know how to set up the plays for his wings.

He is the hub of both the attack and defense and must take the forwards with him on a three-lane rush on attack and bring them quickly back to defense when the puck is lost. Forwards always function better as a line than as individuals.

The center should be good at body-checking; he must have the knack of keeping his arms and shoulders free for stick work. He should be good at avoiding the body checks of the defense, too.

The *wings* of a hockey team are the speedy, darting front-line fighters who skim down the rink along the sides flanking the center in every attacking wave. The wings must be good shots off either their forehand or backhand, aiming for ankle-high openings through the squatting goal-keepers. They must always follow in their own or a teammate's shots and if either of them recovers the puck, he should pass it to an open player if he cannot shoot at the goal himself. On defense they should cover opponents so as to intercept passes and aid in the general defense.

Wings should know how to avoid the severe body checks thrown by husky rivals. Body checks, either given or taken, wear out men quickly for top-speed play. If a wing takes a spill, he should instantly get back onto his feet and into the game, and not pause to alibi.

Wings should be eternally aggressive and good team players. They should always skate in their own territory and be looking for a chance to pass to their open center.

They should know how to get the puck past opponents by starting fast and thus breaking around them, and also by dodging, feinting and jumping the puck through by suddenly flipping it over the opponent's stick. Like the center, the wings dress as lightly as possible, although their hip pads should give plenty of protection.

Defense players should let the attack come toward them; then they should stay in front of it, watching a forward's feet as much as the puck to determine in what direction he is going and then trying to force him to the side. They should never lunge toward a forward with the puck, for that is exactly what the forward wants them to do. Once the defense shows direction, the forward can whiz past.

Defense players should learn the poke check, which

consists of a defense man's suddenly reaching out his stick to wrest or knock the puck away from an adversary. They should learn too the double flat stick, in which two defense players let an opponent with the puck skate almost between them but at the last moment take the puck away from him by dropping their sticks simultaneously to the ice in front of the puck, and let him skate on through.

They should also try to take the puck away from a forward whom they have driven into the side, by sliding their stick under his and lifting it. They should catch the puck in their hand when they can, dropping it immediately and playing it. They should also be alert to recover rebounds from the goal-keeper, or prevent their adversaries from following in and capturing those rebounds.

When they come into possession of the puck, they should break like lightning up the ice on attack or quickly whip the puck to their own wings or center for a scoring dash. When they are up the rink, they should skate back into defensive alignment.

Defense men are often more valuable to a club than a crack scorer. For example, the veteran Eddie Shore, a mild-looking Alberta farmer who played defense for the Boston Bruins during the hockey season, was not only a savage body-checker, but also such a rough one that more than four hundred stitches were taken in his tough hide during his professional career to close wounds inflicted by retaliating opponents. Yet he was so valuable that when a rival team telegraphed an offer for him, C. F. Adams, president of the Boston club, wired back: "You are so far from Shore you need a life preserver."

Mattressed in fifteen pounds of pads, the *goal-keeper* squats in front of his tidy little cage and keeps his eye on the puck, stops shots with his stick, feet, hands, legs or body and then diverts the puck to a teammate.

The goal-keeper has more responsibility than any other player on the team. If a wing or a defense man slips, it isn't necessarily fatal. But if a goalie lets a speeding puck leak through him, the goal is against him and his team; and goals are very hard to get back in ice hockey.

The goalie should be husky, a good skater, keen-eyed as a hawk and nimble as a mountain goat. He should never leave his position unless he is quite certain of reaching the puck before his adversary. He should have enough knowledge of the game, preferably from having played other positions, so that he can predict when and where the puck usually will come.

Although hockey is a low score game, much of the credit for its being such a popular spectator sport is due to the earnest goalie. His breath-fetching saves are far more thrilling than goals themselves.

In ice hockey, a player who does not start when he is a boy has a difficult time advancing. The main qualities of a good player are skating skill, stick-handling and boundless pluck. This latter ingredient is absolutely necessary. As one old-timer put it, "A successful ice hockey player must have a well-chosen grandmother."

CHAPTER 10

SOFTBALL

OUTSIDE the windows of the Farragut Boat Club at Chicago one November afternoon in 1887, gray rain sluiced down in long wind-slanted lines, melodiously pelting the roofs and docks. George Hancock, a member of the club who was marooned indoors, was pacing up and down, impatiently waiting for the shower to cease. But it wasn't a shower, it was a steady downpour. Hancock was bored, so he looked around for something to pass the time.

He spied a broom sitting in a corner. He picked it up, looked at it for a moment, then grasped it by the end of its handle and idly swung it as though it were a baseball bat. Then he looked about him for something to hit and saw an old tan boxing glove lying on a locker.

George Hancock had an idea, an idea so absurd that he laughed aloud as he turned it over in his mind. Carrying the boxing glove and the broom, he summoned several of his companions who were as bored with the rain as he.

"Come on, fellows!" he called. "We're going to play a new game. We're going to play baseball right here in this room. This broom will be the bat and this boxing glove will do for the ball. What do you say?"

The others were willing, so bases were marked off. Soon they all had plunged into the game, shouting and laughing with enjoyment and forgetting all about the rain outside. Thus softball was born. But it was not called softball at first and it was not played outdoors as thousands of American boys play it today. It first became an indoor game, usually played in gymnasiums, and was known as kitten ball, indoor baseball, pumpkin ball, recreation ball, twilight ball, army ball and playground ball. Despite its wide variety of names, the game mushroomed so rapidly that the schools, Y.M.C.A.'s, Y.W.C.A.'s and recreational centers couldn't find enough indoor space upon which to play it; consequently it was moved outdoors as early as 1908. Nowadays, nearly every small town has its fenced-in, floodlighted field.

Softball's greatest growth dates from the depression in the early 1930's when the thousands of people who were out of work found softball a great way to while away the time and make them forget their troubles. It quickly became an ideal sport for baseball-minded boys or adults. In the first place it was inexpensive, for a bat and ball comprised all the equipment needed. Also, a softball field is so small that it can be fitted into any back yard or vacant lot. The shortened base-lines and the rule prohibiting

stolen bases reduced strenuous running, and this was
popular with older people whose legs had begun to slow
up, just as do the legs of veteran big league baseball players.
The playing time of a softball game, approximately forty-
five minutes, is so short that laboring folk or schoolboys
could stop after work or school and have plenty of time
to play a game before the evening meal. For all these
reasons, softball flourished.

Boys who have never played softball will find it about
ninety per cent baseball. The main differences are that
the bases in softball are fifty-five feet apart compared to
ninety feet in the senior-sized baseball diamond and
eighty-two feet in the junior diamond. The softball bat
is shorter, narrower and lighter. A softball is one-half
inch larger in diameter than a baseball and will not go
as far or sting as much. In softball, all pitching is done
underhanded, as baseball pitching was in baseball's in-
fancy.

To strengthen the defense which, many will argue, needs
curbing instead of strengthening, softball did employ
a tenth player, called a short-fielder, who usually was
stationed as a roaming outfielder midway between second
base and center field and snared many a drive that would
have fallen safely between the outfield and infield. However the position was later removed. Only seven innings
are played, and base-stealing is not permitted.

Softball is far from being a sissy sport. In Chicago in
1936 Matt Ruppert, a softball hurler who had pitched

DIAGRAM
OF
SOFTBALL DIAMOND

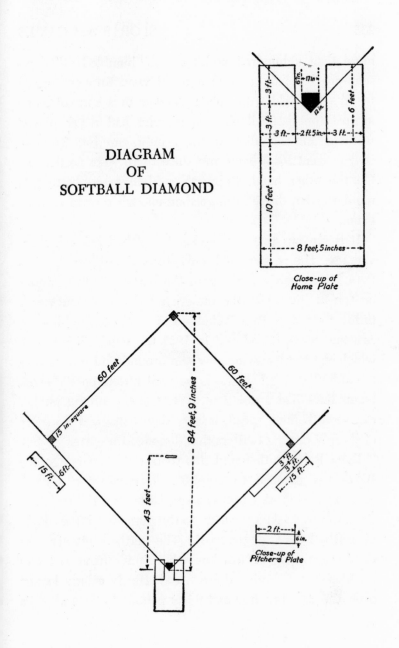

Close-up of
Home Plate

Close-up of
Pitcher's Plate

more than a hundred no-hit games, humbled a famous
semi-pro baseball team in a novel way. Ruppert agreed
to take the field with only a catcher in a softball game
against the baseball champions, who had never played
softball, and he allowed them only one hit. This, of
course, went for a home run since there were no fielders.
On the other hand, Ruppert's softball team, batting in
regular order, drove in more than enough runs to win the
game.

It is obvious that the pitcher in softball has a big advantage. He is stationed only forty-three feet, or less
than fifteen yards, away from the batter—in fact, almost
on top of him. Also the underhand delivery is not easy
to hit. Ever since Paul "Windmill" Watson, of the Phoenix,
Arizona, team, introduced in 1933 the windmill pitch, in
which the twirler swings his arm around and around like
a windmill going backwards, softball hitters on the crack
teams have had a sad time of it. A good softball pitcher
can serve baffling speed, teasing slow balls, and a variety
of sharply darting twisters that disconcert a batter.

Even Babe Ruth found this to be true. Years ago the
Babe was induced to umpire a championship softball
game in New York City. As a special feature the powerful
Bambino was asked to stride to the plate and hit a couple
of softballs out of the park. The softball pitcher was
Hardy Brownell, a farm boy whose underhand fast ball
traveled like lightning down a rod. Hardy calmly looked
over the two-hundred-and-thirty-pound Ruth and then

deliberately shot three fast balls wide of the plate. Babe spat in the dust and looked disgusted. Then Brownell suddenly changed his range and began delivering his thunderbolts over the heart of the plate. But the fiercely-swinging Bambino couldn't touch the ball. He couldn't even see it. After four or five terrific swipes, Ruth took the ball away from the softball catcher and fungoed it into the distant stands.

"I just wanted to see if that ball could be hit!" he explained.

Aside from pitching, the mechanical skills of softball and baseball are very much alike, except for the throwing, which has to be faster in softball since the base lines are shorter. However, this is partially compensated for by the fact that the batted ball consequently reaches the softball infielder more quickly. Choke-hitting is more popular in softball than baseball because of the short pitching distance. Also, the average softball batter likes to stand well back in the batter's box so that he can take full advantage of the extra pitching distance.

PITCHING

The rules for softball say that, preliminary to delivering the ball, the pitcher must come to a full stop, facing the batsman. Both his feet must be squarely on the ground and in contact with the pitcher's plate for at least one second. The ball must be held in both hands, in front of the body, and it may not be held longer than twenty seconds. While he is in the act of delivering the ball, the pitcher must keep one foot in contact with the ground until the ball has left his hand. He cannot take more than one step until the ball is on its way and this step must be forward and toward the batter, and taken simultaneously with the delivery.

The correct softball pitch should resemble a horseshoe pitch. It should be delivered to the batter underhanded and with a follow-through of the hand and wrist past the straight line of the body before the ball is released. The pitcher may use any windup he wishes, provided: he immediately delivers the ball to the batter; he does not use a rocker action (removes one hand from the ball, takes a backward and forward swing and returns the ball to both hands in front of the body); he does not make a stop or reversal of the forward motion; he does not make more than one revolution of the arm in the windmill pitch; and he does not continue to wind up after taking the forward step which is simultaneous with the release of the ball. The use of tape or other substance upon the pitching hand or fingers, or of a foreign substance other than powdered resin upon the ball, is forbidden.

In the underhand softball delivery, it is most important that the pitching arm be swung from the side, parallel to the body. When the ball passes the right leg, the arm should be straight and perpendicular to the ground. The ball should be from two to six inches from

(1) (2) (3)

(4) (5) (6)

A CORRECT PITCH

1. Having taken proper position, the ball held in both hands, facing the batsman, and both feet in contact with the pitcher's plate, the pitcher has bent forward preliminary to starting a one revolution windup in the so-called "windmill" pitch.
2. The hands are separated and the pitching hand has started up in front.
3. Ball reaches its highest point; left foot starts the step.
4. Ball starts backward and down, in delivery.
5. Pitching arm has come forward past the body, ball has just left the hand, and the right foot is breaking contact with the pitcher's plate.
6. Completion of the pitch, with the step and follow-through toward the batsman.

the leg. A distance of more than six inches is illegal. This same delivery is used for all the different "foolers." Grip the ball between the thumb and the first three fingers. The little finger is used to put the twist on the ball and is either left free or placed midway between the thumb and third finger.

The various pitches may be described as follows:

DROP: This is the fastest pitch in softball. It can be a dangerous boomerang, too, since it doesn't spin much; consequently it will go farther off the bat. Throw it with the hand behind the ball. The ball's face is plainly exposed to the batter on this pitch.

SLOW BALL: Grip the ball between the thumb and little finger, knuckling the middle three fingers. Deliver with the same motion as the drop and other pitches. Keep the hand behind the ball, but slow up the pitch.

OUT-CURVE: As the ball leaves the hand, thrust the thumb back and rotate all the fingers to the left.

IN-CURVE: As the ball leaves the hand, thrust the third finger and the little finger up back and to the right, first and second fingers forward and down, the thumb forward and to the right.

UPSHOOT: This is the easiest pitch to throw and also one of the most baffling. As the ball leaves the hand, the little finger and third finger are thrust forward and the first and second fingers slightly upward. The thumb is back, and thus a back spin is imparted to the ball. At the moment of delivery, the hand forms almost a right angle with the arm.

To get the correct follow-through, force the hand to continue on a line horizontal with the ground. If you let your arm rise to shoulder height, you probably will lose

control of the ball. Remember that the right foot should
not leave the pitching mound until the ball has left the
hand. Put as much twist on the ball as possible since a
twisting ball usually is popped up unless met squarely.
Do not throw too many slow balls for they are easy to
hit out of the park. However, use them occasionally to
cross the batter and also to conserve energy. The "international weakness" of softball hitters, as in baseball, is a
pitch thrown high and inside. Do not turn the body side-
way when starting a pitch, nor finish a pitch with the
arm across the body. Neither should the player twist the
forearm outward with the elbow against the body.

A softball pitcher's speed, or threat of it, sometimes
gets umpires into queer situations. Leo Fischer, the Chicago sports writer who has so industriously sponsored
the game, tells of a softball game in Iowa where there
were two strikes on the batter. The pitcher suddenly went
into his windmill windup but instead of exploding the
expected fast ball, tossed a tantalizing slow ball or "floater."
Surprised, the hitter took a fast swing, which he missed,
and then continued around again, blasting the ball on his
second revolution for a home run. One side contended
the batter had struck out on the first pitch, the other
argued that the home run was legal. Completely puzzled,
the umpire wrote to national softball headquarters asking
for a decision.

Softball leaders are constantly experimenting to reduce the heavy advantage of pitching and defense. In

1938 they passed a rule compelling pitchers to wear uniforms of a solid dark color so the batter could better see the ball at night games. They also ruled that a foul tip caught by the catcher on third strike did not retire the batter. The base-running rules were amended to allow a runner's scoring from third base on a wild pitch, passed ball or throw-back to the pitcher. In 1939 the pitching distance in men's softball was lengthened from forty to forty-three feet and the batsman was allowed to run to first on third strikes not caught by the catcher. In 1946 the short-fielder was eliminated, the base lines shortened five feet and batters struck by a pitched ball were given a base. And these are only a few new rules.

Although the two sports have a great deal in common, there was a coolness between baseball and softball men during the depression. Baseball receipts naturally dwindled, as did those of every amusement where admission was charged, while there was a phenomenal rise in newly discovered softball, where admission was free or only a trifling sum. Loyal baseball men thought that softball was the crippling influence and looked upon their softball cousins with something of the same contempt that the old-time cattleman used to regard the sheepman. When the depression lifted and baseball began to boom again, there was less resentment by baseball men.

CHAPTER 11

SWIMMING *and* DIVING

SWIMMING probably ranks close to running, jumping and throwing as the oldest sport of all. We know that even the overhand swimming stroke was practiced by the Romans. Their paintings and mosaics show swimmers cutting through the water overhand, and others swimming with their faces in the water, which suggests the speedy crawl of modern times.

The Greeks and Romans knew a great deal about swimming and diving. Plato declared that in Greece, a man who was not able to swim and dive was as uneducated as one who was ignorant of letters. Caesar was a good swimmer, Cato showed his son how to cross dangerous gulfs, and the Emperor Augustus taught his nephew to swim.

In more modern times, Charlemagne was noted for his swimming stroke, King Louis XI of France often swam in the Seine at the head of his courtiers, and the swimming couriers of Peru traversed hundreds of miles of the

South American continent swimming day and night down the rivers. They were aided only by a light log of wood, and their dispatches were enclosed in turbans on their heads.

Several exceptional swimming accomplishments in history have been recorded. One of the most unusual was that of a famous Neapolitan diver nicknamed *El Pesce,* or "The Fish," who once swam fifty miles without stopping along the coast of Calabria in Southern Italy. Another almost unbelievable episode occurred in 1769: A vessel overturning in a squall off Martinique in the French West Indies was lost. Its entire crew of Europeans were drowned. However, a Carib, after battling the violence of the tempest as well as hunger and thirst for sixty hours, reached land safely. The most modern is, of course, the aquatic spanning in August, 1926, of the foggy English Channel by Gertrude Ederle, a nineteen-year-old American girl, who swam the thirty-one miles between England and France in fourteen hours thirty-one minutes, breaking by more than two hours all previous records established by any of the five men who had swum this treacherous stretch before her. This in spite of the fact that Benjamin Franklin had said that the only way anyone would ever swim the English Channel was on the back with one leg extended vertically and a sail attached to it.

Literature is filled with allusions to swimming. Longfellow's Kwasind, in *Hiawatha,* caught a beaver after a long underwater cruise; Beowulf and Breca swam seven nights in the swollen seas, carrying their swords with them to fight off whale fishes; Dumas' hero Edmond Dantes escaped by swimming from the Chateau to the Isle of Tiboulen; and Leander swam across the Hellespont, the narrow strait that divides Europe and Asia.

Perhaps the most poignant tale ever written about a swimmer occurs in that charming story, *The Tale of James Carabine,* by Donn Byrne, the Irish author. The swimmer was not successful and paid with his life. His name was Bartley McGeehan, known as Swimmer McGeehan, the Swan of Ireland or the Marine Marvel, as he was billed in the circus. He had once swum between Ireland and Scotland over the stormy waters of Moyle.

However, McGeehan was a heavy drinker. When he was on a ship bound for America, he became intoxicated and recounted his feat in the hearing of the captain of the vessel. The captain, a jolly red-faced fellow, scoffed; whereupon a queer look came into the eyes of McGeehan.

"We're two days out of New York," he said. "I'll wager a hundred pounds I'll beat you to the landing post." "Done!" exclaimed the captain, thinking McGeehan was a joker like himself and never once taking the fellow seriously. Carabine tells what followed:

"Before I could get to him he had shied his brown bowler hat into the sea and 'So long, Shamus!' he called to me, and vaulted over the rail. A great green wave swept him onward. Of course there was hell to pay and boats got out, but there was no sign of Swimmer McGeehan. I saw the last of him. . . . The plunge in the water must have sobered him, and the strength in the waves told him where he was. But he didn't throw up his hands or call for help. He just bored in. God be good to the Swimmer McGeehan . . . he died game!

"The sea captain came up to me later and his face was white. 'That was a madman,' he said. 'Madman or not,' said I, 'we shared the same bed for a year, and when there was only a crust between us, we shared it. He was my dear friend.' 'I'm sorry. I'm damned sorry,' said the sea captain and he went and shut himself up in his cabin and I saw no more of him until we came to Castle Garden. Then I went to him to pay the bet my friend lost. The big man broke down and cried, and wouldn't touch a penny of the money. . . . He was a decent fellow . . . but I wished he hadn't tried his joking on my poor friend."

SWIMMING TECHNIQUE

THE CRAWL: The safest and easiest place to learn to swim is in a swimming pool. Go to the shallow end and stand where the water is about chest deep. Put your hands on the curb. Open your mouth and draw in a short breath. Hold it in your lungs until you count five, then blow it out through the mouth. Do it once more, remembering to draw it in and blow it out quietly.

Then draw in another short breath, close your mouth and place your face in the water between your arms. After counting five, blow your breath out through your mouth under water and raise your head. Be sure the breath you take is a short one; you will have trouble exhaling a long breath under water. Never hurry. Do everything quietly.

Try it again, but this time open your eyes when your face is in the water so that when you start expelling your breath through your mouth (many swimmers also exhale under water through the nose), you can see tiny air bubbles racing from your mouth down through the water. After you have blown the air all out, raise your face out of the water.

If your eyes hurt, blink them a few times; do not rub them to get the water out. Should some water get in your nose, duck your head, wrinkle your nose and blow the water out through *both* nostrils, not one at a time. And don't blow too hard. Just short quick little sniffs.

The next step is floating on your stomach. It will prove to you that your body rides like a cork atop the water. Stand in chest-deep or even shallower water, and grasp the ladder in both hands, preferably on a rung a foot or so beneath the surface (or place your hands on a step under water). Take a short breath, put your face in the water and lie down on top of the water on your stomach. Do not be in a hurry to come up. Notice how the water lifts your feet up, and how lightly you float!

Repeat the stomach float but this time as you lie, stomach down, in the water, kick your feet behind you. A swimmer's feet, like the propellers of a motorboat, are what send him through the water. Don't bend your knees but hold your legs stretched out almost straight, swinging them loosely from the hips. The feet should be toed in. Their motion through the water should make them work around each other. As one foot goes down the other should be lifted up. The downbeat of the kick should be emphasized in the crawl. Don't spread the feet too widely or splash too much. Don't hold them rigid and pound the water. Relax and make the feet pump steadily and smoothly. This is called the flutter-kick and relaxation is its key.

Repeat this, and with your face in the water; then turn the face sideways (don't lift it) out of the water until your mouth is barely above the surface. Take a short quick breath, turn your face back in the water a quarter turn past the perpendicular, and hold it there until you count five. Meanwhile blow your breath out under water through your mouth and turn the face out of water again for another breath. Keep kicking your feet loosely from the hips and turning your face in and out of the water for fresh breaths. The face is always turned to the same side for the breathing, and each swimmer selects the side that seems most comfortable for him.

Turning your head a quarter turn past the perpendicular while expelling your breath under water gives balance to the stroke. Assuming that you breathe on your left side, this is how it works: When you turn your face out of the water to breathe, your left side is raised; consequently a freer stroke can be executed. However if, when turning your face back into the water, you stop it at the perpendicular, your right side is not raised, for you are breathing on your left side only. However, turning your head past center to the right raises your right side and balances the stroke. Breathing is the most difficult part of the crawl stroke. For this reason it cannot be emphasized or practiced too much.

Now let us learn to move about the shallow end of the pool. Using both hands, take hold of what is known in every swimming pool as a flutter board (almost any heavy board will do). Lie on your stomach, breathe and flutter-kick exactly as you did when you held to the submerged ladder; let your legs propel you across the pool. As you glide along you can imagine you are in a glass-bottomed boat. Open your eyes under water and watch the bubbles creaming from your mouth as you blow out your breath, or watch the tiny squares of white tile on the bottom of the pool slip past under you. If you become tired, stand up and rest, then do it again.

The arm stroke is next. To practice it, stand in waist-deep water and lean forward until your chin touches the surface. Then, holding the palms of your hands down, throw your left arm straight forward above the surface. Let the left hand drop in the water about a foot in front of your left ear, let it sink six inches under water and *then* pull it straight down and back until it passes the perpendicular under the middle of your body. Now do the same thing with your other arm, alternating your arms so that as one is thrown forward above the water, the other is pulled back under the water.

Don't forget that your hand always goes into the water

first. Always bend your elbow when you lift your arm out
of the water and remember that the bent elbow always
comes out of the water before the hand. Walk about the
pool, practicing this arm stroking.

Now do it with your face in the water, turning your
head up to breathe each time your left arm has finished
its pull, and expelling your breath under water when
you again submerge your face. Walk about the pool
practicing this.

Now you are ready to swim. Lie on your stomach with
your face in the waist-deep water and start your kick.
At the same time begin your arm stroke and your breathing. The result will be that not only are you swimming,
but instead of using the "dog paddle" stroke that so many
boys learn first, you will be using the speedier, more graceful and less fatiguing crawl, the stroke employed by all
the champions in the free-style events.

Don't try to do all the steps outlined above in one day.
Practice one thing at a time. It would be much better to
take at least a day or more for each separate maneuver,
doing it over and over. Also, before you try something
new on the following day, first carefully rehearse the
steps you have already learned.

To achieve steady improvement, boys should swim every
day. However, from thirty to forty-five minutes in the water
is enough for each session.

The *backstroke* is even easier than the crawl. Since
you are swimming on your back, you can do all your

exhaling as well as inhaling above water. Also, the kick and arm motion for the backstroke is closely related to those of the crawl, but the backstroker does them in reverse.

Perhaps the first step is learning to float on the back, one of the easiest maneuvers of all. Stand in waist-deep water with your feet spread, stretch your arms out horizontally to maintain balance, take a good breath of air, close the mouth and gradually arch the body backward until your shoulders are under water. Then, push with your feet off the bottom of the pool, holding the body in a straight line. Don't bend at the hips. Make every movement slowly, without jerking. As the legs rise to the surface, stretch them out. The idea is to make the body lie horizontally on top of the surface and if a little water ripples over your face as your back first settles into the water, don't be alarmed. Just keep holding your breath and straightening your spine; your mouth, nose, chest and toes will quickly rise and stay above the surface. Then you can take a fresh breath.

When you get ready to stand up again, sit down hard, lean forward, push your feet to the bottom of the pool, stand up and lift your face out of the water.

To start the backstroke, simply float on your back. However, instead of holding the legs still, kick them much the same as you did in the flutter-kick for the crawl, holding them almost straight with only a slight bend in knee and ankles, swinging them loosely from the

hip, and never letting them go up and down more than
a foot. In the backstroke, the propelling force comes
from the slash of the feet upward. Concentrate on relaxation, trying for a whippy sensation of the ankles.

The chin is cupped in the lower neck and the head
held up enough that the swimmer may see the action of
his kicking feet. Don't ever throw your head back so far
that you can see the ceiling of the pool. Then comes the
alternate arm stroke; the left shoulder is lifted and the
relaxed arm is swung loosely *out* and *away* from the
body so that no water will fall on the face. When the arm
passes the shoulder, the hand falls palm down half a foot
under the water. Then the oarlike forward pull begins;
the arm, with elbow kept straight, sweeps sideways through
the water at the depth of half a foot, toward the feet.

Meanwhile, when the left hand drops into the water,
the right shoulder lifts and the relaxed right arm is
thrown back in the same maneuver as that just described
for the left. The two arms are always kept opposite, but
aided by the thrashing feet, they maintain such a constantly smooth pull that the body is motored steadily
backward through the water as though equipped with an
outboard engine.

Perhaps the top swimming coach in America is English-
born Matt Mann, whose University of Michigan teams won
several national collegiate championships and who coached
the American Olympic team to the world's championship at
Helsinki in 1952. After retiring as Michigan's coach, Mann

was hired by the University of Oklahoma. Mann tells swimmers who use either the crawl or the backstroke that the maximum leverage in the arm pull is obtained when the hands "grip" the water so that the body passes by the anchored hands. He contends that power is lost and wasted when the hands are pulled too fast through the water and too much pressure exerted. "The swimmer should always have the feeling of going past his hands," Mann declares, "not of bringing the hands back to the body."

The *breast stroke* is not nearly so fast as the crawl or backstroke, nor has it as much utility. However, a breast stroke race, both butterfly and surface, of one hundred yards is swum by high schools; in collegiate meets the distance is increased to two hundred yards. Both strokes are also used in the medley relay in which each of four contestants swims one-fourth the distance, the first boy swimming backstroke, the second surface breast stroke, the third butterfly and the fourth the front crawl stroke. Therefore a brief study of the breast stroke is in order.

The breast stroke differs from the crawl and backstroke in that both arms stroke a duplicate maneuver simultaneously, as do both legs. In executing this stroke don't fight the water or take the strokes too hastily.

To start, lie flat on your stomach in the water, thrust the chin forward, and keep the face above the surface. Both arms should be drawn into the chest until the elbows are nearly at the side; the hands point forward with palms facing outward. From this chest position, push the arms straight forward almost, but not quite, to their full length and drop your face into the water.

Then sweep the forearms back and around a quarter circle under water until they are at right angles to the shoulders, never farther back. Take a breath during this maneuver to lift the face out of the water. Then relax the arms, and turn the hands inward. Drop the elbows to the side and bring the hands back in front of the chest for the next stroke.

Now for the leg action: While both arms are pulling hard, bend the knees and draw the legs up behind you, holding the soles of your feet together. When the arms finish their long pull, the gathered legs strike out powerfully backward. The toes meanwhile have been turned out so that the flats of the feet are exposed to the water during the kick, and more pressure, and consequently more forward propulsion, is generated. Then bring the extended legs together again and relax them as you prepare to start the whole movement over.

It is important to remember that after the powerful leg kick, the swimmer relaxes with hands together under his chin in the starting position and legs strung out together behind him. Thus he rides through the water, getting the full benefit of the ride forward from the vigorous leg drive. He should not be in too much of a hurry to stop the glide and begin the arm motion, for he should get the full momentum out of the glide.

Racers in the breast stroke use the butterfly arm movement to gain increased speed. This differs from the con-
ventional style in that immediately after the leg drive,
the arms, when returned to their forward position, are
brought back *above* the water instead of under it, and
upon falling in the water start to pull. In the butterfly
this arm pull is *straight down* instead of sweeping around.
There is no glide in the butterfly as there is in the
regular breast stroke. Also, in the butterfly a breath is
taken every two strokes instead of every stroke. During
the arm throw forward above water, keep the elbows
slightly higher than the rest of the arm and keep the
arms relaxed.

DIVING

BEGINNERS: First learn to dive sitting down.
Sit on the edge of the curb of the pool where the water
is about waist deep; your feet should be on a lower rung
of the ladder under water. Drop your chin on your chest,
extend your arms over your head until you can feel
them pressing both ears; then lock your thumbs. Take
a short breath and hold it, bend forward until your
hands almost touch the surface of the water; then push
off with your feet, making your hands and head enter
the water first. Never have your eyes open at the moment
of coming in contact with the water. Close them just
before striking the water and open them again after you
have entered the water. When you get ready to come up,

gather your feet under you and stand up in the water. Practice this dive several times before passing to the next step: the dive off one knee.

The knee dive is executed exactly like the sitting-down dive except that the diver starts from one knee at the side of the pool, and keeps the toes of the other foot curled over the curb so that he cannot slip. Then he leans forward toward the water and, just as he is losing his balance, he *pushes off vigorously* with the foot which is gripping the curb. He does not look up, but keeps his chin on his chest until he enters the water. He practices this many times, concentrating on a strong push off the foot just as he falls forward into the water.

The final step for beginning divers is the stand-up dive in which the diver stands on both feet on the side curb, and makes the toes of his feet grip the curb so that he won't slip. Keeping his chin tucked in on his chest, pressing his ears with his extended arms and locking his thumbs, the diver bends his knees, leans forward and just as he feels himself falling into the water, *pushes hard* off *both* feet. Immediately after the push, he *lifts his heels* behind him so his body will be tilted upon entering the water, thus preventing his striking flat upon the stomach. After the diver learns to push off and lift the heels, he can practice holding the feet together with the legs stretched out loosely behind him. He maintains this position until he reaches the limit of his dive and starts back up. He is in no hurry to come up. He holds his form until he gets the last bit of forward momentum from his submarine ride.

Too much jumping into the water feet first, especially from a height, is apt to be harmful. Often the rush of water into the nasal cavities may cause acute infections of the sinuses, the middle ear and the mastoid.

SPRINGBOARD DIVING: More loft, and consequently more grace, can be attained when the diver uses a springboard. Standing somewhere near the middle of the board, the diver keeps his body erect and relaxed; the arms are swung loosely at his sides. He approaches the end of the board with two or three short springy steps. He should then take a short hop of a foot or two upward with one knee raised and land *lightly* on the balls of his feet on the end of the board. (Never stamp a board.)

After the tip of the board has dipped to its lowest point from the diver's weight, the diver gets the maximum of whip from the rebound of the board by immediately pressing hard with the balls of his feet and springing strongly up and out, getting all the lift possible out of arms and shoulders. He does not bend the waist or knees at the spring. He aims to strike the water only six feet beyond the tip of the board. The dive is finished by bringing the hands together, tucking in the chin, keeping the legs together and the toes pointed, and maintaining this position until the feet are under water or the hands encounter the bottom of the pool.

The body should enter the water at an angle of seventy-five to ninety degrees. The knees and elbows should not be bent, nor should the feet be separated; toes are pointed outward. The diver does not allow either his shins or calves to splash, nor does he twist the body sideways upon entering the water.

Following are the most common fancy dives:

SWAN: This dive is made with the arms stretched out horizontally sideways, the palms up, head thrown back and chest expanded in order to give the impression of a bird in flight. An important feature is the back arch, obtained by lifting the heels from the hips. This maneuver slants the body forward in the air so it can glide into the water cleanly and noiselessly. If there is too little back arch and heel lift, the diver will have to jackknife just before hitting the water in order to keep from striking flat. The graceful swan position is held until just before the water is entered, whereupon the head is lowered and the hands position quickly brought together in the locked-thumb. The water should not be entered too far beyond the board. Six feet is a good distance.

JACKKNIFE: In this dive, the body is bent in the middle at the top of the lift from the board and the hands are dropped until they deftly touch the toes or that portion of the top of the foot where the shoelaces cross. The head is back, the legs straight and the toes pointed so that the diver at the climax of the jack looks as if he were doing setting-up exercises in the air. After the jackknife movement in mid-air, the legs are thrown back and the body straightens at the hips and drops noiselessly into the water. The knees are never bent. Since height is such a necessity, the take-off walk is slower, the hop shortened and the spring off the board is made with the body almost vertical. The diver's entrance into the water is made only three or four feet beyond the tip of the board.

BACK DIVE: The diver walks to within inches of the end of the board, turns around with his back to the water, stands on the end of the board with both heels touching over the water and his toes, pointed out, gripping the end of the board strongly. He gets good balance by extending his arms horizontally in front of him. The spring off the tip of the board is straight up. Height should be the aim, and when the body reaches its zenith, the head is thrown back, the chin hoisted, the chest lifted and the back arched. The head throw and back arch are most important. A limber back, pulling the head down to meet the heels, is most necessary. The feet must not come up too soon. When the diver is in the midst of his head pull, he throws his hands up and back to aid the pull, and his feet follow the body into the water with legs straight and toes pointed. Entrance is made five or six feet beyond the board.

CHAPTER 12

TENNIS

D ESPITE an undeserved reputation for effeminacy, probably caused by its etiquette, tennis measures up to any sport in its demands upon skill, speed, stamina and gameness. The etiquette of tennis is more rigid than that of any other widely played American sport. A tennis crowd sits dignifiedly and sedately, applauding only at correct intervals and then with a pleasant patter of handclaps. The spectators do not raise parasols at matches, nor move around during actual play, nor boo players or officials. Tennis players always wear white clothing.

In England, player and spectator conduct is even more conservative. While the English have a decided sense of humor, they will not tolerate comedy in tennis if it conflicts with the sport's conventions. In the *Atlantic Monthly* of October, 1936, R. Norris Williams, the American national champion of 1914 and 1916, described this oddity in English spectator behavior which he especially noticed at cosmopolitan tournaments:

262

To them [the English] the tennis court is not a stage for antics or humor. Therefore, when one of the greatest players of his day, a Frenchman, became so exasperated with his bad playing that he sat down in the middle of the court and sobbed like a child, it caused more than a little consternation. When a Spaniard, on missing a sideline volley, would vault the net, rush to the backstop of his opponent's court, pick up the offending ball and bite it repeatedly, there was hardly a laugh. When a well-known Austrian count defaulted because his opponent's shadow bothered him, it created more indignation than entertainment. Nor were the qualities of Rumania's best-known player ever fully appreciated. He was the trick stroke artist of the tennis world. His most outstanding shot was a serve which he would hit over his shoulder as he walked over the baseline with his back to the court. He was banking on the theory that his opponent wouldn't be expecting a serve and would not be able to return it.

Good tennis players begin to practice at an early age. The American Bill Tilden, perhaps the greatest player of all time, began playing at the age of six. The late Suzanne Lenglen of France, probably the world's outstanding woman player, started when she was eight.

The tennis uniform is a comparatively simple one. Every boy probably can secure white trousers or shorts, a white shirt with half sleeves, heavy white woolen socks and white crepe rubber-soled shoes. He will need also a sweater or a sweat shirt or jacket to wear while not playing. The racket he selects should be strong and well-balanced, neither too heavy nor too light. However, a too heavy bat is to be guarded against more than a too light one. A big handle affords a better grip than a small one. The purchase of a good racket is an economy. Try them all and select the one that feels the most comfortable.

A tennis court is built so that it lies north and south; thus the sunshine will come in from the sides and not blind the players. The court is laid out on high well-drained ground; advantage is taken of any natural shelter from the wind. No trees should be planted too closely to the west boundary where the shadows will fall on the court. It is essential that plenty of room be left at the sides or ends. This is the outstanding fault of the average court in America. There should be an open space of at least twenty-one feet behind each baseline and at the sides of not less than twelve feet.

If singles are being played, there is one player on each side of the net; if doubles, two on each side. The game is started by one player's standing at the baseline and putting the ball in play by serving it over the net into the diagonally opposite service court. There the opponent hits it back after it has bounded once. The idea is to win the point by driving the ball at a high rate of speed past the opponent, or lobbing it over his head, or placing it where he cannot return it before it has bounded twice, or causing him to hit the ball outside the court or into the net.

After the service and first return, the ball may be taken in the air. The first player winning four points takes a game, and the first player winning six games wins a set.

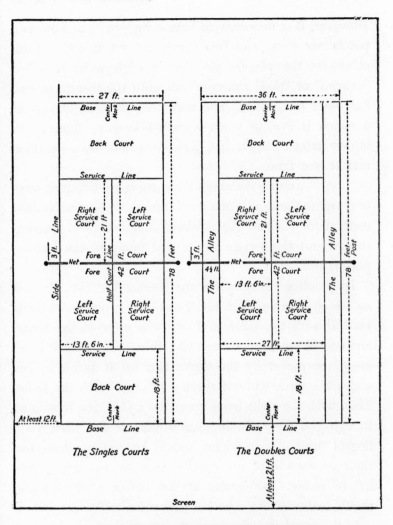

DIAGRAM OF TENNIS COURT

However, it is necessary to have a margin of at least two points per game and two games per set in either case; otherwise the players play on through what is called "deuced" or "tied" games or sets until the margin of two has been established. The maximum number of sets in a match is five, or when women take part, three. Boys under sixteen should not play more than two or three sets at one time.

GRIPS: Although there are many different ways of grasping the handle of a tennis racket, there is a standard method for each of the forehand and backhand ground-strokes and the service stroke that many of the leading players use.

To practice the grip for the forehand stroke, lay the racket on a table, then tilt it until the wooden frame is vertical with the table, and only the edge of the frame and end of the handle touch the table. With the left hand grasp the racket by the throat and lift it a few inches above the table without altering its angle with the table. Then with the right hand grasp the end of the handle as though you were shaking hands with it and close your fingers firmly. Your fingers should be resting along the right or outside of the handle, your thumb around the left or inside. The leather at the bottom of the handle should be touching the heel of your palm.

In the backhand, the opposite face of the racket is used for striking. Shift the hand a quarter of a turn backward or counterclockwise on the handle until the knuckles are pointed upward and the thumb is underneath and you'll have the proper backhand grip. If you wish, you may slide your thumb up the back of the handle as a brace. All hitting is aided if the palm of the hand is behind the racket handle, and placing the thumb up the back of the handle on the backhand stroke insures having the palm behind. The forehand grip may be used both for forehand groundstrokes (shots hit after the ball has bounced once) and volleys (shots hit off the ball in the air, before it bounds). Similarly, the backhand grip may be used for both backhand groundstrokes and volleys.

The grip used for service (service is the method of putting the ball into play) is one-eight shift of the hand backward or counterclockwise, or, in other words, a grasp of the handle exactly halfway between the forehand and backhand grip.

Between strokes, hold the racket across and almost touching your chest, supporting it with the left hand on the spliced throat. Relax the right hand grip on the handle a bit between strokes to prevent cramping the hitting hand, but tighten it at the instant of striking the ball.

FOOTWORK: The position of the feet determines the direction of the strokes in tennis, so footwork is enormously important. When executing the forehand strokes, face the right sideline. This puts the left foot nearer the net. When executing the backhand stroke face the left sideline and have the right foot advanced nearer the net.

Stay well up on the toes. René LaCoste, frail young

Frenchman who won Wimbledon championships in 1925 and 1928 and American titles in 1926 and 1927, says he improved one point a game the day he decided always to start on his toes, thus enabling him to put himself in position more quickly and consequently to place his feet correctly.

The *forehand drive* is the basic stroke of tennis. To lift the game out of the "pat ball" stage the player must develop a drive that not only will propel the ball deep into the opponent's court, but also will give pace to the ball so it will travel on a level, like a low golf drive, and not in a high arc.

Do not try to hit too hard. First learn to put the ball carefully where you want it, using correct form. In practice hit with correct form or do not hit at all. Never waste time on the court.

Let us pretend our opponent hits a ball that bounds to our forehand. What are we going to do? First, we should remember always to attack the ball and not stand still and let it attack us. We must quickly move our body a little to the left of the ball's line of flight. With our left foot nearest the net, we face the right sideline. Our left side is toward the net so that our feet, arm swing and shoulders will be lined up parallel with the flight of the ball. We keep our body well away from the ball so that we do not cramp the movement of our hitting arm.

We concentrate next on the backswing. Bending our elbow, keeping it low and holding the racket handle at right angles to our forearm, we slowly swing our hitting arm far back behind our body and then, without stopping it, loop it forward again as we start the long forward hitting stroke. Simultaneously, as the bounding ball nears us, we drop our weight on our back foot, then shift it forward to the front foot just as we strike the ball as it falls from the top of its bound. We must remember to meet the ball with the racket a little in front of our body, swinging with the whole body in the stroke, and taking a full follow-through that ends with the racket over the left shoulder. Above all, we must watch the ball from the time it leaves our adversary's racket *until it hits the strings of our own racket*. Seventy-five per cent of the missed shots in tennis are caused by taking the eyes off the ball in the last moment of striking.

The racket should meet the ball flat, being held parallel to the backstop. The elbow of the hitting arm should be only slightly bent and the arm itself comfortably extended from the body. The arm and racket should turn slightly over the top of the ball, pulling it downward and imparting top spin. The hitting plane, like the strike in baseball, is anywhere between the knee and shoulder, although one should strive to meet the ball at about belt-buckle height.

To hit left, pull the front foot slightly to the left and without too much backswing, meet the ball in front of the left hip, throwing the weight into the shot and not stepping away from it. To hit down the middle, shift the front foot more to the right and meet the ball directly in front of the stomach. To hit right, shift the front foot still further right and carry the racket lower and farther back, meeting the ball near your right hip. Remember always that the position of the feet determines hitting direction. Line them up in the direction the ball is to be sent.

To add speed to the forehand drive (which should not be attempted until accuracy and form have been reasonably mastered) learn to meet the ball at a slight run, bringing the body and shoulders forward in the act of striking, as Tilden did. René LaCoste says speed is obtained not by a rapid movement of the racket, but by a long and supple movement, carefully executed.

The drive should drop somewhere between the service line and the baseline, the closer to the latter the better. Allow a slight margin of safety for the height of the net, and the side and back lines. Never take your eye off the ball to see the place where you intend to hit it, or to spot your opponent. Even though you know your adversary is following his stroke to the net, forget him and concentrate on watching the ball. "First get in your mind's eye where he is and where you mean to hit the ball," was the sage advice of the Dohertys.

BACKHAND DRIVE: Never run around a ball hit to your backhand to play it on your forehand. This leaves most of your court wide open. Learn to play as willingly and as well on your backhand as on your forehand. The superlative backhand of Don Budge, husky young California who won four Davis Cup singles matches in 1937 and 1938 and also American titles, was his principal point-winner until he strengthened the rest of his game.

The technique for the backhand drive is largely the same as that for the forehand. It is merely reversed. If you are a right-hander, your right side faces the left sideline, your right foot is the front foot and you play the ball on your left side. Remember that the grip is changed a quarter of a turn backward on the handle of the racket with the knuckles on top, and that you use the opposite side of the racket from that used by the forearm. The weight shifts from the rear to the front foot a trifle *before* the ball is struck. By turning a little more toward the left before striking, one can learn to shoot down the line.

The backhand requires backswing. Reginald F. Doherty kept his elbow touching his right side on his backhand backswing, and both Dohertys hit their left ears with their rackets while swinging back. Tilden got speed on his backhand by turning the top of his body much more than he did on his forehand. LaCoste says the secret of hitting hard off the backhand is to bring the right shoulder very far back and to have the palm behind the handle of the racket. He declares this is assured by running the thumb up the back of the handle although he admits some very fine players do not reinforce the stroke with the thumb.

If the ball comes to you too high, it has to be undercut.

SPORTS and GAMES

272

Tilden and the Dohertys undercut their backhands when
the ball bounded high but hit the others with the racket
nearly flat, employing only a slight top spin. This latter
is the best backhand stroke if you can maneuver away
from the high bound. Do not try for too much top spin
and keep the ball low.

SERVICE: The speedy slice service is most
practical. Face the right side of the court as for the forehand drive, and stand with the left foot a few inches back
of the baseline close to the middle of the court. The right
foot should be about a foot back of the left. Remember
that the service grip is halfway between the forehand and
backhand grips.

Drop the right shoulder and bend the body far back
with nearly all the weight on the rear foot. Then toss the
ball upward four or five feet, forward and a little to the
right, swing your racket backward, upward and forward
in one long smooth movement, and hit the ball in the
center of the racket as high above the head as you can
comfortably reach. The weight of the body starts shifting
from the back to the front foot as you swing your racket,
and you finish with the body weight thrown onto the left
foot, and follow through with the racket, which just misses
the left knee. As in all strokes, keep the eye on the ball
until it hits the strings.

The angle of the racket face, which passes outside and
slightly over the ball in this service, imparts spin to the
ball and pulls it within the opponent's service court.

Moreover, upon bounding, it breaks low and away from the receiver and is hard to handle. Left-handed receivers find it especially puzzling. The downswing of the racket will be from right to left and the wrist used more so than in the forehand and backhand drives. By putting a little spin on the ball, you can hit it hard and still pull it within the service court.

The Americans, Maurice McLoughlin and Bill Tilden, and Gerald Patterson, big Australian who won two Davis Cup singles matches from the British in 1919, probably owned the most severe services of all time. Tilden and Patterson, because of their height and reach, which gives the effect when they serve of dropping the height of the net six inches, often hit their first balls flat and with unplayable speed, but smaller players, like the American Bill Johnston and the Australian Norman F. Brooks, had to depend upon the slice to pull the ball into court.

The Golden Rule of service is not to try to kill the first ball, but always to put it in court. Tilden says your aces must equal your double faults or your service is a handicap. The Dohertys always held that it is best to make a certainty of a moderately good first serve than a mere possibility of a very fast first serve. Their idea was to make their opponents move to take their service, which they directed to the sides of the service court, and preferably to the backhand.

Avoid footfault. After both feet come to rest prior to the serve, it is a fault if you change your position by walking or running or if you jump into the air, or step on or across the service line before the ball is hit. After you have played awhile, learn other services. If you like to go to the net after service, remember to get a fast start by leaning forward, like a dash man on the track, before striking the serve.

VOLLEY: If modern tennis is superior to that of the old-timers, it is probably because of more aggressive net play today. The stroke most used by a player at the net is the volley, which means hitting a ball in flight before it bounds. A player who has advanced to the net behind a forcing stroke is in a commanding position to win the point outright with a well-played volley because at the net there are so many more angles for placements that should render the fastest opponent helpless. Beginners should go to the net at every opportunity so they may learn the volley along with the groundstrokes.

The body and feet are placed the same for volleying as for groundstrokes provided there is time, and there usually is more time than you realize. Lack of time makes the volley a difficult stroke because you may not have time to place the feet correctly. In this case you should instinctively hurl your weight onto the foot nearest the ball, right foot for forehanders and left foot for backhanders. Always play volleys on the balls of the feet. Keep the feet spaced so you can move and bend easily.

A short swing and very little follow-through are the rules in volleying. Never stroke or top them. Always keep

the racket head higher than the wrist. Meet the ball with
the wrist well locked and the racket face flat, in a sort of
half push. The ball rebounds from the strings of your
stiffly held racket back into the foe's court and meanwhile,
if you have slanted your racket at an angle away from
your opponent, you can cause this rebound to go to an
unguarded spot in his court for an outright placement.

The volley should always be played down, but if you
are forced to take it low, bend your knees to squat and
meet the ball where you can see it at eye level, keeping
the head of the racket up and using the same action as
for a high volley. Since the stroke is largely pushed, it is
all the more necessary to have the palm behind the handle of the racket.

A good volleyer tries to win the point with one decisive
stroke; otherwise the opponent may pass him. To be a
good volleyer, one should be able to smash lobs well.

Borotra, the popular French player who attacked so
ruthlessly at the net, was probably the finest volleyer in
the history of the game. Vincent Richards, who played
on five American national championship doubles teams
from 1918 through 1926, was a very fine low volleyer.
Wilmer Allison, the Texan who won the American singles title in 1935, volleyed beautifully, stroking the ball
more than is usually considered sound.

FOREHAND SMASH: This is an overhead stroke,
taken between the service line and net, and hit downward with full power so that it bounces beyond the op-

ponent's reach. It is used primarily to kill at a stroke all short lobs. Lobs are high balls lifted over an adversary at the net.

The smasher must know how far away from the net he is standing when hitting. The farther away, the higher he must hit the ball. However, if he takes the stroke somewhere between the service line and the baseline, he should play safe and aim to get the ball back deep.

The technique of the smash is similar to that of the serve: body facing the right sideline and the ball being hit from overhead. However, the smash is stroked with more speed and less spin than the serve, because spin cuts down the speed and also makes the stroke more difficult to hit.

René LaCoste says confidence is a tremendously important factor in smashing. He also holds that a player who is about to smash must follow the ball more closely with his eyes than in any other stroke. Bill Tilden warns that the tendency on a smash is to net the ball; therefore do not hesitate to hit deeply.

LOB: This is a soft stroke by which the ball is lifted over an opponent's head at the net. If mixed with aggressive passing drives, it is a good way to encompass a great net player. Tilden and LaCoste could never have handled Jean Borotra's wolfish net play had they not been able to drive him back, exhaust him and discourage him with slow lobs that floated maddeningly over his head.

There are two kinds of lobs, (1) the low lob, used only

against a foe close to the net, in which you arch the ball just high enough to clear his head, and stroke it flat so it will rebound away from him to the backstop, and (2) the high lob, used when you are trying to recover position after an effective forcing stroke by your adversary. This type of lob is defensive. It is often undercut and goes very high, dropping to within a yard or two of the baseline and bounding straight up. It is a hard ball to smash, as the Dohertys point out, for the higher a ball goes the harder it is to kill since there is longer waiting and therefore more chance of nervousness. Also, the higher the ball, the faster it falls; therefore it is more difficult to time.

To execute the lob, grip the racket as if for a ground-stroke and do not shorten your swing. Take a full backward swing but carry your racket lower. Try to mask the stroke so the foe will not guess your intent. Hit the ball upward with a loose wrist and a slow complete action and remember to strike it exactly in the center of your racket as the ball reacts better there.

LOB VOLLEY: This is a difficult stroke, used principally in doubles when all four players are at the net. To execute it, a player replies to a volley by lobbing low over an adversary's head. The difference between this stroke and the regular lob is that the ball isn't allowed to bound. It is a dangerous play because if your opponent reaches it, he very likely will score a point on a smash. It is better to hit the ball out, when attempting this stroke,

than to risk its being reached by an opponent. The lob
volley calls for a firmly held racket and an especially
strong wrist. The Dohertys occasionally scored points in
doubles with this stroke and Henri Cochet, the Frenchman, was very good at it in singles.

TRAP SHOT: This stroke, also called the half-
volley, should never be undertaken except when a ball
is hit at one's feet and one has no alternative but to try
and return the ball on a pickup or lose the point. The
Dohertys executed it by turning the body sideways, as
for the ordinary strokes, holding the racket firmly, and
slightly overspinning the ball by bringing the head of the
racket through in an upward direction. They used a rigid
wrist, a short swing, and no follow-through. The weight
of the body should be on the left leg on the finish of the
forehand stroke and on the right leg when the backhand
is finished.

George Caridia, an English player prominent back in
1900, is generally conceded to have had the most skill at
trap shots although Cochet and the American Vincent
Richards were good.

CHOP: This is a stroke hit from the vicinity
of the baseline, employed to break up a driving game.
The ball is hit with medium speed and heavily undercut
with lots of wrist action. Upon striking the court, a ball
that has been chopped will bound weakly almost straight
up in the air as though pulled back by a string.

The best way to strike a chopped ball is with a flat

racket. A player shouldn't exaggerate spin, whether it be chopped or topped. Speed is the first essential in a stroke. Spin is valuable if it is not overdone at the expense of speed and form.

The chop is one of the oldest strokes known. That it was used in court tennis is indicated by the following quotation from the *Edinburgh Review* of January–April 1875:

> What is the precise process by which a stroke comes to be heavily cut? Observe closely the way in which the player at this end holds his racket. . . . He holds his weapon obliquely, and gives the ball a sort of slanting wipe, which makes it spin with a shrill whistling whisper.

Beginners in tennis should learn the correct strokes and practice lots against a wall, trying for a full, unhurried swing with correct body action. Start moving into position as soon as you see which way the ball is coming, keep a racket's reach away from it at all times and stand to one side, waiting until it bounces opposite your forward foot. Take your backswing before the ball bounces, pausing at the end of it to insure aim and timing.

As a player gains experience, he can move to other things, practicing his backhand equally with his forehand and weak strokes as well as strong ones. Always try to maintain form. Stay on your toes and think about gaining correct court position. Expect every ball you hit to be returned. Try for everything hit at you. Finally, always try to place your ball, not just get it back.

After he has played for some time, and his strokes become natural, a player should think more and more of tactics, making the opponent do most of the running. It's a good idea to get in tournaments. Always treat opponents and officials with respect.

The main idea in tennis as in so many other games is to force your opponent to make errors.

TACTICS

The growth of tennis tactics is most interesting. In the game's early years, players clung to the baselines, letting the ball bound low before hitting it with lift and top spin off the popular stroke invented by H. F. Lawford, an Englishman who played in the 1880's. Finally players began to storm the net, defeating advocates of the Lawford stroke.

Later, the net players themselves were beaten by opponents who by great diligence and practice made themselves masters of strokes at both the net and baseline. Tilden was the great exponent of this "all court" vogue which Dr. Helen Irene Driver says demands facility with the following strokes: forehand and backhand drives and chops, two kinds of service, volley and overhand smash for net play, lob for defense against net play and the half volley or trap stroke as weapon for balls hit at the feet.

COURT POSITION: After hitting a stroke in tennis, do not stand and watch the ball, but always hurry to one of two safe positions in the middle plane of the

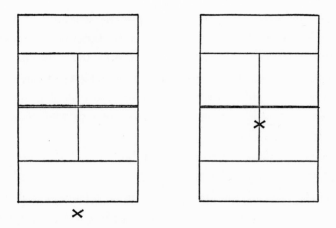

COURT POSITIONS FOR SINGLES

Hurry to this spot if you plan to play the next stroke from base line.

Hurry to this spot if you plan to play your next stroke from the net.

court. Never linger along a sideline. If you plan to play the next stroke from the baseline, hasten to a spot about a yard behind the middle of the baseline so you can run in on the next shot. Reginald Doherty, the older of the famous English brothers, was reckoned slow of foot, but he was always very fast at returning to his baseline position after each stroke.

However if you plan to make your second shot from the net, race forward following the line of flight of your first stroke to a spot two or three yards from the net and there await your adversary's return. Although the idea in net play is to win decisively with the first stroke or risk being passed, if the volleyer at the net fails to win this stroke outright, and sees his opponent reaching and returning it, he may quickly retreat to the middle of the court where the middle line runs into the service line. From there he is in a position to race forward again to play another volley or run back for a lob. And if it isn't a lob, he should always charge the net and play another volley.

Never remain, after you have hit a ball, in that part of the court between the service line and the baseline, because most of the balls hit by your opponent will fall there at your feet, where they are hardest to take. In tennis, a player should aim to take the ball from the net or baseline; there should be no halfway point.

Try to do all your running before you hit a ball so you will have time to get set correctly for the shot. Always try to advance on the ball instead of running backward for it.

In receiving service, a beginner should stand at a spot where he can comfortably move forward and take the service just as it is dropping from the top of its bound. His lateral position should be a stand a little to the left of the middle of a line stretched between the best services his opponent can hit to the left and right extremity of the service court. The reason he plays slightly to the left is because one's forehand stroke is usually more dependable than one's backhand.

When serving in singles, stand just behind the baseline as near as possible to the middle of the court, where you will have a shorter ball to hit, can better command both corners, and where you are centrally placed and therefore better able to play a well-placed return by your opponent.

Reginald Doherty and Norman F. Brooks, the Australian, were artists at footwork and court position. They made the other fellow do the running. The cook of a neighbor who lived near a court where Brooks occasionally played after his retirement from international competition said, "I like to see that old man stand in the middle of the court and keep the young folks on the run."

SINGLES

The best tennis players are those who think in action. Not only do they study their adversary's game before the match, if possible, but also examine it for a weakness while they are playing. If they discover he is poor on overhead balls, they lob to him repeatedly. If he is weak on low balls, they give him chops. If he has a weakness on his backhand and, realizing it, runs around the ball to play it off his forehand, they hit down the line to his forehand to open up the court for their next shot, which should be to his backhand.

Some players even store up a discovered weakness in an opponent; for instance, as did Jean Borotra in a match against LaCoste at Wimbledon. Noticing that LaCoste could not pass him with his backhand, Borotra wisely refrained from attacking LaCoste there until the games were tied at four all. Then Borotra broke LaCoste's service by suddenly placing four quick returns to LaCoste's backhand and came to the net each time to volley LaCoste's weak returns for points, after which he won his own service and the set, 6–4.

A good player finds out, as soon as possible, what his opponent's favorite shot is, then *does not* give it to him. After Larned, at the age of forty-one, had defeated McLoughlin in the 1911 national singles championship finals, a friend tried to console McLoughlin by saying: "You didn't play your game today." "You're right," the California Comet replied, with a rueful grin, "I didn't play my regular game but I played just as well as Larned let me."

When serving, if you plan to rush to the net after striking the ball, hit it with a great deal of spin, preferably near the center line to compel a backhand reply and also to avoid a cross-court return. If you are not running in after the serve, try to put your first ball near the sideline to pull your opponent out of position and thus open up his court for your return. When returning service the best return from the right-hand court is deep down the line to the server's backhand so you can come up to volley the return; from the left-hand court a drive across court to his backhand.

If your foe runs in on his serve, never take your eye off the ball but try to hit a low, fast-attacking stroke that will force him to hit the ball up, or a slow across-court shot that just skims the net and falls at his feet as he rushes in.

If he does not follow his serve to the net, try a deep return to his backhand if his service is well hit, or if it is weakly hit, a hard aggressive forcing shot across court or

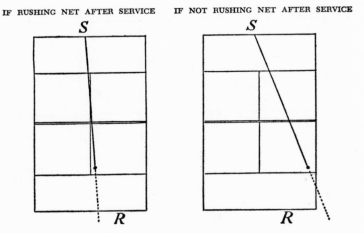

SERVICE POSITIONS FOR SINGLES *

Hit ball with lots of spin, preferably near center line to compel backhand reply, and also to avoid a
cross-court return.

Try to put your first ball near sideline to pull opponent out of position
and thus open up his court for your
return.

* Symbols: S, server; R, receiver.

to his backhand, and follow it to the net. When lobbing
in singles, aim for the foe's backhand so if he runs around
to take it off his forehand, he will open up his court.

Always go to the net after making a deep stroke that
puts your opponent on the defense, or when compelled
to take a short ball, or whenever you can get there before
your adversary strikes the ball. While at the net should
you fail to hit a decisive shot and be caught there, don't
hesitate to gamble and jump to the side on which you
think he will try to pass you.

It is difficult to play against an opponent at the net
when you are at the baseline. When confronted with this

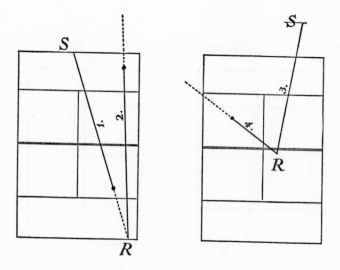

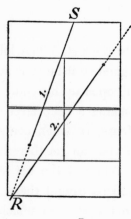
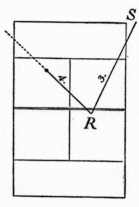

Best return from *right-hand* court

(*First position*) Hit deep down the line to server's backhand so   (*second position*) you can come up to volley his return.

Best return from *left-hand* court

(*First position*) Drive across court to his backhand, then   (*second position*) rush to net to volley his return.

RETURN OF SERVICE IN SINGLES

situation, LaCoste advises hitting a fast deep ball along a sideline to that side from which he volleys more poorly. He advises, too, that the player mix in lobs and short diagonal balls that fall close to the net.

Never change your tactics when winning. Likewise, if you are losing try something new even though it may be foreign to your usual style of play. For instance, change from a baseline to a net game, or from a driving game to softer strokes, and vice versa.

Do not let an erroneous decision unnerve you, as Allison did in a Davis Cup match in 1932. He had match point on Borotra and then won the vital point on the Frenchman's double fault, only to have a linesman call the service in; the error upset Allison so that his game collapsed and he lost. René LaCoste confesses that his secret for being calm is to force himself to appear calm until calmness actually comes to him.

It is important also to know how to conserve energy in tennis. Bill Tilden says there are four ways: (1) cutting out all unnecessary steps, (2) not hurrying between points, (3) refusing to chase absolutely hopeless shots, and (4) always putting your first service in court.

In singles, a player can risk hitting harder than in doubles because, with only one player arrayed against him, he has a better chance of scoring with his speed.

DOUBLES

Doubles is a battle for the vital net position; therefore a good doubles player should be able to volley well. Dou-

bles calls for more finesse and less speed than singles, for
lower hitting over the net to compel the opponents to
volley up, and for more lobbing inasmuch as it is hard to
pass two foes at the net with drives. These lobs should
be tossed down the middle, or better yet a little to the
left of the middle, between the two adversaries, so they
may be confused as to which of them should take it. Al-

DOUBLES *

SERVICE   LOBBING

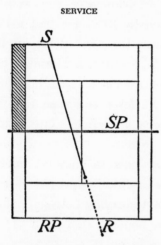

Server should stand two yards away from middle of court so that he can better cover cross-court returns to his alley (shaded section). Server should shoot for middle line so that receiver can't pass his partner at net or pull server out of position with sharply angled cross-court return.

In doubles, don't try to pass your foes at the net, but toss a high lob deep down the middle over their heads, thus forcing them to the base line and enabling you to charge to the vital net position, ready to volley or smash decisively for the point.

* Symbols: *SP*, server's partner; *RP*, receiver's partner.

ways be alert to shoot a stroke down the "weak middle," the open territory between your opponents.

At the net you and your partner should always stay parallel and, as the Dohertys advised, "work as one great wide man of the same width consistently, and not like a concertina, now wider and now narrower." It is always important to protect the "weak middle" in doubles. For example, if your opponent is forced to the right, you must also move right to cover him. Never leave too large a space between you.

Service is an even bigger advantage in doubles than in singles because it gives the important net to the server, who should never fail to take it after each serve. The server in doubles should stand a couple of yards to the right or left of the middle of the baseline instead of squarely in the middle so he can better cover cross-court returns in the additional four and one-half feet of alley. He should also serve as nearly as possible to the middle line so the receiver cannot pass his partner at the net or pull the server out of position with a sharply angled cross-court return.

The server in doubles should be responsible for all balls down the center or across court and for all lobs over his own head. The partner of the server should stand a yard from the net (and even farther back if the server's second ball is weak), a little nearer the sideline than the middle. He takes all strokes down his sideline, all lobs in his half of the court and should be alert to step across and kill easy shots near the net.

The receiver of service can reply in various ways; he can whip a low stroke down the often vulnerable center, or a low stroke across court near the sideline which the server may have to hit up to the receiver's partner at the net, or a low well-placed shot down the sideline into the alley inside the server's partner (a good shot to make if the service is hit near the sideline), or a high lob to the rear middle of the court. Return of service is conceded the most difficult stroke in doubles.

The receiver's partner should play at the baseline if the server hits a severe ball; otherwise, and for all second services, he may stand in between the service line and the net ready to volley, and his partner quickly joins him at the net after hitting the return. Probably the safer formation is for both receivers to stand back, although they should both be good lobbers in this case.

The Dohertys, back in 1903, introduced a brilliant defensive stratagem that noticeably turned the tables against the practice of the serving pair rushing to the net for a kill. The Dohertys posted the receiver's partner at a modified net position that enabled him to go on the offensive and volley any poor return from the server as the latter moved up to the net. The Dohertys broke so many services with this maneuver that the Australians quickly adopted it and have used it widely through the years, winning a much higher percentage of Davis Cup doubles victories than any other nation.

If all four players are volleying at the net, do not watch

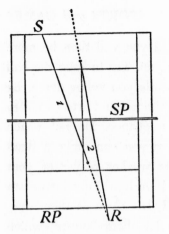

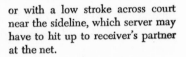

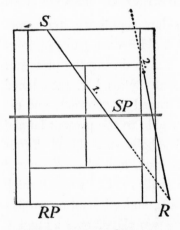

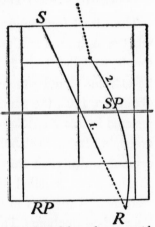

Reply to service with a low stroke down the often vulnerable center, outside server's partner,

or with a low stroke across court near the sideline, which server may have to hit up to receiver's partner at the net.

Or, if the service is hit near your sideline, with a low, fast shot down the alley inside server's partner,

or with a high lob to the rear middle of the court.

RETURN OF SERVICE IN DOUBLES

your partner. Watch the ball and you will then be more
ready to hit it when it comes to you. Try to keep the ball
low, making the foe volley up while you volley down. Be
alert for opportunities to rush to the net and attack. Volley
and smash whenever you get a chance. Do not poach
on your partner's territory unless you can make a decisive stroke. Try to discover the weaker player of your
opponents and center your attack on him. Lobs hit to you
should not be allowed to bound. Hit them as they drop.
However, if you are forced to let them bounce, which
means you have given the important net to your adversaries,
your return should be a high lob.

ORIGIN AND DEVELOPMENT OF TENNIS

The direct forerunner of modern tennis was the somewhat complicated and grandiose old French game of court
tennis, so-called because at one time during the period of
its extreme popularity only royalty played it. Introduced
about A.D. 1000, the game was waged on an ornate and expensive indoor court somewhat akin to the present jai-alai
arena, but far more elaborate. The balls were played off four
cement walls, each thirty feet high, and also off several
elegant annexes called dedans, grilles and galleries, which
were netted recesses in the walls, and off slanting projections called tambours. The game was played over a sagging
net on a concrete floor space of one hundred and ten by
thirty-eight feet with the players using cumbersome over-
sized rackets which our modern champions scornfully liken

to a cross between a landing net and a poached egg spoon.

England derived court tennis from France, and adopted the French rules and system of scoring. They also took over the nomenclature, such as deuce, otherwise *à deux* and the name of the game itself, which Professor W. W. Skeat, a learned biographer, in 1896 discovered originated from the French *tenetz,* the imperative of *tenir,* which was an exclamation French players called to one another just before putting the ball in play, meaning "Take heed" or "Mark" or "Play." However, court tennis did not flourish in England, where only royalty played it, as it did in France, where as early as 1600 there were twenty-five hundred courts and the game was played widely by everybody.

The present counting system of tennis goes back to the ancient Italian game of *pallone* in which points were counted 15, 30, 40 and game, instead of 1, 2, 3 and 4. *Pallone* probably descended from the ball games of the Romans, who got them from the Greeks, who say they got them from the East, which gives an idea of how difficult it is to excavate the roots of this ancient game.

Although nowadays tennis is one of the quietest games known, in the period of its popularity in France it was one of the noisiest. All the French players shouted so shrilly at one another that Tissot, surgeon-major of the French Army, in 1780 recommended the game for its healthy effect upon the throats and lungs of the players. However, as J. J. Jusserand, a scholar, pointed out in 1901, "many of these shouts, so beneficial for the throat and lungs . . .

consisted largely of big round oaths," so that the French tennis ordinances, drawn up in twenty-four articles in Paris in 1592, reminded players in the first paragraph that they should play "in order to recreate your body and exhilarate your mind, without swearing or blaspheming the name of God." Moreover, the ordinances provided that in the case of a prize match, players would be fined five *sols* for each oath.

Then came the doom of court tennis. By 1750 gambling had largely killed the sport in both France and England. Players were so flagrantly "bought off" that everybody became disgusted with the game and abandoned it. The sport probably got no encouragement from the French Revolution, either; in fact it was in an abandoned tennis court that the French National Assembly boldly defied King Louis XVI by passing the famous "Tennis Court Oath." The sport never has revived and although played sporadically nowadays by the wealthy class, there are said to be only sixty-five courts in the world today and, as Frank G. Menke points out, probably not more than ten thousand people in the United States have seen a game of court tennis.

However, considerably before the sport's demise, it had begotten a popular outdoor offshoot in England. Shorn of its expensive indoor splendor, the game was transferred to hundreds of broad English lawns where the only expense was for rackets, a few six-penny balls, a net and some streaks of whitewash to mark out the lines.

An extract from Nichols' *Progresses of Queen Elizabeth* proves that even in its antiquated form, tennis was played outdoors in England in the sixteenth century. To quote from Strutt's translation, "When Queen Elizabeth was entertained at Elvetham, in Hampshire, by the Earl of Hertford, after dinner, about three o'clock, ten of his lordship's servants, all Somersetshire men, in a square green court before Her Majesty's window, did hang up lines, squaring out the forms of a tennis court and making a crosse line in the middle. In this square they, being stript of their doublets, played, five to five (five on each side) with hand-ball, 'at bord and cord,' as they terme it, to the greate liking of Her Highness."

As the centuries spun away, this sturdy English offshoot kept developing and changing until by the nineteenth century people were stretching a cord between two trees and hitting the ball back and forth over it with bare hands, gloved hands, wooden bats and rackets. Then in 1872, Major Walter C. Wingfield, a British Army officer, after extensive experimenting, put lawn tennis into practical shape, borrowing from handball, the lawn games, court tennis, badminton and paume. The game called for play over a net five feet high near the middle and seven feet near the posts that supported it; the ball was struck after it had rebounded, always with an upward forehand stroke. English sportsmen became delighted with it and gradually it was speeded up by an adoption of present-day dimensions until in 1877 the present English championships started and the American in 1881.

The game is said to have spread to America via Bermuda. One of the guests at a garden party given by Major Wingfield in 1873 was another British Army officer home on furlough from Bermuda. When he returned to his post soon after, he took several sets of tennis equipment with him. Meanwhile, in Bermuda, Mary Outerbridge, a visiting American girl, played the new game and liked it so well that she brought a set to her home on New York's Staten Island, and although it was held up at the docks by perplexed customs officials, it was finally admitted without duty and thus lawn tennis was introduced to the young nation that has since been more successful than older nations in the Davis Cup competitions, the symbol of the world tennis championships.

RECENT HISTORY

In keeping with their disposition, the English tennis vogue has been conservative baseline driving, a cautious and graceful style that America was content to follow until approximately 1900. Then Dwight F. Davis and Holcombe Ward, a youthful United States doubles team, introduced a twist service that gave them time to charge to the net and turn off their adversaries' returns with severe volleys or smoking smashes. It was said of Davis, a left-hander who later put up the famous Davis Cup for international tennis supremacy, that he killed lobs harder than anybody who had played the game up to his time, and this new-found American aggressiveness swung the early advantage to the United States for three years after the turn of the century.

Perhaps the foremost singles player in America then was Malcolm Whitman, the rangy blond United States champion of 1898, 1899 and 1900, who seems to have been something of a prototype of Bill Tilden, the modern American tennis giant. Whitman had a consistently good all-around game with a backhand that nearly matched his forehand, a wonderfully sure volley, a severe overhead, enormous reach and well-thought-out court tactics. His closest rival was William A. Larned, a brawny, tanned six-footer who was a graduate of Cornell and played in a flannel rowing hat. Larned was primarily a baseliner, like the English. His game was to keep the other fellow on the run while he stood like a stage director pulling the strings, and before he retired he had won seven American national championships, the last in 1911 at the age of forty-one when he overwhelmed his adversary in straight sets.

In the first international lawn tennis competition, the Davis Cup matches of 1900, the United States defeated the British Isles decisively, 5 to 0, with Davis himself winning two singles matches and teaming with Ward to gain the doubles in straight sets. However in the next competition, in 1902, the Americans were hard-pressed to win, but Whitman's fine singles play carried them through, 3 to 2, although a new British doubles team, the peerless Doherty brothers, Reginald and Hugh, made its introductory appearance and thrashed Davis and Ward three out of four sets.

The Dohertys, a couple of fluent-stroking Englishmen who played with baffling coolness, were masters of finesse. Many experts ranked them as the greatest doubles team of all time. They launched a British dynasty that was supreme for four years. With Hugh "Little Do" Doherty, the soundest groundstroker of his day, triumphing in eight consecutive Davis Cup singles matches from 1903 through 1906, England overwhelmed the United States in Davis Cup play, winning fourteen of fifteen matches and losing the fifteenth by default; they also drubbed Belgium 5 to 0 in 1904. During this period the Dohertys were never beaten in Davis Cup doubles and Hugh Doherty never lost a Davis Cup singles match, although Larned twice carried him to five sets.

With the retirement of the Dohertys, Australia came to the fore with Norman Brooks and Anthony Wilding and ruled international tennis from 1907 through 1911 and intermittently until 1914 when World War I interrupted and took the life of Wilding, who fell in action. Brooks, a shrewd left-hander who played in a sharp-visored cap and used a loose racket with gut knotted to produce an erratic bound, has the longest record of Davis Cup competition, from 1907 through 1920, during which he won nine of fourteen singles matches and was on the winning side in six of eight doubles encounters.

Meanwhile in the United States the game was undergoing a revolutionary change with the eruption on the American tennis scene of Maurice McLoughlin, a young red-headed Californian of charming personality and sportsmanship who hit harder than any player the world had seen up to his time. Speed was the keynote of McLoughlin's game. Serves and smashes seemed to explode from his racket and Americans "ate him up." Actually Red Mac's game was not well-rounded. Opponents began shooting everything to his faulty backhand and the gallant Californian was through after winning United States singles titles in 1912 and 1913 and blasting Brooks and Wilding in Davis Cup singles matches in 1914. However McLoughlin's influence was vast, for many young American players began to model their games on his motif of blinding speed.

Then in 1920 began the longest of all international tennis overlordships—an American one—that of the Walloping Williams, lanky William Tilden of Philadelphia and diminutive William Johnston of California. Johnston, who weighed only one hundred and fifteen pounds and was just twenty when he won his first American national championship in 1915, was the first to come into prominence. Probably the greatest tennis player of his inches and pounds the world has ever seen, Johnston had the misfortune to play in an era when the unbeatable Tilden was at his best. It is not generally realized that

Johnston won eleven of fourteen Davis Cup singles matches from 1920 through 1926. Together he and Tilden, supported at times by youthful Vincent Richards and the veteran R. Norris Williams, won the Davis Cup seven years in a row for America.

The dominant tennis figure of all time probably was Tilden, a gaunt, stoop-shouldered, fretful man who didn't lose an important singles match from 1920 through 1926 and won seventeen of twenty-two Davis Cup singles matches, thirteen of them consecutively, a record that has never been equaled. Technically, Tilden had the most flawless game the modern tennis world has ever seen. Included in his unparalleled equipment was ability to strike his drives flat, heavily undercut or with top spin, a dozen different services, speed fully as devastating as Mc-Loughlin's, skillful variation of length and pace of stroke, uncommon fleetness of foot, extraordinary reach, the stamina of a greyhound and a keen tennis brain that, chesslike, operated a couple of strokes ahead of his opponent.

But what further set Tilden apart from other players was the strange fascination he seemed to hold over his opponents and the spectators alike, a fascination so strong that even when Tilden lost the public felt he was still the better player. Also the fact that he was a law unto himself made him a novelty as he fussed at judges and linesmen, unostentatiously gave a point to his foe if a linesman missed a decision, or courteously lofted a high

lob if an opponent sprawled on the court. He liked to
help young players and even in a tournament never
tried to annihilate a novice, because he knew the value
of instilling confidence. He loved nothing better than to
come dramatically from behind. For instance in 1925
René LaCoste led him 6–3, 12–10 and three times had
match point in the third set, only to have Tilden pull
his game together and, with brilliant strokes that shone
like jewels cut and polished by a master artificer, blow
LaCoste off the court. Tilden had several close calls like
this and seemed deliberately to seek and to enjoy all of
them.

But every dynasty must tumble some day and age
finally caught up with the Americans. One of the many
nations which had never won the Davis Cup was France.
She had made modern tennis possible by originating and
developing court tennis but had never been a power in
international play. The confidence the French had always seemed to lack was provided them when Suzanne
Lenglen, a French girl, starting in 1919, won five world
women's championships in a row at Wimbledon. Like
Jeanne d'Arc, graceful buoyant Suzanne was a wonderful inspiration to her tennis-playing countrymen, who
had systematically begun to play in tournaments all over
the world. René LaCoste, studious and able baseline
player who like a mechanical ball machine got everything
back; Jean Borotra, who wore a blue beret and became
the greatest net player and also the most popular player

of modern times; Henri Cochet, wiry little French Titan
who was probably the greatest French singles player of
all time with eleven of fourteen Davis Cup singles victories, ten of them in a row; and Jacques Brugnon, a
fine doubles man, made up the unstoppable French array
and eventually they overthrew the creaking Americans
and went on to win the Davis Cup for the six years from
1927 through 1932.

Then Great Britain, after twenty-seven years of frustra-
tion since the retirement of the Doherty brothers, returned with Fred Perry and Bunny Austin to sweep the
Davis Cup four years from 1933 through 1936; and the
United States, led by another of its aces developed in
sunny California, young J. Donald Budge, broke through
for triumphs in 1937 and 1938. After that Budge, like
Tilden, Cochet, Ellsworth Vines (another Californian who
had won United States national championships in 1931
and 1932), and Perry, turned professional, leaving the
amateur field to younger players.

Australia broke through in 1939 with Adrian K. Quist
and John E. Bromwich to sweep the Davis Cup for the
first time in twenty years. Then World War II struck and
for seven long years there was no Davis Cup play. Finally,
in 1946, play resumed and the United States triumphed
four years consecutively behind players like Jack Kramer,
Frederick R. Schroeder, Jr., Frank Parker and Pancho
Gonzales.

But starting in 1950, Australia won five times in six

years. Frank Sedgman, her shock-haired ace, swept six straight singles wins and three consecutive doubles encounters in 1950–51–52. Lew Hoad and Kenneth Rosewall propelled the Aussies to later international triumphs over the Americans. Nowadays, the fastest tennis is played by the professionals, a trend that completely reverses the situation that existed through the first 60 years of the game, detracting from the great popularity amateur tennis had enjoyed from the days of Davis, Larned and the Dohertys.

CHAPTER 13

TRACK *and* FIELD

EADERS of Donn Byrne's *The Tale of James Carabine* know that man is a tougher and more durable animal than the horse. Although the story is largely fiction, the incident is based upon fact, for several such races have been run in England the last two or three hundred years, almost all of which ended as did this one.

In introducing Carabine, his fighter-hero, Byrne wrote as follows of this celebrated race:

It was Carabine who pulled my uncle through that famous match of his for a bet of two thousand guineas with Piers Fleming, that in a six-day race he on foot would beat Piers Fleming's beautiful mare Lalla Rookh (by The Jackdaw out of Killala Girl), with any jockey Piers wanted up. . . . James Carabine was at that time fighting his way to the top, and my uncle told him of the wager.

"Sure you'll do it on one foot," said James Carabine.

They started off from Donegall Place in Belfast at five on a June morning, with Captain Head, the lightweight cross-country rider, upon Lalla Rookh, my Uncle Valentine in shirt and shorts with the green cricket cap upon his head and James

Carabine with him. The mare trotted off and Carabine and my Uncle Valentine started in a long swinging walk. Though my uncle was fairly fresh at the end of thirty miles, Carabine would let him go no farther.

"We'll stop here the night," said Carabine.

"But the mare'll be in Dundalk," said my Uncle Valentine.

"Let her," said Carabine. And he bundled my Uncle Valentine into a hot bath and pummelled his legs, and after dinner, saw that he went to bed. When my Uncle Valentine rose in the morning Carabine was gone ahead, but Tubby Sweeny the footballer was by his side.

"I'll be with you the twenty miles to Dundalk," said Sweeny.

"Have you heard anything of the horse?" asked my Uncle Valentine.

"Devil the word," said Sweeny.

At Dundalk Carabine was waiting. He went over every inch of my uncle's feet and legs.

"Where's the horse?" said my uncle.

"A bit ahead," said Carabine.

"How far?" asked my uncle.

"A trifle," said Carabine. "About thirty miles."

When they passed through Dublin, Piers Fleming was waiting. He was a thin shifty man.

"Valentine," he said, "give it up and all bets off."

My uncle was going to agree, but Carabine broke in. "Oh, no," said Carabine. "Across my dead body, Mister Valentine."

"Ha," said Fleming. "This isn't for you. This is a matter between gentlemen."

"You may always be a gentleman, Mister Fleming, but Mister Valentine stopped being one in Donegall Place. He is now only a pedestrian and foot-runner and under my charge," said James Carabine.

On the fourth day they passed the game little mare, lame, with Flory Head leading her. They had done one hundred and forty-nine miles in the time. In Waterford Town on the fifth day, they got a message from Fleming, withdrawing his horse and paying forfeit.

Although the feat was that of a full-grown athlete in training and obviously should not be attempted by any boy, there is a fine lesson for boys in that race. First, it should prove to a boy that his body is strong and that if he wants to become a runner he need not fear injuring it, provided he passes a physical examination before he runs a step in training, and does not overtax his strength thereafter. Next, it illustrates the futility of overstrain and the wisdom of starting out carefully and conserving strength. Although the average athlete would have begun at a brisk trot and tried to cover forty or fifty miles the first day, Valentine MacFarlane's commencing gait was a long swinging walk. Although he felt like going farther, his trainer wisely stopped him after he had covered an ordinary distance. Finally, notice how Mac-Farlane went to bed that first day almost immediately after eating his evening meal, thus storing up valuable energy for the next day's going. That is precept number three. Without plenty of sleep, at least three hours of it before midnight if possible, no boy is going to go far in athletics.

Overstraining is simply trying to do too much. A boy's constitution will not stand nearly so much physical effort as a man's in spite of the fact a boy's competitive spirit flares just as brightly. No boy under sixteen should attempt to run farther than one mile or compete in more than two hard races in one meet. Younger boys do not have to go through the rigid training program intercollegiate athletes undertake because a boy's muscles are naturally more supple and his body in better general physical condition, thanks to the surprising amount of out-of-door walking, running, jumping, swimming, pulling, pushing and stooping boys do every day. Boys under sixteen should concentrate on acquiring form in their events rather than gaining razor-edge physical trim. A short period of special drill and speed sharpening is all they need before a meet.

Boys should not be afraid that running will give them a weak heart or shorten their lives. Statistics prove that longevity has favored the athlete. In 1904 John M. Gaines and Arthur Hunter made a study for the New York Life Insurance Company of the eight hundred and eight men who won athletic letters at Yale from 1863 to 1904 and discovered that the athlete was not only a better physical risk than the average insured person of his time, but also a better risk than the general run of college men of the same classes. In 1928 the Metropolitan Life Insurance Company's statistical department completed and published a study of the longevity of athletes at ten leading American colleges and universities and found that athletes outlived insured people (who had passed strict physical examinations) by from 6.5 to 8.5 per cent and that after the age of forty-five, track athletes outlived those of any other sport.

In the old days, an announcement by a boy that he wanted to try out for a distance event on his school track team brought a gasp of horror from his parents and his friends. But Tom Jones, veteran cross-country coach at the University of Wisconsin, recently announced that only one man died of the ninety-two Wisconsin runners who had lettered at the four- to five-mile distance since 1905, and that one was killed in an automobile accident! In 1910 an old-fashioned doctor advised Clarence DeMar, the marathon runner, that he would die from heart trouble if he kept on running. Two years later the doctor himself died from a heart attack and DeMar was still running marathons when he was over sixty years of age. So any normal boy can expect to improve his health by running. It is important, however, to undergo at first a careful physical examination to establish this normalcy, and then not to overstrain yourself after you start your running career.

CONDITIONING: Common sense is the secret of track and field training, as in all athletic training. No matter what the age of the contestant, nine hours of sleep in fresh air each night is absolutely necessary. Athletes should dress warmly in cold weather and not walk barefoot on cold concrete floors. Nor should they go outdoors with uncovered hair freshly wet from a shower bath. Boys can drink all the water they wish except two or three hours before competition. They also should eat regularly three times a day and not be finicky about foods. Any wholesome food is all right and a boy's mother is the best trainer he can have. Don't avoid meat. Meats are excellent; they provide energy and replace waste. In fact, it is sound not to avoid deliberately any food. Potatoes, bread, fruits, cereals, hot biscuits, oatmeal, bananas and ice cream are all good, for they give a great deal of energy in a small time. It is most important to eat regularly and slowly, chew well and rest a little before and after each meal, if possible. Eat at least two and one-half to three hours before competition, and be careful not to stuff. Shower baths should be taken after exercise and should be short, rarely lasting more than four or five minutes. Use warm water and soap first, then finish with a clean warm spray and finally with a cold one, toweling vigorously.

Rubdowns are seldom necessary. In the hands of unskilled volunteers, and this includes ninety per cent of boy masseurs, they only take up time and may actually be harmful. "A good man doesn't need one and a poor man isn't worth one," is the way one old-time coach puts it. Probably the best part of a rub is the ten-minute rest one gets while lying relaxed on the rubbing table. If a spike wound is at all deep, the athlete should be rushed to a physician or a hospital or infirmary so that antitetanus serum can be injected to prevent lockjaw. Shin

splints or pains radiating along the shinbone, usually
caused by running too fast before arriving in condition
or by running on too hard a surface, can best be cured
by rest. When the sufferer resumes workouts, he can
avert a recurrence by running on grass for a few days.
Spiked shoes should fit snugly, toenails must be cut short
to prevent bruising, and blisters cared for by the method
described in the chapter on baseball. Cinder burns, caused
from falling down, should be washed with soap and
water, cleansed with an antiseptic and painted with
mercurochrome. Pulled muscles, sprained ankles and other
more serious injuries, or any injury that does not readily
respond to treatment, should be referred to a physician.
Above all, avoid colds and constipation. Runners are
seldom constipated and early learn the habit of regular
elimination.

In track and field, as in all sports, boys under sixteen
should use such junior paraphernalia as the eight-pound
shot, the junior high-school discus, and a light bamboo
vaulting pole around which they can readily wind their
fingers. The boy who struggles with senior equipment
will find it difficult to learn form. Boy hurdlers should
do their racing over two-foot or two-and-one-half-foot
barriers spaced not more than nine yards apart, and
should never run a hurdle race of more than 120 yards.
The running program for under-sixteeners may consist
of flat races of 75 and 120 yards, a hurdle event of 60
yards and a quarter-mile relay in which each of four

runners travels 110 yards. All field events save the hammer may be tried.

Boys over sixteen, who usually come in the senior high school category, may compete over the same measurements and in the same events as the collegians with the following exceptions: exclusion of the hammer throw and two-mile run; reduction of high hurdles to three feet three inches; reduction of the length of the low hurdle race to 180 yards with the fences set twenty yards apart. Also the weight of the senior-high discus has been diminished to three pounds nine ounces.

There is ample opportunity for American boys to get track and field competition in college or university. In the spring, almost every state has its grade school, rural school and county school meets for youngsters, not to mention the county, district, conference and state meets for high-school students. The intercollegiate teams start their program with indoor meets in January, February and March, and in April send their fastest relay combinations and special-events men to the large outdoor relay carnivals originated in America such as the Pennsylvania Relays, established in 1895 and held annually at Franklin Field, Philadelphia; the Drake Relays at Des Moines, Iowa; Kansas Relays at Lawrence, Kansas; Texas Relays at Austin, Texas; West Coast Relays at Fresno, California; and the Colorado Relays at Boulder, Colorado. Meanwhile all the schools engage in dual and tri-meet competition, and close their programs in May with the various conference competitions followed by the two national collegiate meets, the I.C.A.A.A.A.[1] and N.C.A.A.[2] in June. Club teams, composed of amateurs and college graduates, also compete in full programs in the East, terminating in the National A.A.U. indoor games in March and the National A.A.U. outdoor games usually held in July. In tryouts for Olympic competition every fourth year, high schoolers, collegians and crack club athletes all compete together in one class to form the strongest American team possible. The weakest point in the American system is the fact that after graduation, there is very little competition available for the average college athlete who does not live in the East, the only section that sponsors a widespread program the year round.

Track and field events get you outdoors, improve health, are not as dangerous or as expensive as other sports, require very little equipment, and can be indulged in any time of year one wishes. Moreover, running is the basis for nearly every other sport on the calendar and therefore part of the training routine for each.

A few brief directions for individual events follow:

SPRINT: This includes all flat races through 300 yards. In America, the average dash is from 50 to 70 yards indoors and 100 and 220 yards outdoors, with metrical distances usually substituted for yards each Olympic year, since Olympic races are in meters. Also,

---

[1] Intercollegiate Association of Amateur Athletes of America.
[2] National Collegiate Athletic Association.

there is a 300-yard dash on several indoor programs. There are three parts to a sprint: the start, run and finish. Starting blocks are required and are one-tenth second faster than starting without them. The sprinter first kneels and puts his fingers on the starting line, letting his feet find their most comfortable position and then setting his blocks there. Ordinarily, the knee of the rear leg will be even with the instep of the front foot, which will be four to nine inches back of the starting mark. When the starter calls "Take your marks!" the sprinter places his front foot in the front hole, planting his spikes firmly, then kneels and puts his hands on the starting mark. After that he places his rear foot in the back hole and relaxes. At the command "Get set!" his hips are raised until the rear knee is about six inches above the ground and the weight is on the arms and front foot. His eyes are focused on the ground three or four yards down the lane. When the pistol cracks, he goes whether he is ready or not. He pumps his arms vigorously and falls off naturally into his first strides, which should be short and fast. Gradually he raises his body and increases his stride in the first twenty yards. The rest of the race is usually run with the body bent forward and the chin tucked in. The sprinter picks up his feet with high knee action and is careful not to overstride. His feet should not be in contact with the ground in front of the head, and his knees should not be bent. The arms should swing backward an inch or two past the hip and will carry straight if the sprinter will keep his thumbs up. He does not make the final stride a broad jump at the string but maintains form and runs right through the twine, as though the race were five yards farther, leaning over and turning the shoulder into the worsted to get an extra few inches. After breasting the string, raise the arms and take another thirty or forty yards to slow gradually to a stop, thus taking the weight off your shins. If a sprinter stops too suddenly after he finishes, he is apt to get shin splints.

440 YARDS: Top collegiate runners sprint this race from start to finish. If boys train properly for it, not shirking hard work, they can sprint it nearly all the way, too. The idea in training is to have the quarter-miler enjoy his preparatory work. Only one day a week should be devoted to over distance, say 500 yards on Tuesday. The rest of the workouts should be at odd distances, 250's, 300's, 350's, running a different lane of the track with a different curve problem each day.

As early season training, boy quarter-milers should run cross-country with no time being taken, never going more than two miles. After two or three weeks of this, they can do "ins and outs" on the grass, going 150 yards at three-quarters speed and then jogging 300 in between. Exercises are excellent. Boys should do at least three daily, toe-touching, sit-ups and push-ups. They stretch and strengthen your leg and stomach muscles and develop the upper body. A little weight-lifting is also good. Before doing starts with the gun, boys should first do five or six mechanical starts on the grass, gradually loosening the starting muscles.

Most high-schoolers sprint the first 50 yards of a 440 race, then relax, lower their arms slightly and without slowing down swing into a smooth and rhythmic action called floating. The knees should not be lifted too high. Try for a slight hip movement where the feet are never more than a few inches from the ground from one stride to the other. At about 300 yards out, drive for home, gradually lifting your arms (but not your shoulders) and shortening the stride a little. Don't jump suddenly from one action to another, or tension results.

It's a good idea to know what you can do, after testing it in practice, and plan your pace for each 110 yards of the race, especially if the race is run in lanes. If it isn't run in lanes, the fast start is necessary to obtain favorable position.

880 YARDS: The training for this event should consist largely of under-distance work such as 220's, 440's and 660's, particularly on the warmer days. A 1,320-yard run once a week, say on Tuesday, is good for over-distance. The runner should also practice starting. If you are training for the 880, run over-distance on the colder days and cross-country in the fall. Try to learn a good form. If the head is held correctly, the correct body angle usually will take care of itself. Keep your eyes set on a spot ten yards down the track and the tendency of head and body to tilt forward will follow naturally. Don't kick

up behind higher than the knee. To prevent this, drive harder off your toes. Run the first quarter about three seconds faster than the second. If the track is wet or the day windy, it is best to follow pace preferably in second or third position. When passing an opponent, do so with a rush. The idea in this is to impress him and also establish a slight lead. Don't let anybody pass you on the back stretch, final curve or homestretch of the last lap, if you can help it. In the last 150 yards lean forward, get up on your toes, raise your knees and pump your arms.

ONE MILE: Cross-country in the fall is an ideal conditioner for this race. In the spring the runner can concentrate on speed and pace and interval running. Try to develop a fast kick through the final 350 yards. Don't be afraid to drop gently down on the heel in this race, for it is restful and takes the strain from the calf muscles. Don't start off like a dash man. The world's greatest milers today distribute their pace evenly. For instance, if you are trying for a 4:40 mile, your laps would probably average close to 70 seconds each. Collegiate runners who shoot for the 3:59 mile average close to 60, 60, 60 and 59 seconds. The last lap should be the fastest. The third lap is a good one in which to widen your lead. Most of your competitors will be resting then.

The great college milers do lots of interval running and it will help high school milers, too, especially during the training season. Gail Hodgson, Oklahoma's fine miler of 1958–60, ran ten 220's in 26 seconds each, jogging a

220 in between each one he ran and never slowing to a complete stop. On other days he would run ten 440's in 57 to 58 seconds each, cutting across the track on the grass at a jog in between and never slowing to a complete stop. Occasionally he would do four half-miles in 1:59 or 2:00 each, jogging a 440 on the track between each and never slowing to a complete stop. This continuous running at intervals of a fast and slow pace is an excellent conditioner but the high schooler should reduce the rigidity of Hodgson's practice jaunts. Plan your schedule with your coach.

The wise runner, in crowded company, will want to glance around him occasionally to study approaching traffic that may result in his being trapped by methods described above. So while "Don't look back!" and "Don't run wide on curves!" is good general advice, there are times when a runner must disregard these adages.

Don't lean. Learn to run upright, using a short, economical stride.

HIGH AND LOW HURDLES: The purpose in hurdling is not to stay in the air too long. Start from a crouch. The eyes should be fixed, first, on the spot where the first leg will strike as it comes out of the starting holes and thereafter on the top edge of the hurdle ahead. Don't jump with both feet together but take the hurdle in the middle of your stride. Bend the body at the hips, when taking the hurdle, to keep yourself in a falling position that will force you down on the other side quickly. The foremost leg should be raised straight to the front and swung over the hurdle so that the heel just clears the top while the body is well forward. Then snap the leg sharply downward. There are two main styles used during this procedure: extending both arms forward simultaneously; or bending the arm on the side of the foremost leg and letting it ride close to your side. Don't hurry the back leg. To discourage jumping, keep the back leg on the ground as long as possible. After the back foot clears the hurdle, reach out with it on the first stride. After clearing the last hurdle, drive hard off the back leg and, taking short fast strides, as in the start of a sprint, run on through the string, remembering to use the shoulder turn as in the finish of a dash.

In the low hurdles form is not so essential. The contestant need not lean forward so sharply, he can bend his foremost leg more and he can whip his rear leg through faster. Speed between the sticks is important in the lows. High-school boys will do well to practice starting over the first hurdle only and also to practice clearing hurdles placed twelve yards apart in five strides instead of three. To prevent skinning and bruising the legs, the early practice can be done over a light bamboo bar suspended the correct height.

RELAYS: In the 440- and 880-yard relays, it is wise to start the fastest man on the number 1 leg and get a lead. This puts pressure on the other teams, forcing them to make errors such as mishandling the baton or running out of the passing zone. However in the mile relay it's best, usually, to start your second fastest boy first, your third fastest at number 2, your slowest boy third and your fastest boy at number 4. Later in the season, as the strengths and weaknesses of both your own foursome and those of your rivals becomes more apparent, your relay personnel can be switched to take advantage of this knowledge.

The best touch-off method for the 440, 880 and mile relays is that coached for forty years by Clyde Little-field, the University of Texas coach. It's a low pass. The number 1 runner clutches the stick in his left hand and upon finishing his leg, passes the bamboo with his extended left arm to the number 2 man, who is standing on the back line of the touch-off lane. This is a palm-down style and the exchange is made at hip level. The receiver extends his right arm back and makes a V between his thumb and fingers. The last three runners will take the baton in their right hands. The second and third runners quickly transfer the baton from right to left hand without losing stride but the number 4 runner, or anchor man, doesn't do this since he has nobody to pass to.

In the 440 and 880 relays, the receiver of the baton watches his teammate only until he approaches at a certain distance, then holding his right arm back low and extended with the thumb and fingers forming a V, takes his sprinting start, shifting his eyes off the approaching teammate onto the track ahead. Thus it's a blind pass on his part and it's up to the passer, holding the baton at its lower end, to thrust it into the V formed by the receiver's palm.

The exchange should be timed perfectly so that the two sprinting boys never get any closer than is necessary to pass the stick. The touch-off has to be completed within the 20-yard zone at the finish of each leg. Failure to do this, or running any leg without a baton, means disqualification. If the race is run in lanes, runners in lanes other than the inside one should tread almost on the inside or left-hand chalk line to reduce the distance.

In all relays of one mile or more, the runner receiving the baton does not take his eye off his teammate coming in until he receives the baton. And he should keep his eye on it until he feels it securely in his hand.

POLE VAULT: First grasp the pole with both thumbs up as if to climb it. Carry it along your side, tilting the plugged base slightly upward to aid the balance, and with uniform strides run hard. This run varies between 80 and 110 feet and the stride should be carefully measured. The vaulter should carry the pole and run through the pit so a correct starting line can be ascertained and the vaulter will not miss his step. Without slackening stride, stab the base of the pole in the take-off box and with a vigorous leap, leave the ground, hanging to the pole like a pendulum. Swing the feet up and over the bar, pull up with the arms, make a half turn of the body until you are upside down in mid-air

and push down on the pole. This final powerful pushup
of the arms not only sends the pole back and prevents
its knocking off the bar, but also shoots the head,
shoulders, arms and hands over the bar. The vaulter
should fall facing the runway, landing on his feet and if
necessary rolling on the shoulders to help take up the
shock. It is best to use pits of wood shavings, for sand
is sometimes hard on the ankles. The lower hand may be
raised to the upper just as the pole is planted but the
upper hand must not be raised, nor the lower hand placed
above it. Arm pull is the reason American vaulters are
now vaulting 15 feet. Today vaulters go as high as speed
will take them, and then use arm power to propel them
even higher. Therefore a pole vaulter should go to the
gymnasium and practice front and back flips, rope pull-
ups, handstands on the horizontal bar and giant swings.

HIGH JUMP: Any boy can use the old scissors
form of running from the side and clearing the bar with
the inside leg while the body is in a sitting position. However, you can jump much higher with the Western form
as popularized by Harold Osborn, former world record-
holder from Illinois. Here is the description of that form:
To locate a take-off spot, stand so you can just touch the
bar with the tips of your fingers with the arm held horizontal to the ground. Your feet will then mark the take-
off spot. Running at an angle of 45 degrees to the bar,
take three short walking steps of four feet each (where
your first check mark will be drawn), then four running

bounding steps of six feet each, a total of 36 feet. On the step just before the take-off, drop your body into a slight crouch. If there is any lean to the body here, it should be backward. Meanwhile the speed of the body is carrying you forward over the bar.

A terrific drive upward with the *outside* leg (which goes over the bar first) along with the spring of the inside leg and a hand drive with the inside arm, carries the body up. The outside leg, in making this swing up, is not straight.

The inside or take-off leg comes off the ground with a hard drive. Its foot or ankle hits the outside leg hard just back of the knee or calf. The back goes over parallel with the bar. The landing is made on the inside foot and both hands. Keep your eyes on the runway until the fifth step, then shift them to the bar. The most common fault is leaning into the bar when you should be leaning back. Warm up well before jumping, jump but twice a week, and work hard for form at a low height.

Probably the most popular high-jumping form among collegians today is the *straddle*. In it, the jumper approaches the bar at an angle of 40 degrees, taking an average of six or seven strides with the only check mark made at the start of the run. The last three strides are longer and at increased speed. Plant your foot at almost a right angle to the bar. Try not to turn toward the bar until your take-off foot leaves the ground.

Your free leg should be slightly bent and swung upward as a pendulum. Try to kick it away from the line of run, almost parallel to the bar. You will probably lean slightly toward the bar. Drive your head, shoulders and chest well above the bar, then while dropping the right side of your body toward the landing pit, rotate your head and hips to assist clearing the bar with the left side of your body. Lift the left leg while turning the toes up, turn your head back to the direction of the run and rotate the hips to insure clearing the bar.

Since most high-jumping landing pits nowadays are built high, you will not have far to fall and shouldn't dread landing on your back. Think only about clearing the bar.

BROAD JUMP: It isn't the frog in your legs that makes a broad jumper, but rather the speed of the take-off run. The world's record of nearly 27 feet is held by Jesse Owens, the American Negro who is also Olympic record-holder in the dash. Practice sprinting, running from 100 to 120 feet. Learn to set your marks so you will not miss your step. Brightly painted ice picks which jab into the ground easily and are hard to blow down make good markers. Measure back twelve paces and make a mark, then measure back twelve more paces and make a second mark. Starting with both feet together on this second mark, you should be going at full speed when your jumping foot hits even with the first mark. You can test this by running down the take-off at top speed, hitting the board and running on through the landing pit without jumping. If your jumping foot strikes eight inches in front of the board, move your marks back eight inches. If your jumping foot lacks six inches reaching the board, peg the marks up six inches. Run at top speed until three steps from the board, then slacken speed slightly so you can crouch and stamp the board hard. The good broad jumper will see the board mainly out of the corner of his eye and will be looking chiefly at the landing pit at a paper marker set at the distance he wishes to jump. The higher you draw your knees, the longer your feet will remain in the air. Practice a hitch-kick or extra stride in the air by throwing your rear leg forward, then kicking it backward, then doing the same thing with your take-off foot, which should start forward as the other leg comes backward, resulting in a scissors action. Try to land with the feet pretty well together. Use sprint shoes with a sponge rubber heel taped or glued inside the shoe to prevent stone bruises. Don't jump for distance oftener than once or twice a week and then take only five or six jumps. Fill up the landing pit after each jump. Jumping in the hole left by the preceding jump may cause a pulled muscle.

If you start on your right foot, raise your right arm a foot higher than your left to maintain balance. If you take off on your left foot, do the opposite. When landing, don't try to pitch forward but turn to one side, rolling off your elbow out of the pit.

Stone bruises on your heel will ruin your check marks and throw you off your step. However, any trainer can make a papier-mâché cup that will fit over the heel and prevent this.

SHOT-PUT: "The main idea in the shot-put," advises John Jacobs, Oklahoma track coach, "is not to stand too close to your instrument after your follow through." Always practice in the regulation seven-foot circle, the front arc of which is a toeboard four inches high. However, the toeboard may be left off while practicing to avoid skinning the foot and ankle.

Parry O'Brien, the University of Southern California champion, perfected the shot-put form everybody uses today. When he developed it, O'Brien weighed 225, was six feet three tall and could run 100 yards in almost ten seconds. His reflexes were very quick. He developed tremendous strength in his arms, back and legs through a well-planned program of weight-lifting. No shot-putter today can stay up with the leaders unless he does weight-lifting at least twice a week.

O'Brien's form stresses a quick explosion and the application of force to the shot over a longer distance and for a longer time. Turning his back on the direction he is throwing, he assumes a back-facing stance, holding the shot well back of the jawline and resting it on the neck just back of the ear. He stands erect with his chest well out and up. His right foot is pointed toward the rear of the ring, 180 degrees from the direction of flight. His back is turned to the center of the toeboard and his eyes are fixed on a point about ten feet behind the ring.

Fixing the eyes so keeps the shoulders and hips in line.

From this starting position he takes a deep dip over his bent right leg, his back almost parallel to the ground. This gives him a very long lift.

As he begins to move across the ring, his left foot kicks straight up and across the ring with the knee pointing toward the ground. This high kick gives him more speed across the ring and keeps him lower over his right leg. His body is still facing backwards. His right foot is planted in the center of the ring but has now come around about 35 degrees. The left foot forms a slight angle with the toeboard, the toes being jammed against the toeboard and pointed along the line of flight.

Still maintaining his back-facing position, O'Brien explodes in a combination of power and timing, swinging the shoulders and hips to the orthodox forward position. This movement is a right-to-left rotation of the hips and shoulders, plus an upward thrust off the right foot and back muscles. Maintaining the same hip and shoulder position and speed across the circle are key factors. A fast thrust, wrist and finger snap and a good follow-through over the left leg complete the throw.

O'Brien's training program includes lots of running to strengthen the legs, sprinting for speed and the valuable weight-lifting that is absolutely essential to obtaining the increased strength all shot-putters must have.

DISCUS: First learn how to spin the discus so it will always stay level and keep in its glide. Hold it flat in the palm, keep the hand relaxed and well spread, but with as little of the fingers as possible folded over the edges. The hand is cocked at the wrist. The back of the discus hand is always up. Stand low and relaxed and swing the discus back and forth in the plane in which you expect to throw. Place your free hand under the discus to balance it each time it comes to the left shoulder. Make your backward swing fairly long and don't start too rapidly.

The discus form has changed from the old-style full turn to a turn of one and a half body revolutions. Instead of starting with the left side facing toward the direction of throw, the athlete has his back toward the direction of throw with both feet at the back of the circle. Thus he will have a full eight feet to spin, since he is pivoting on his left foot. This is a big help, giving him another quarter turn to generate more speed.

As you start your turn, shift your weight to your left foot with the knees slightly flexed. The right arm swings back through the turn with the left arm cocked across the chest. Start the spin on the ball of the left foot, throwing your right leg around your left with the knee well bent. Push off with your left leg, using a tremendous thrust to gain momentum. Your right foot should land in the center of the circle and your left slightly to the left of the line of flight. Now start the long pull. Your left arm starts to pull, your hips begin to rotate in advance of the right arm. Your left leg is almost straight, your right

leg is well bent, your weight is over your right leg. As
you come around for the final release, the discus will
drop slightly below hip level. The right hip leads the
arm but when the throw is completed, the momentum
of the throw will bring the right foot around so that both
feet are near the front of the circle.

Running, sprinting and weight-lifting are important in
training for this event. It can be practiced without fear
of injuring the arm but a three-day layoff before competition is advisable.

Throw low into the wind, throw high with the wind.
If the breeze is crosswise, raise the side of the discus
that is into the wind.

JAVELIN: To grasp the javelin, hold the palm
upward and place the spear in it. The thumb should
lie along the shaft and the index finger should rest against
the edge of the whipcord binding. The chief throwing
fingers are the thumb and index. During the run, which
is usually 50 to 60 feet, the spear is carried slightly higher
than the shoulder with the point turned inward and downward. The spear is held loosely until the last three strides,
when pressure is put on the thumb and index finger and
the javelin is pulled back to arm's length.

The actual throw is a long overhand pull without any
side twist, during which the body and then the shoulder
are put in before the arm. The wrist is snapped just as
the spear is whipped over the head. Many throwers use
a crisscross step on the last stride, side-stepping to the

left with the left foot, turning the body slightly to the right and shifting the right foot to the rear of the left. As soon as the javelin has left the hand, the feet are reversed, and the weight is shifted to the right leg. This leg is brought in front of the body to check the forward movement across the scratch line. Tail drag is the most common fault and is usually caused by pointing the javelin too high or holding onto it too long. The javelin is an event for the little fellow as well as the big. Some of the best international throwers are one-hundred-and-thirty-five-pound Japanese who make hurls of more than 230 feet.

CROSS-COUNTRY

This sport originated in England, where it flourishes unabated from September to April and where a whiff of nippy autumn air is a challenge to thousands of Britishers of all ages who run simply for pleasure and exercise during the cooler months. In America, where the colleges and clubs run from four miles to 10,000 meters, the sport is newer. Especially is it new in our high schools, where two-mile cross-country runs in October and November have become popular in the East and some of the midwestern states.

The charm of this race lies in the fact that the runners get away, for at least one season in the year, from the monotony of cinder track running, for the cross-country courses are routed out in the country over hills, grass,

roads and stone fences, where contestants constantly encounter different running surfaces and changing autumnal
scenery that help them forget the mental and physical
fatigue of the race. The sport is also a prime conditioner
for track men. Distance men who run cross-country in the
fall will beat the other half-milers and milers in the
spring. A thorough physical examination followed by a
moderate but intelligent training program of from six
to eight weeks, should be a required precaution. Runners should gain back the following day all weight lost
during practice. Sleep and an occasional after-lunch nap
are marvelous stamina builders for the challenge of cross-
country racing.

In his training the cross-country runner should try for
an easy relaxed style involving a short stride, more upright body carriage, an absence of kick-up behind and
an occasional dropping down on the heel from the ball
of the foot to rest the calf muscles. He should breathe
through both mouth and nose for he will need all the
fuel he can get, and he should warm up carefully each
day before undertaking even a practice jaunt, wearing
full-length sweat clothing if the day is at all cool. He attacks hills with a short stride, leaning over and pumping
his arms a bit more. Runners should not run too fast
uphill, but they can increase the pace going down if they
employ long fast strides and are careful to land on the
ball of the foot.

The ideal cross-country shoe is a light one with short

spikes and a small rubber heel glued or sewn to the outside of the shoe, although tennis slippers will do. Basketball shoes are too heavy. Wool socks are good for the
cushioning effect they give and a frequent change of
socks often prevents foot troubles. If the runner wishes,
he may toughen his feet by soaking them in salt water
after the shower bath, or in a solution including one cup
of formaldehyde in two gallons of water, or he can paint
the toes with tincture of benzoin. Carrying a stop watch
is risky since it may not keep time accurately because of
the constant shaking. It is best to let the coach or an experienced sideliner hold the watch.

Runners should train in all kinds of weather, wearing
long spikes, if possible, if the course is muddy. If the
footing is good, you will make your fastest time on rainy
days because the air is clean and contains more fuel, and
the sun gives you no trouble.

On extremely cold days, cotton gloves, long-sleeved
jerseys and even light drawers are good although the
coldest weather won't hurt bare legs. Some runners daub
melted paraffin or cocoa butter over them to keep out
the cold while others pin newspapers inside their shirts.

It is wise to know the course thoroughly before running it. If possible, go over it in an automobile or walk
it the day before the race, studying it carefully. Try to
keep a map of it in the head and have the short cuts
figured out. Always run in as straight a line as possible
and you will save as high as 40 or 50 yards in a single

race. If you are to race on a foreign course, adapt your training to it. If it is a hilly course, do a lot of hill running in your own country. If there are no hills there, run up and down your stadium. The same thing applies to flat running, or to races held on grass or asphalt. You should practice running on the flat the week before the race.

In a race, the ambitious contestant will want to stay fairly close to the leaders. He should be careful not to kill himself off at the start. He should let somebody else lead if the course is wet or the wind is blowing against him, and should watch the ground for good footing and keep a wary eye on his opponents to prevent being spiked or boxed. However, if the pace is too slow, he will want to take the lead. When fatigue strikes, the runner will need to call upon all his pluck. He must try to forget weariness by thinking of form and concentrating upon running as effortlessly and relaxed as possible. When the pace whips up at the start of the last half-mile, he remembers that he can always go a little farther and faster than he thinks he can. Mental fatigue always comes before physical fatigue; in fact more races are lost through inability to resist mental fatigue than for any other reason. How many times have you heard a defeated runner ruefully exclaim after a race: "I could have run faster. I just didn't put out. I felt so tired I didn't know I had so much strength left."

Cross-country is a team sport, too, and many a meet has

been won by what the English call "packing," whereby one team sticks together and the good runners encourage the poorer ones, until the final dash home.

After a run of any kind contestants should not stand around in the cold, but should don sweat clothing, and walk a bit in the fresh air. Then they should hurry into the warm soapy shower bath and, no matter how freezing the weather, finish with the tingling cold shower that closes the pores, increases muscular tone and gives a glorious feeling of perfect condition.

CHAPTER 14

VOLLEYBALL

VOLLEYBALL is an American adaptation
of an Italian game that originated in the Romanic countries
back in the Middle Ages. From Italy, the sport was introduced in 1893 to Germany, where it was known as
faustball, and two years later an American, William G.
Morgan, then physical director of the Holyoke, Massachusetts, Y.M.C.A., grafted some well-thought-out variations
of his own onto the basic essentials of the German game
and called his game "mintonette."

Morgan's chief innovation, and it is an important one,
was the idea that the ball should be volleyed in the air
and never be permitted to touch the floor. This seems to
have been an entirely new feature, since in *faustball* two
bounces of the ball were permitted. Also, Morgan's introduction of a net was new, since in the older game the
ball was played over a rope. Otherwise the two games are
quite similar. The German rules call for a court fifty
by twenty meters, a rope two meters (approximately six
and one-half feet) high extending through the middle of

the playing rectangle, five players on a side and a ball seventy centimeters in circumference, which roughly corresponds to the ball Morgan introduced.

At the suggestion of Dr. Alfred T. Halstead of the faculty of the International Y.M.C.A. College at Springfield, Massachusetts, the name of Morgan's game was changed from mintonette to volleyball, and like all games, the sport has also undergone several rule changes. For instance, before 1921 the ball could be played in the air an unlimited number of times. In the old days, the net was only seven feet high, there was no rotation of players, and reaching over the net to play a ball was not penalized. All these rules have since been modified although the form and spirit of the game have remained unchanged.

Y.M.C.A.'s in the United States quickly adopted and promoted volleyball and soon it spread to foreign countries. Today it enjoys considerable vogue in South America, Australia, India, the Philippines, Russia, Siberia and the Orient. During both World Wars the sport was widely played by American soldiers. Experiments have been conducted to improve the rules and in America today the game is played so widely on playgrounds, in school intramural leagues, gymnasiums and in recreation centers that it has been estimated that four and one-half million people now play volleyball.

There are many reasons for the popularity of the sport. It is not only a good game for boys of all ages, but it is a sport a boy can play until he is seventy since it requires very little sprinting. Even dubs who never played it before get fun out of it. Volleyball is not expensive, for a ball and a net comprise the only equipment needed. It is a year-round game and can be played either indoors or outdoors. Since there is no personal contact, it offers very little chance for bodily injury. Not only can it be played on a small court surface, but since the ball is not allowed to touch the floor, the surface of the court doesn't need to be especially prepared. In fact, the game is played on the beach in the mild climates of southern California and Brazil.

Volleyball is perhaps the best game ever devised for correcting the "student stoop" since, if the net is kept high and the two-handed return used, it compels players to keep the head and shoulders up and back, the spine straight and the chest thrust out. It is a good game for the spectator, too, since he can sit close to the small court and keep the ball in constant view, and yet it is hard for a spectator to watch it very long without acquiring a strong impulse to pull off his coat and join the players.

Good-will tours of Europe by American volleyball teams after World War II helped international relationships, believes Harold T. Friermood, former secretary-treasurer of the United States Volleyball Association. "The best type of international relationship is that which evolves from face-to-face contact," he declared. "When people have an opportunity to meet and talk about their work, their recreation, their families and their philosophies of life and the day-to-day problems that they encounter, this is perhaps the best kind of groundwork for establishing substantial relationships among people around the world."

Volleyball rules are so simple that anyone can quickly learn them. The court is sixty feet long by thirty feet wide and divided by a net eight feet above the floor. The

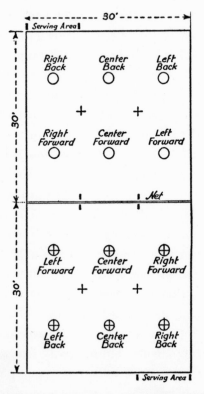

DIAGRAM OF VOLLEYBALL COURT, WITH PLAYERS
IN POSITION AT START OF A GAME

inflated ball used is small and light and round, weighing
between nine and ten ounces, and is only about half as
big and heavy as a basketball. The net is three feet wide
and eight feet high but may be lowered one foot for
junior play. Taking their positions on opposite sides of
the net, the two six-man teams toss a coin to determine
which shall serve.

Service is always hit by the right back, who stands in
the serving area and bats the ball over the net with one
hand. Volleyball is entirely an aerial game and after the
serve the ball is volleyed back and forth across the net.
The object of the game is never to let the ball touch the
floor inside one's own court. Players cannot grasp and
throw the ball, called holding, but must hit it cleanly.
Points are usually scored by driving the ball to the floor
of the opponents' court, or by forcing the opponents to
hit it out of bounds or into or under the net. A maximum
of three hits is permitted each team in returning a ball
over the net and the best teams cleverly use up all three
hits. A player in the rear line lifts the ball up to a front-
line player, who in turn feeds a high fluffy pass close to
the net to another front-line player, who leaps up and
smashes the ball, usually with the heel of an open palm,
over the net into the other court. One man may play a
ball twice during a volley but not twice in succession.

Players of the offensive team rotate one position, clock-
wise, after each lost service, which makes for versatility.
Each contestant is obliged to play each position in turn.

A game is won when either team scores fifteen points, provided the winner has at least a two-point margin. For instance, when the score reaches 14–14, the game must be
won at 16–14 or by the first two-point margin that can
be established after the 14–14 tie, such as 17–15, 18–16,
etc. Points may be scored only by the serving team.

The following terminology will aid beginning players:

STOPPER: The defensive player, usually a
back-line man, who first hits the ball after it has been
batted over the net by the opponents. The stopper will
usually hit his pass, called a stop pass, high to the set-up
man in the front line.

SET-UP MAN OR BOOSTER: The front-line player
who makes the second or set-up pass of the series. The
set-up man usually receives the ball from a rear-line
stopper and feeds it up near the net to the spiker.

SPIKER: The net man who makes the third
or climax hit—a smash or placement that is often unreturnable—in each volley. Such a hit is called a spike.

SERVICE

Service is the method used to put the ball in play
and since only the serving team may score in volleyball,
service is tremendously important. Moreover only one
serve is permitted, which puts an added value upon
control.

UNDERHAND SERVE: This is the most reliable
and popular serve. Although it is not as speedy as other

forms, it is the easiest to control, and control means just as much to the volleyball server as to the baseball pitcher. Stand behind the service line, left foot forward, right knee bent, weight over the right foot and lean slightly forward. The ball lies in the partly extended left hand, which is held waist high and toward the right side of the body. The act of serving consists simply of striking the ball with the right hand off the left hand, at the same time straightening the body, shifting the weight to the left foot, stepping forward with the right foot and following through with the right arm and hand.

OVERHAND SERVE: This serve is used by some experienced players. While not nearly so accurate as the underhand method, it is much faster and may better be curved. The stance is the same as for the underhand serve, except the ball is held head high or higher, and the hit is usually made with the fist or off the heel of the palm. At impact, the body is carried forward by a strong thrust off the right foot. Overhand serves usually cross the net low and fast, and if executed correctly are often unreturnable.

SIDEARM SERVE: This is the least-used method of all. The stance for it is about the same as for the underhand style, save the body is not crouched so much and the ball is held shoulder high and struck with a side-arm sweep of the right arm.

In all three methods, spin may be added by striking the ball on one side or the other, but beginners will find this difficult. Try for overspin with the underhand serve, and for underspin and side cuts with the overhand serve. The fist or heel of the palm may also be used in the underhand or sidearm methods, if desired.

PLACEMENT OF SERVICE: When the opponents' spiker is at the center of the net, it is a good idea to serve deep to the left back, thus increasing the diagonal distance to which the stop pass will have to be hit toward the set-up man, who will be the right forward if the spiker is right-handed. When the spiker is playing the left forward position, it is wise to serve deep to the right back so the set-up man playing the center forward position will have to turn his back to the spiker when handling the feeding pass. Sometimes a short serve to the setter-upper himself will disconcert him or make it more difficult for him to stop the ball and boost it up in the same stroke. This service, difficult for beginners but worthy of cultivation, is especially good when the set-up man is in the right forward position.

PASSING

The ball should be played whenever possible off the tips of the ten stiffened fingers, which are spread and cupped so that only the finger and thumb tips actually come in contact with the ball. With ten points of control on the ball instead of two, far greater accuracy is possible, holding is almost totally obviated and the spin can better be taken out of a ball, making it easier for the next man

to handle. In bringing the ball up from back court or
setting it up for spiking, use the ten-point method. Don't
strike the ball with the palm of the hand, or with the heel
of the palm in these situations if it can be avoided.

A ball hit low will have to be handled underhanded.
The feet should be spread, body crouched low and both
hands should be used. However on balls taken above the
shoulders, spread the feet comfortably, relax the arms,
which are held with elbows at sides and hands just in
front of the face, and, using the ten-point method, try to
make contact with the ball on its rear and sides with all
the fingers and thumbs to assure control. Keep the eyes
carefully on the dropping ball and meet it with an upward thrust of the taut fingers and thumbs, at the same
time straightening the body with a slight jump to add
force. Never touch the ball with the palms on this pass.

Of course, on terrifically hit or sharply cut balls, a
player will want to use more finger surface. On one-
handed passes, usually emergency shots, use the fingers
and thumb if possible and try to send the ball high.

After the players in the rear court have taken the shock
off the pass from the foe and fed it up high to the booster
or set-up man, it is the latter's job to lift the second pass
high to the spiker at the net. Set-up men can make or
break a volleyball team because their pass has to be just
right if the spiker is to do his savage work effectively.

The set-up man must drop the ball on the hitting side
of the spiker, half a foot to two feet from the net, depend-

ing upon where his spiker likes it best. He will want to toss the ball from ten to fifteen feet high so the spiker will have more time to gauge it. He should also make the ball drop halfway between himself and the spiker so the latter will have room to take one or two short steps and a jump prior to rising into the air to kill the pass. Even if the set-up man has to go several feet for the pass from the stopper, he should try to take it facing the spiker, for this will help the accuracy of his pass.

SPIKING

The spike in volleyball corresponds to the smash or kill in tennis and badminton. Usually the spiker jumps into the air close to the net and, hitting with all his power, slams the ball to an opening in the defensive half of the court. Thus he seeks to deliver an unreturnable shot. He should always direct his blasts at an opening, or at the left side of an opponent, and not hit blindly.

The important thing in spiking is to time the ball in order to get above it with the hitting hand just as it drops near the top of the net. It is important also to hit the ball about one foot in front of the spiking shoulder just as it is dropping down on the left shoulder, so the downward angle will be assured. Some spikers hit with a long swing of the full arm, others with the arm bent, employing both forearm and wrist in a powerful stroke.

HAND POSITIONS: Several hand positions may be used in spiking: (1) The flat-hand stance in which the fingers are kept together and the wrist loose. In this style the center of the ball is hit with the base of the fingers and the tips of the fingers are applied to the top of the ball to aid its being pulled down at an angle. (2) The rigid-hand form in which the fingers are clasped tightly together with the extended thumb held against the side of the main joint of the first finger as a brace. The ball is clubbed down with the heel of the palm and the fingers may make contact with the top of the ball. (3) The spread-finger form in which the ball is played off the full length of the fingers. This style gives good control but because it makes no loud slapping sound, sometimes arouses the suspicion of the referee who is on the watch for holding. However it is a perfectly legal form. (4) The first position with wrist relaxed, a style that adds power but shortens the reach and lacks control. Stances (1) and (2) described above are the most popular.

As soon as he sees that his back-court man, or stopper, has successfully handled the stroke from the opponents and will be able to feed the ball up to the set-up man, the spiker takes a quick look at the defensive court to pick out unguarded holes into which to hit the ball. The spiker should take only a few short steps prior to his jump into the air. He should stand with his left shoulder to the net, facing his set-up man. Of course the taller he is and the higher he can jump, the better.

He should be more than just a terrific hitter. Finesse should be mixed with power in spiking. For instance, a crafty spiker will mix soft drop shots and cross-angled shots with his thunderbolts. Occasionally, when he sees that his set-up pass has been lifted a bit too strongly and is dropping close to the net but *on the foe's side*, the spiker may jump into the air and bluff to spike the ball, thus tricking his front-line opponents into backing up and letting the ball drop safe. If the ball is dropping on top of the net, the spiker can swing his arm more nearly parallel to the net and slice the ball to one side.

The center forward stands about a yard from the net and the remaining two forwards about three yards from the net. All the players stand a little to the left of the center of their positions on the court to take advantage of their right-handedness. All defensive players should be crouched, on their toes, their feet spread comfortably, arms waist high with fingers spread and eyes eternally glued on the ball. Each forward stands with his side to the net, for this position gives freer movement, lets him take passes from his teammates or shots from his opponents with little change of facing, and lessens his chance of touching the net on a stroke since he isn't faced towards it. All players look to the server.

DEFENSE

FORMATIONS: Against a spiker who customarily hits hard to the back of the court, use a retreated formation, dropping the left and right backs in each corner, the left and right forwards about four yards back of the net and pulling the center back well up. Against a spiker who likes to angle the ball downward sharply to the floor, use a more closely knit formation, with the left and right forwards and backs pulled forward and drawn more to the center of the court, and the center back stationed about a yard from the end line.

The outstanding development of volleyball in recent years has been blocking, the name given to that maneuver where one or two defensive men jump into the air when the spiker jumps and, presenting their hands over the top of the net as a fence, block the spiker's terrific smashes almost before they start. Thus they force the hard-driven ball to rebound back to the spiker's side of the net and deprive him of his point.

Blocking is ordinarily effective only when the set-up pass to the spiker is falling within inches of, or right on top of, the net. It is difficult to block a ball that is set up two or three feet from the net on the spiker's side.

The blocker should use both hands, hold them two or three inches apart and keep them two or three inches from the net. He must hold his hands straight up and down in the vertical plane, for if his fingers are angled forward, the ball will trickle down on his side of the net instead of on the spiker's. If two defensive players block together, and this is preferred to only one man blocking, they should rise as one man, timing their leap so the fence formed by their four hands is presented above the top of the net just as the spiker smashes the ball.

A smart spiker will try to outguess a blocking team by flicking cross swipes to the unguarded flanks, or by tapping gentle drop shots just over the hands of the blockers and inside of the rear defensive line. Teammates of a spiker who is threatened by a block should be alert to stop the deflected smash exploding back in their faces and again feed it to their spiker. Occasionally a team which has as a set-up man a converted spiker, can switch the set-up pass to him instead of to the spiker, crossing up the blockers.

The rules forbid more than two players' blocking together, although there was no limit and many teams used three prior to the rule change in 1938.

Boys in the lower teens will enjoy volleyball far more if they use the modified rules for juniors. These rules provide for a net seven feet in height, a lighter ball of six or seven ounces, service from the center of the offensive court instead of from the distant corner, two serves instead of one, and teammates of the server being permitted to assist a short serve over the net. There is no limit on the number of hits a team may use to play a ball over the net and one player may hit the ball twice in succession. The size of junior courts is forty by twenty feet if six boys play on each team, fifty by twenty-five feet for teams of nine players each, or sixty by thirty feet for teams of twelve players each. These changes are recommended by the United States Volleyball Association, and are incorporated in the official rules.

CHAPTER 15

WRESTLING

$\mathbf{B}$ECAUSE of the want of science and sincerity in American professional wrestling today, the sport now enjoys far less reputation than it did in ancient times. Amateur wrestling in American colleges and high schools is steadily advancing but the professional sport sorely needs the advertisement of a real world's champion and the national interest and glamour that go with him. It needs honest matches between him and the best men in his craft.

There is no questioning the age and universality of this sport. Wall paintings found in the temple tombs of Beni Hassan, a village in middle Egypt, show that the Egyptians five thousand years ago not only knew nearly every hold we know today, but also several others we have never seen.

In 708 B.C. wrestling became an event in the Olympic Games of ancient Greece. Milo of Croton, a giant who won the Olympic laurel six times without ever falling on his knees, was perhaps the first wrestling champion of which there is authentic record. Milo had other talents, too. No one could rush or push him off an oiled plate, so firm was his stand. Also it was claimed for him that he ate, at one sitting, seventeen pounds of meat and bread and washed it down with five quarts of wine. He was wrestling and eating champion of Greece for twenty-four long years and the Greeks must have grown tired of seeing the big fellow around, because once when he slipped and fell on his hip while advancing to receive one of his many crowns, the people booed him. Wrestling is so extremely healthy that its champions go on forever and the American public, like the ancient Greek public, finally becomes bored with seeing the same faces in the ring year after year.

In Japan the most popular form of wrestling is not jiujitsu, but *sumo*, which started in 23 B.C. and is still watched by tremendous crowds. The champion *sumo* wrestlers weigh three hundred pounds or more and wear nothing but ornamental loin cloths. Their matches are held in small soft-sanded rings marked off with rice straw, and unfair play is scrupulously avoided. The idea in *sumo* is to push an opponent out of the ring or throw him to the ring floor. The slightest touch of knee or finger to the ground is a fall. The sport is charmingly unique in that when one of the contestants is ready to strike, he stands up with a shout, but if the other calls out *"Matta!"* (which means "Not yet!") the action is postponed and both then go outside the ring for a sip of water and a

sprinkle of salt, the original meaning of which was purifi-
cation and prayer for success and personal safety.

Nearly all countries had their ancient form of wrestling, such as the colorful *glima* of the Icelanders, the
schweitzer schwingen of the Swiss, the Cumberland of
the Irish, and the rough Lancashire style of the Scotch.
Graeco-Roman wrestling, still popular in foreign countries and still on the Olympic program, stipulates that
legs cannot be used for attack or defense and that every
hold must be above the belt. Wrestling is older than
civilization in India and China and has been popular in
Germany for centuries. In fact, several of our crack American wrestlers were husky men of German extraction: Eu-
gene Sandow, Max Luttbeg, Frank Gotch, Joe Stecher,
Ray Steele and Dick Daviscourt.

In America the prevailing mode is catch-as-catch-can,
in which only the strangle hold is barred. It's a different
fashion from the free style form used in the Olympic
games, consequently American teams seldom win in Olympic wrestling, having had so little experience in the style
used. All American wrestling was amateur at first. Friendly
scufflings were held outdoors at picnics and fairs like the
backwoods bouts of young Abraham Lincoln. However,
soon the best wrestlers went on tour, meeting all comers,
and the sport widened.

The American corn-belt states have always produced
great wrestlers. One of their first was Clarence Whistler
of Omaha, Nebraska, who was perhaps outstanding among

the early champions. After Whistler came Tom Jenkins of Cleveland who ruled until he ran afoul of another corn-belter, an Iowa farm boy named Frank Gotch. After defeating Jenkins, Gotch vanquished opponent after opponent until he won more than one hundred matches and retired in 1915. The irritable Gotch is usually conceded to be greatest of all the American champions, although some fine wrestlers, among them Joe Stecher, Earl Caddock, Ed "Strangler" Lewis and Stanislaus Zbyszko, held the world's title after him. None of them, however, held it for more than three years at a stretch.

The term "world's champion" is often a misnomer. A few years ago Zbyszko, the great Polish champion who twice won the so-called world's championship by vanquishing the best wrestlers in America, was offered ten thousand dollars to go to Bombay and wrestle Gama, the champion of India. Although few people had ever heard of Gama, who was a Jew turned Mohammedan, Zbyszko was amazed when he faced him across the ring. He saw a man fifty-five years old who was only five feet seven inches tall and weighed two hundred and sixty pounds. The man had not the faintest ripple of fat on his body. The bout was all over in eight seconds and later the surprised Zbyszko said it was like wrestling some wild animal, and that he felt if he got up and tried to fight back he would be killed in the ring.

In 1929 "hippodrome" wrestling, in which the contestants kicked, butted heads, slapped faces and threw one

another out of the ring, was introduced by the flying tackles of Gus Sonnenberg, the Dartmouth football player,
and entertainment, rather than wrestling skill, became
the aim. Today the cleverest and most earnest wrestling
in America is that of the colleges and high schools. The
state of Oklahoma is at present the leader. Oklahoma
State University at Stillwater, coached for two decades by
the old master Ed Gallagher and later by Art Griffith and
Myron Roderick, has won twenty and tied a twenty-first
national collegiate wrestling championship in the twenty-
nine tournaments held. And the Aggies' most determined
challengers have been University of Oklahoma teams
coached by Port Robertson who have won three national
championships in the last nine years and during that period
have defeated the powerful Aggies nine times, tied them
four times and lost to them only four times.

Younger boys need not engage in a routine training
program. They are naturally in good physical trim. However high-school or intercollegiate wrestlers need a long
period of conditioning. They should start shortly after
school begins in the fall, doing easy jogging on the road
and wrestling on odd days, carefully practicing and re-
practicing the fundamental take-downs, rides, escapes and
falls. Calisthenics are good, particularly bridging, which
is helpful to both the intestines and neck.

It is not good for you to wrestle immediately after eating, or if you have a cold, or if you are injured. Do not
wrestle too long, or on hard floors. Never wrestle with

long fingernails or while wearing rings, buckles or wrist watches. It is unwise to wrestle a boy much heavier or much lighter than yourself.

Watch out for skin infections. Stanley Stasiak, Polish heavyweight, died from blood poisoning caused by skin infection contracted from an unclean wrestling mat. Wrestlers should wrestle only on clean mats and mat covers. Keep your fingernails trimmed; long nails are blood poisoners. Spitting, or blowing the nose on the mat or on the floor, is a filthy habit which can endanger the health of others.

It is well to wrestle with a head harness, as did the boy wrestlers of Greece more than two thousand years ago, to protect the ears. Ear injuries, usually caused by head scissors and head locks, are common, for the skin of the ear is easily separated from the cartilage it protects, much as the skin of a peach is rubbed off the fruit. This separation causes swelling and internal bleeding (not visible on the surface) between the skin and cartilage. If this fluid blood is not drawn off by a doctor using a carefully asepticized hypodermic needle and syringe, blood clots will form. These rapidly harden into solid tissue and the ear will be "cauliflowered," a name for an ugly condition that is permanent and can be repaired only by a competent plastic surgeon.

Above all, don't try to lose a pound of weight. Sweating and abstinence from foods and liquids are not only harmful to heart, muscles and kidneys, but will badly

weaken the wrestler for his event. Wrestle at your normal
weight, whatever it is.

RULES

LENGTH OF BOUTS: In collegiate and high-school
dual meets, matches shall be nine minutes in length,
divided into three bouts of three minutes duration each.
The first three-minute bout starts from the neutral position with both contestants on their feet. A fall in this
opening two-minute bout ends the match. If neither contestant secures a fall in this bout, the referee shall stop
the bout and toss a coin, and the winner of the toss may
elect to go behind or underneath in the referee's position
on the mat at the beginning of the first three-minute
bout. If no fall occurs during this second period, the
referee places the contestant who started the second period
in the position of advantage underneath and the final
three-minute period begins. If no fall occurs during this
period, the referee awards the bout on a basis of individual
match points scored by each contestant. This point system
gives three points for a near fall, two for each take-down
or reversal and one each for a predicament or escape. In
dual meets, if the point score is tied, the bout is declared
a draw. In tournaments, in case of a tie, two extra two-
minute periods are wrestled with each contestant taking
his turn in the position of advantage, and if the bout is
still tied a jury of two judges and the referee selects the
winner by secret ballot, giving the victory to the man who

showed superior wrestling ability during the overtime period.

REFEREE'S POSITION ON THE MAT: This is the position wrestlers take at the start of each three-minute period and when they roll off the mat. The *defensive wrestler* assumes a stationary position with his hands in the center of the mat. He should keep both knees on the mat and they must not be spread greater than the width of the shoulders. The legs must be parallel with the toes, turned neither out nor under in an exaggerated position. The heels of both hands must be on the mat not less than twelve inches in front of the knees. The elbows should not touch the mat.

The *offensive wrestler* must be on his knees at the side of his opponent with his head along the midline of his opponent's back. The palm of his encircling arm should be placed loosely against the defensive man's navel at the waistline, and the palm of his other hand should be placed loosely on the back of the opponent's elbow. Both of his knees should be on the mat outside of the defensive wrestler's near leg. His knee should not touch the near leg of his opponent and should be even with, or ahead, of the defensive man's foot.

Falls bring premium points and are secured when one contestant holds the other's shoulders, or area of both shoulder blades, on the mat for two full seconds.

Dual meets are decided by team scoring. Competition is held in eight classes, 123 pounds, 130, 137, 147, 157,

167, 177 and unlimited weight. In national collegiate and some conference tournaments and dual meets, bouts are also wrestled at 115 and 191 pounds. Scoring is five points for fall, forfeit or default, three for decision and two each in case of draw. In tournaments, four places are scored on a 10–7–4–2 basis with a one-point bonus given for each fall, forfeit or default.

High school weight classifications are 103 pounds, 112, 120, 127, 133, 138, 145, 154, 165 and unlimited. High school dual meet bouts are six minutes long and consist of three bouts, each of two minutes' duration. In high school tournaments, if two contestants are tied, the extra periods are only one minute long.

Illegal holds in college matches are the hammerlock above the right angle, twisting hammerlock, front head-lock, straight head scissors, over-scissors, flying mare with the palm up, full (double) nelson, strangle holds, all body slams, toe holds, twisting knee lock, the bending, twisting or forcing of the head or any limb beyond its normal limits of movement, locking the hands in a double arm bar from a neutral position and any hold used for punishment alone. In high school matches, all the above holds are barred and in addition the double wristlock and all headlocks without the arm and leg included.

High school and intercollegiate wrestlers must make an honest effort to secure a position of advantage and when one contestant has secured it, he must make an honest effort to gain a fall.

Let us assume a practice bout has started and you are facing an opponent in the center of the ring.

STANDING

OFFENSIVE POSITION: The standing position is the first thing to learn. If you want to carry the action to your adversary, and that is the brand of wrestling that usually gets the nod from the judges, try this offensive stance:

Spread your feet about a yard apart and bend your hips slightly until you are crouching. The lower you hold your center of balance, the harder it is to turn you over although you don't want to get so low you can't move around quickly. Stand on the balls of your feet, not too much on your toes, or your opponent can jerk you forward on your face. Don't stand too flat on your heels or he may shove you over backwards.

Now extend your right hand (if you are right-handed) and grasp, lightly, your opponent's left hand, forcing it upward a few inches. At the same time drop on both knees to the mat, into your opponent's left leg about knee high. Grasp and engage this leg at the knee with your right arm, make a balance on the mat with your left hand, then suddenly pick up his left foot with your left hand and force him to the mat. This is an effective coming out stance and should bring you many a take-down.

DEFENSIVE POSITION: Let us assume your opponent is rushing you hard and you find it difficult to defend yourself. How can you prevent his throwing you down?

The answer is that you lower your body balance. Always face him, and squat on one or both knees. Keep the body bent slightly forward, arms extended and ready, eyes watching every move he makes. Now you are set for his charges. No matter how fast he is, he will find it hard to rush you and turn you over. He cannot flank you because you are describing a smaller circle and should be able to turn faster than he. He cannot pick up your legs, nor can he use an arm drag. And if he comes too close, you can pick up *his* legs and take *him* down.

The next time you are wrestling, invite someone to rush you. See how easy it is to fend him off, even if he is speedier and stronger than you are. If you choose to go into your shell and wrestle defensively, any opponent will find you difficult opposition. However, when a wrestler is on the offensive he is apt to fall prey to a take-down hold and perhaps a pin-hold (one that pins his shoulders to the mat for a fall), if he attacks too recklessly.

The maneuvers detailed below will be described from one side only although any hold works from either side and should be practiced from both sides to gain skill.

TAKE-DOWNS

HEAD SNAP AND ANKLE PICK-UP: Place your right hand on your opponent's neck and your left hand on his right elbow. Drive toward him off your left leg and snap his head down toward his left knee. Grasp the heel of his left foot with your left hand and jerk it forward. Or if it is impossible to jerk it forward, hold it firmly while continuing to drive his head down toward his left knee and complete the take-down by forcing him back on his buttocks.

DOUBLE LEG TACKLE: Place your right hand on your opponent's neck and grasp his right elbow with your left hand. Drive in deep on both knees, at the same time snapping his head forward with your right hand. Release his right elbow and encircle his right knee with your left arm. Lift with your head, bringing it to the outside of his right leg. With your right hand, grasp the back of his left knee and pull in sharply. At the same time drive your head against his right leg and carry him in a circular motion to his left, upsetting him on his buttocks for the completion of the take-down.

BREAKDOWN

ARM AND HEAD BREAKDOWN: Starting behind your opponent from the referee's position on the mat, slide your left hand from his left elbow to his left wrist. Lift on his right thigh with an inside crotch pry, driving his head against his left armpit. At the same time pull outward on his left wrist and force him to the mat under control.

REVERSES

WING: From the underneath position on the mat, lock your opponent's right elbow with your own right elbow. Pull his right arm, which is around your waist, under you and roll on your right side. You have now rolled him under you and have only to turn toward his feet, release his arm and whirl on top of him for the reversal.

SWITCH: From the underneath position on the mat, reach across and plant your left hand on the mat in front of your right shoulder. Drive off your right foot, sit through and land with your buttocks on the mat even with your left hand. Reach over your opponent's right arm, drive forward and catch the inside of his right thigh with your right hand. Drive your buttocks away from him and turn into him to complete the reversal.

ESCAPE

THE STANDUP: From the underneath position on the mat, when the referee blows the whistle, come to your feet, grab both of your opponent's hands, which encircle your body, with both your hands and pull his arms loose so you can escape.

FALLS

CROTCH AND HALF-NELSON: More wrestlers are pinned with this hold than any other. To apply it, break down your opponent flat on his stomach or side, then clamp on a half-nelson. This means that you thrust your nearest arm under his arm and back over his neck to force the top part of his body over on his shoulder. Slide off his back and, working from the side from which you applied the half-nelson, thrust your other hand deeply under his crotch, grasping his buttocks and bear-hugging him. Pull his ends together, push down hard with your right shoulder and lift up with your left. If you concentrate your weight on his forced-down shoulders, you should soon have him.

If he tries to push you off with his outside hand, grab it with the hand you have under his crotch and hold it, at the same time pushing down with all your weight on his chest. Extend your legs and spread them to prevent his rolling to either side.

Wrestling is healthy. No other sport so brings into play the vital organs of the body. The constant stretching and twisting of the body tends to strengthen the muscles needed for good digestion. Likewise wrestling is an effective blood circulator and body builder. Wrestling is not dangerous. Ed "Strangler" Lewis, a former heavyweight champion who wrestled nearly a quarter of a century, declares that only two wrestlers have ever been killed in an American ring. What other American contact sport can show such immunity?

INDEX

ABOUT THE AUTHOR

Harold Keith is a man of many parts. His interest in the Civil War and, in particular, the fighting in the West led to his writing a novel for older boys and girls—*Rifles for Watie*. This book won the Newbery Medal in 1958.

Mr. Keith is well known throughout the country in the field of sports. He has been director of sports publicity at the University of Oklahoma since 1930.

A native Oklahoman, Harold Keith was born at Lambert, Oklahoma. He was educated at Northwestern State Teachers College at Alva, Oklahoma, and at the University of Oklahoma where he received his B.A. and M.A. degrees in history.

As an undergraduate athlete at Oklahoma in 1928, Harold Keith was a long-distance runner. He won the Pennsylvania Relays 3000-meter steeplechase at Philadelphia. In 1945 he returned to competition and won the 3¼-mile Oklahoma A.A.U. cross-country run.

In 1950 Mr. Keith won the Helms Athletic Foundation Award as the outstanding sports publicist in the nation.